7 Ben

1966.

THE CHERRY-TREE

THE
CHERRY-TREE

A Collection of Poems chosen by

GEOFFREY GRIGSON

PHOENIX HOUSE
LONDON

Set in 11 pt Joanna type, printed and bound
at the Aldine Press, Letchworth, Herts, for
Phoenix House Ltd, 38 William IV Street
Charing Cross, W.C.2

First published 1959

For Anna

CONTENTS

TO THE READER

Poetry comes from playing the best game of words which has ever been invented.

But the game is many games in one. It can be played to explain why we live or die; to present the strangling of a forlorn duchess, to picture a woodpecker chipping its nest into an oak-tree, to record pleasure in clouds riding or melancholy at leaves dropping. It makes puns. It changes the look of words and pretends they belong to another language:

> Gnoses mare, Thebe trux.
> Vatis inem?
> Causan dux.

It can be sad, glad, serious, frivolous, trivial, gentle, tough, extravagant. And played with words, its ideal is to fit the words into patterns of sound and meaning, each of which by its rhythm, does not easily wear out and will bear, and insist upon, being read again and again.

Being read – yes, by yourself, and aloud. After all, poems are made aloud. They are read over and over by the poets who are making them, and using that apparatus by which words are announced and pronounced. Poems are not made 'by ear', entirely. Poets have good ears, which help them to invent the rhythms of a poem; but also they have good chords of speech-making, which they control so that words fit so excellently to each other, and make such excellent blocks or filagrees of controlled speech (i.e. poems).

Reading your favourite poems aloud (where no one else can hear you, since reading poems in that way seems irresistibly comic to other people) turns them by their linkings and their rhythm, line after line, into your own possessions – until you find yourself, without intention, knowing whole poems, or special pieces, by heart, as we say; which should also mean by love.

Reading them by yourself – alone as well as aloud: I think that is how poems should be read   until, at any rate, we can share them with someone we love. 'The skies were mine', said Traherne after talking of the corn which was orient and immortal wheat, 'and so were the sun and moon and stars, and all the world was mine; and I the only spectator and enjoyer of it.' Poems do become in that way affairs as personal as orient and immortal wheat, skies, sun, moon, and stars and all the world were to Traherne. Made alone by the poet, they are read as lonely, individual, importantly private acts, just as we each think and feel and dream alone in other ways. (Some comic, witty, satirical, or nonsensical poems, all the same, are not so private. They are the ones – riddles, limericks, epigrams, or *The Dong with a Luminous Nose* – in which fun or a point needs to be shared, and which we enjoy best with friends or our family.)

I have always liked – and now offer – a large book of poems of all kinds, arranged according to mood and subject; a book of so many poems that there is room inside it for endless exploration and new discovery. Sometimes (or so I have found) the reader at first will refuse to read a particular poem, perhaps because he does not like its title, or the equal length of the lines or the solid mass of the poem. It may be in dialect, or some immediate trick of the rhythm, the 'way it runs', may put him off. Then one day he will read that poem after all, not quite knowing why he does so; and to his surprise and delight will acquire another personal possession. Here there are more than 550 poems or pieces of poetry – more than 550 such opportunities, which should last a good while.

Why – to go on to the first of a few particular remarks – has this book of poems been called *The Cherry-Tree*?

Cherry-trees are delightful, are neither everyday nor remote. At least they are different in winter, spring, summer, and autumn. Poems are sad as well as happy ('If you listen to David's harp, you shall hear as many hearselike airs as carols', said the Lord Verulam, very truly). The cherry-tree is bare in winter, puts on leaves and delightful blossom in spring, is hung with shining fruits, which are both tender and solid, and will grow if we plant the stones. Also the cherry-tree exudes a gum. Into the bargain remembered cherry-tree poems include old ones from the Middle Ages, such as the *Cherry Tree Carol* (page 127) or the lines which compare life to a cherry fair (page 321) which is a fair held among the cherry orchards, and modern ones such as the poems by A. E. Housman (page 47) and Robert Bridges (page 47). There isn't really a better tree for poems, though I have to allow that it would fit them better still if only the white cherry flowers were strongly and delightfully scented, or if cherry leaves were aromatic.

The poems, as you come to them, will not be explained (the meaning of very unfamiliar words may be given, but it would be unkind to deprive anyone of the delight of looking words up in a dictionary). Also you will not find dates after the name of the poet at the foot of the poem. If I like a poem, I do so without regard for when it was written – or even for the poet it was written by. Yet as far as the poets go, I may come to like a particular poet because different pieces by him have a quality in common; in which case his name is really the name of that quality – the quality Shakespeare, the quality Tennyson, the quality Hopkins or George Peele. But I come to regard him as a friend as well (unless he is altogether too great a poet); and his name below a poem becomes a friendly introduction or even a guarantee.

Time When is not so important. Still, it is often pleasant to know that a poet a thousand years ago could feel much as we do, and compose his word-feelings in a way which affects us even now; or it is pleasant to know that poets who lived as many hundreds of years apart as

T'ao Ch'ien in China and Shakespeare in London, or as Tu Fu and Thomas Hardy, could make poems out of similar warmth or sadness or delight or dislike. The Index of Authors (and anonymous poems) will therefore give the dates of this incidental poetic history, where they are known, and a few other details.

Also it is a good thing to go from one poem to another by the same writer. If you read something by Marlowe or Yeats and like it, you can see at a glance from the Index of Authors what other poems there are in *The Cherry-Tree* by Marlowe and Yeats, and so on. And when you find that a special poet moves you to a special degree, the next step is to go from an anthology such as this one to his Collected Poems.

Since we do not always have cause to remember, or do not always like, the whole of a poem, and since it is good to know about poems too long to include, I give some especially golden passages by themselves. Dots after the last word will show that an extract is an extract. But in that same Index of Authors you will always find the name of the poem it has been taken from. When the authorship of a poem is unknown, I have left the poem bare without tacking to it that word 'anonymous', which always seems slightly disreputable, as if it were the poem's fault and shame to have no acknowledged begetter.

Some books print old poems in the old spelling. I think this is generally a mistake, unless you are interested more in the history of poetry than in poems. A living poem or line out of a past age only looks like an antique with incrustations in such spelling, as if we valued it for its quaintness or ancientness alone. We do not remember, or say over to ourselves, great lines in curious original orthography:

Cover her face: Mine eyes dazell: she di'd yong.

So the spellings in *The Cherry-Tree* are modernized for the most part – though it is necessary to except a few poems out of the Middle Ages, in which modern and different words, instead of modern and familiar spelling, would have to be substituted; which would be wrong.

Very rhythmical verse makes up most of the book — verse which by rhythms grand, bold, subtle, delicate, obvious, and less obvious, stamps or insinuates itself into our affection and memory. But I have also included a number of translated poems — especially, since English is not our only literature in the British Isles, some from Irish and Welsh. Of these I should have given more if only Irishmen or Welshmen — or Englishmen — had translated a great many more to choose from, and had done so efficiently. It is odd, don't you agree, that we should have translated many more poems from the Chinese than from all the literature of our own fellow islanders (I have included Chinese poems as well, I should add).

Otherwise this *Cherry-Tree* presents some of the best of English poetry, familiar and unfamiliar, by writers named and nameless, made in the run of more than five centuries. Because people you know do not seem to value poems, do not think despondently that either the writing of them or the reading of them is going to die out. It never will. People have more to do with poetry than they realize.

Shakespeare makes Lorenzo say in *The Merchant of Venice*:

> *The man that hath no music in himself*
> *Nor is not moved with concord of sweet sounds*

(poetry is as much a concord of sounded words)

> *Is fit for treasons, stratagems, and spoils;*
> *The motions of his spirit are dull as night,*
> *And his affections dark as Erebus:*
> *Let no such man be trusted.*

But I doubt if such an absolute monster exists — either for poetry or music. I have never met one; and I doubt if there is a day in the life of anybody, a banker, or a bank-robber, a Beauty Queen or a maker of hydrogen bombs, a plumber, a milkman, an ironmonger, a man-murderer or a cat-murderer, a prime minister or a scraper of skins, an editor, a miser, a magnate, a clipper of poodles, or a very unpoetical chief of staff, during which he is not affected, in some direct way or another, by a poem of some kind.

Also great poems are stones in a pond of time and existence; their ripples run out to people who never read them or hear of them.

The poems in this book are divided into many groups or sections. Each group has its own title; and as well, its own decoration or illustration. Most of these engravings are from books of the first hundred years of printing, chosen not because they are so old, but because they are at once rhythmical, simple, and tactful. They were meant to go with a printed text, to provide pauses or comment, but not to be superior to what the text was saying.

REMINDER

Extracts from poems or plays are marked by dots at the end. The sources of such extracts will be found in the Index of Authors.

1. IDLE FYNO

Idle Fyno

Poems, remember, are made of words, and can each be a game of words and rhymes. They can be words put together for twisting the tongue, they can even be riddles, in which sense is hidden inside nonsense, or one sense inside another sense. Some of the nature riddles in this first part of The Cherry-Tree (you will know others of the same kind) may be very old, having been passed down by word of mouth for hundreds of years. They are not always hard to guess, but often they will emphasize something particularly beautiful or noticeable, or they will use beautiful or curious notions and words to describe an ordinary thing we all know. Since riddle poems are as old as the English language, I have put into a later part of The Cherry-Tree – on page 97 – a modern version of one of the riddles which the first Englishmen in England used to ask fourteen hundred years ago.

In game poems we do not have to obey dictionaries. We can make up words, names, and situations. We say there are musical weasels or that Jumblies exist with green hands; we say *fara diddle diddle dyno*, or change 'garden' into 'garding' to rhyme with 'Mrs Harding'. Which is a very pleasant freedom.

TWO RIDDLES

i

Highty, tighty, paradighty, clothed in green,
The king could not read it, no more could the queen;
They sent for a wise man out of the East,
Who said it had horns, but was not a beast.

ii

Little Nancy Etticoat with a white petticoat,
And a red nose;
The longer she stands, the shorter she grows.

(A holly tree; a candle)

INFIR TARIS

Infir taris,
Inoak nonis,
Inmudeelsis,
In claynonis.
Cana goateati vi?
Cana maretots?

TWISTER TWISTING TWINE

When a twister a-twisting will twist him a twist,
For the twisting of his twist he three twines doth intwist;
But if one of the twines of the twist do untwist,
The twine that untwisteth, untwisteth the twist.

Untwirling the twine that untwisteth between,
He twirls with his twister the two in a twine;
Then twice having twisted the twines of the twine,
He twisteth the twice he had twinèd in twain.

The twain that in twining before in the twine
As twines were untwisted, he now doth untwine;
Twixt the twain inter-twisting a twine more between,
He, hurling his twister, makes a twist of the twine.

John Wallis

Ragged-and-Tough.

Not Ragged-and-Tough,
But —
    Huckem-a-Buff,
First cousin to Ragged-and-Tough.

Not Ragged-and-Tough
Nor Huckem-a-Buff
First cousin to Ragged-and-Tough,
But —
    Miss Grizzle,
Maiden aunt to Huckem-a-Buff
First cousin to Ragged-and-Tough.

Not Ragged-and-Tough
Nor Huckem-a-Buff
First cousin to Ragged-and-Tough
Nor Miss Grizzle, maiden aunt to Huckem-a-Buff
First cousin to Ragged-and-Tough,
But —
    Goody Gherkin,
Grandmama to Miss Grizzle
Maiden aunt to Huckem-a-Buff
First cousin to Ragged-and-Tough.

Not Ragged-and-Tough
Nor Huckem-a-Buff
First cousin to Ragged-and-Tough,
Nor Miss Grizzle, maiden aunt to Huckem-a-Buff
First cousin to Ragged-and-Tough,
Nor Goody Gherkin, grandmama to Miss Grizzle
Maiden aunt to Huckem-a-Buff
First cousin to Ragged-and-Tough,
But —
    Little Snap,
Favourite dog of Goody Gherkin
Grandmama to Miss Grizzle
Maiden aunt to Huckem-a-Buff
First cousin to Ragged-and-Tough.

Not Ragged-and-Tough
Nor Huckem-a-Buff

First cousin to Ragged-and-Tough,
Nor Miss Grizzle, maiden aunt to Huckem-a-Buff
First cousin to Ragged-and-Tough,
Nor Goody Gherkin, grandmama to Miss Grizzle
Maiden aunt to Huckem-a-Buff
First cousin to Ragged-and-Tough,
Nor Little Snap, favourite dog of Goody Gherkin
Grandmama to Miss Grizzle
Maiden aunt to Huckem-a-Buff
First cousin to Ragged-and-Tough,
But –
    the Whip,
Which tickled the tail of Little Snap,
Favourite dog of Goody Gherkin,
Grandmama to Miss Grizzle,
Maiden aunt to Huckem-a-Buff,
First cousin to Ragged-and-Tough.

SEE, WILL, 'ERE'S A GO

Civile, res ago,
Fortibus es in ero.
Gnoses mare, Thebe trux.
Vatis inem?
Causan dux.

MOLLIS ABUTI

Mollis abuti
Has an acuti,
No lasso finis,
Molli divinis.
Omi de armis tres,
Imi na dis tres:
Cantu disco ver
Meas alo ver?

Jonathan Swift

INTRAMURAL AESTIVATION, OR SUMMER IN TOWN, BY A TEACHER OF LATIN

In candent ire the solar splendor flames;
The foles, languescent, pend from arid ramcs;
His humid front the cive, anheling, wipes,
And dreams of erring on ventiferous ripes.

5

How dulce to vive occult to mortal eyes,
Dorm on the herb with none to supervise,
Carp the suave berries from the crescent vine,
And bibe the flow from longicaudate kine!

To me, alas! no verdurous visions come,
Save yon exiguous pool's conferva-scum, –
No concave vast repeats the tender hue
That laves my milk-jug with celestial blue!

Me wretched! Let me curr to quercine shades!
Effund your albid hausts, lactiferous maids!
O, might I vole to some umbrageous clump, –
Depart, – be off, – excede, – evade, – erump!

Oliver Wendell Holmes

THE JUMBLIES

i

They went to sea in a Sieve, they did,
  In a Sieve they went to sea:
In spite of all their friends could say,
On a winter's morn, on a stormy day,
  In a Sieve they went to sea!
And when the Sieve turned round and round,
And everyone cried, 'You'll all be drowned!'
They called aloud, 'Our Sieve ain't big,
But we don't care a button! we don't care a fig!
  In a Sieve we'll go to sea!'
    Far and few, far and few,
      Are the lands where the Jumblies live;
      Their heads are green, and their hands are blue,
      And they went to sea in a Sieve.

ii

They sailed away in a Sieve, they did,
  In a Sieve they sailed so fast,
With only a beautiful pea-green veil
Tied with a riband by way of a sail,
  To a small tobacco-pipe mast;
And everyone said, who saw them go,
'O won't they be soon upset, you know!
For the sky is dark, and the voyage is long,
And happen what may, it's extremely wrong
  In a Sieve to sail so fast!'

Far and few, far and few,
   Are the lands where the Jumblies live;
  Their heads are green, and their hands are blue,
  And they went to sea in a Sieve.

iii

The water it soon came in, it did,
  The water it soon came in;
So to keep them dry, they wrapped their feet
In a pinky paper all folded neat,
  And they fastened it down with a pin.
And they passed the night in a crockery-jar,
And each of them said, 'How wise we are!
Though the sky be dark, and the voyage be long,
And happen what may, it's extremely wrong
  In a Sieve to sail so fast!'
   Far and few, far and few,
   Are the lands where the Jumblies live;
  Their heads are green, and their hands are blue,
  And they went to sea in a Sieve.

iv

And all night long they sailed away;
  And when the sun went down,
They whistled and warbled a moony song
To the echoing sound of a coppery gong,
  In the shade of the mountains brown.
'O Timballo! How happy we are,
When we live in a sieve and a crockery-jar,
And all night long in the moonlight pale,
We sail away with a pea-green sail,
  In the shade of the mountains brown!'
   Far and few, far and few,
   Are the lands where the Jumblies live;
  Their heads are green, and their hands are blue,
  And they went to sea in a Sieve.

v

They sailed to the Western Sea, they did,
  To a land all covered with trees,
And they bought an Owl, and a useful Cart,
And a pound of Rice, and a Cranberry Tart,
  And a hive of silvery Bees.

7

And they bought a Pig, and some green Jack-daws,
And a lovely Monkey with lollipop paws,
And forty bottles of Ring-Bo-Ree,
  And no end of Stilton Cheese.
    Far and few, far and few,
      Are the lands where the Jumblies live;
    Their heads are green, and their hands are blue,
      And they went to sea in a Sieve.

vi

And in twenty years they all came back,
  In twenty years or more,
And every one said, 'How tall they've grown!
For they've been to the Lakes, and the Torrible Zone,
  And the hills of the Chankly Bore;
And they drank their health, and gave them a feast
Of dumplings made of beautiful yeast;
And every one said, 'If we only live,
We too will go to sea in a Sieve, –
  To the hills of the Chankly Bore!'
    Far and few, far and few,
      Are the lands where the Jumblies live;
    Their heads are green, and their hands are blue.
      And they went to sea in a Sieve.

Edward Lear

WHAT'S IN THE CUPBOARD?

What's in the cupboard? says Mr Hubbard;
A knuckle of veal, says Mr Beal;
Is that all? says Mr Ball;
And enough too, says Mr Glue;
And away they all flew.

GHOSTESSES

I saw the ghostesses,
Sitting on the poetesses,
Eating of their toastesses,
And fighting with their fistesses.

8

THE DYER

As I went by a dyer's door
I met a lusty tawnymoor,
Tawny hands, and tawny face,
Tawny petticoats, silver lace.

ANNIE BOLANNY

Annie Bolanny,
Tillie annie go sanny,
Tee-legged, tie-legged,
Bow-legged Annie.

W

The King sent for his wise men all
  To find a rhyme for W.
When they had thought a good long time
But could not think of a single rhyme,
  'I'm sorry', said he, 'to trouble you.'

James Reeves

FERRY ME ACROSS THE WATER

'Ferry me across the water,
  Do, boatman, do.'
'If you've a penny in your purse
  I'll ferry you.'

'I have a penny in my purse,
  And my eyes are blue;
So ferry me across the water,
  Do, boatman, do.'

'Step into my ferry-boat,
  Be they black or blue,
And for the penny in your purse
  I'll ferry you.'

Christina Rossetti

RIDDLES

i

It is in the rock, but not in the stone;
It is in the marrow, but not in the bone;
It is in the bolster, but not in the bed;
It is not in the living, nor yet in the dead.

ii

The land was white,
    The seed was black;
It'll take a good scholar
    To riddle me that.

(The letter R; print on a page)

BEG PARDING

'Beg parding, Mrs Harding,
Is my kitting in your garding?'
'Is your kitting in my garding?
Yes she is, and all alone,
Chewing of a mutting bone'

I STOLE BRASS

Policeman, policeman, don't take me,
    Take that man behind that tree;
I stole brass, he stole gold —
Policeman, policeman, don't take hold!

CROSS-PATCH

    Cross-patch,
    Draw the latch,
Sit by the fire and spin;
    Take a cup,
    And drink it up,
Then call your neighbours in.

LET'S GO TO BED

'Let's go to bed', says Sleepy-head,
'Let's wait awhile', says Slow,
'Put on the pot', says Greedy-gut,
'We'll sup before we go.'

The sun's perpendicular rays
Illumine the depths of the sea;
The fishes, beginning to sweat,
Cry 'Damn it, how hot we shall be!'

W. L. Mansel

THE SWAN

Swan swam over the sea,
Swim, swan, swim.
Swan swam back again:
Well swam, swan.

THE WEASEL

One morning a weasel came swimming
All the way over from France,
And taught all the weasels of England
To play on the fiddle and dance.

RIDDLES

i

On yonder hill there is a red deer,
The more you shoot it, the more you may,
You cannot drive that deer away.

ii

As I went over London Bridge
Upon a cloudy day
I met a fellow clothed in yellow.
I took him up and sucked his blood,
And threw his skin away.

iii

In marble halls as white as milk,
Lined with a skin as soft as silk,
Within a fountain crystal-clear,
A golden apple doth appear.
No doors there are to this stronghold,
Yet thieves break in and steal the gold.

(*The rising sun; a blood orange; a hen's egg*)

AS I WALK'D BY MYSELF

As I walk'd by myself,
And talk'd to myself,
　Myself said unto me,
'Look to thyself,
Take care of thyself,
　For nobody cares for thee.'

I answer'd myself,
And said to myself
　In the self-same repartee,
'Look to thyself
Or not look to thyself,
　The self-same thing will be.'

A SHROPSHIRE LAD

I am of Shropshire, my shins be sharp:
Lay wood to the fire and dress me my harp.

THREE MORE RIDDLES

i

At the end of my yard there is a vat,
Four-and-twenty ladies dancing in that:
Some have green gowns, some a blue hat:
He is a wise man who can tell me that.

ii

As I went over Tipple Tyne
I met a troop of bonny swine,
Some yellow-necked, some yellow-backed.
They were the very bonniest swine
That ever went on Tipple Tyne.

iii

Wee man o'leather
Gaed through the heather,
Through a rock, through a reel,
Through an auld spinning-wheel,
Through a sheep-shank bane;
Sic a man was never seen.

(Flax in flower; a swarm of bees; a beetle)

There was a lady loved a swine.
'Honey', said she,
'Pig-hog, wilt thou be mine?'
'Hunc', said he.

'I'll build for thee a silver sty,
Honey', said she,
'And in it softly thou shalt lie.'
'Hunc', said he.

'Pinned with a silver pin,
Honey', said she,
'That you may go both out and in.'
'Hunc', said he.

'When shall we two be wed,
Honey?' said she.
'Hunc, hunc, hunc', he said,
And away went he.

A RIDDLE

Four stiff-standers,
Four lily-landers,
Two lookers, two crookers,
And a wig-wag.

(*A cow*)

EPITAPH ON JOHN KNOTT

Here lies John Knott:
His father was Knott before him,
He lived Knott, died Knott,
Yet underneath this stone doth lie
Knott christened, Knott begot,
And here he lies and still is Knott.

IPECACUANHA

Coughing in a shady grove
  Sat my Juliana,
Lozenges I gave my love,
  Ipecacuanha —
Full twenty from the lozenge box
  The greedy nymph did pick;
Then, sighing sadly, said to me —
  'My Damon, I am sick.'

George Canning

COWBOY

I'm wild and woolly
And full of fleas;
Ain't never been curried
Below the knees.

I'm a wild she wolf
From Bitter Creek
And it's my time
To h—o—w—l, whoop—i—e—e—ee.

THE MULE IN THE MINES

My sweetheart's the mule in the mines,
I drive her without reins or lines,
  On the bumper I sit,
  And I chew and I spit
All over my sweetheart's behind.

MY MAMMY WAS A WALL-EYED GOAT

My Mammy was a wall-eyed goat,
My Old Man was an ass,
And I feed myself off leather boots
And dynamite and grass;
For I'm a mule, a long-eared fool
And I ain't never been to school —
    Mammeee! Ma-ha-mam-hee!
    Heee-haw! Mamaah!
    Ma-ha-mee!

THE HARNET AND THE BITTLE,
A WILTSHIRE TALE

A harnet zet in a hollur tree —
A proper spiteful twoad was he;
And a merrily zung while he did zet
His stinge as shearp as a bagganet;
  'Oh, who so vine and bowld as I?
  I vears not bee, nor wapse, nor vly!'

A bittle up thuck tree did clim,
And scarnvully did look at him;
Zays he, 'Zur harnet, who giv thee
A right to zet in thuck there tree?
  Vor ael you zengs so nation vine,
  I tell 'e 'tis a house o' mine!'

The harnet's conscience velt a twinge,
But grawin' bowld wi' his long stinge,
Zays he, 'Possession's the best laaw;
Zo here th' sha'sn't put a claaw!
  Be off, and leave the tree to me,
  The mixen's good enough for thee!'

Just then a yuckel, passin' by,
Was axed by them the cause to try;
'Ha! ha! I zee how 'tis!' zays he,
'They'll make a vamous munch vor me!'
  His bill was shearp, his stomach lear,
  Zo up a snapped the caddlin' pair!

Moral

All you as be to laaw inclined,
This leetle story bear in mind;
For if to laaw you ever gwo,
You'll vind they'll allus zarve 'e zo;
You'll meet the vate o' these 'ere two:
They'll take your cwoat and carcass too!

J. Y. *Akerman*

bittle: *beetle*; zet: *sat*; bagganet: *bayonet*; thuck: *that*;
mixen: *midden, dung-heap*; yuckel: *woodpecker*; lear: *empty*;
caddlin': *quarrelsome*.

i

Fhairshon swore a feud
    Against the clan M'Tavish;
Marched into their land
    To murder and to rafish;
For he did resolve
    To extirpate the vipers,
With four-and-twenty men
    And five-and-thirty pipers.

ii

But when he had gone
    Half-way down Strath Canaan,
Of his fighting tail
    Just three were remainin'.
They were all he had,
    To back him in ta battle;
All the rest had gone
    Off, to drive the cattle.

iii

'Fery coot!' cried Fhairshon,
    'So my clan disgraced is;
Lads, we'll need to fight,
    Pefore we touch the peasties.
Here's Mhic-Mac-Methusaleh
    Coming wi' his fassals,
Gillies seventy-three,
    And sixty Dhuinéwassails!'

iv

'Coot tay to you, sir;
    Are you not ta Fhairshon?
Was you coming here
    To fisit any person?
You are a plackguard, sir!
    It is now six hundred
Coot long years, and more,
    Since my glen was plundered.'

'Fat is tat you say?
    Dare you cock your peaver?
I will teach you, sir,
    Fat is coot pehaviour!
You shall not exist
    For another day more;
I will shoot you, sir,
    Or stap you with my claymore!'

'I am fery glad,
    To learn what you mention,
Since I can prevent
    Any such intention.'
So Mhic-Mac-Methusaleh
    Gave some warlike howls,
Trew his skhian-dhu,
    An' stuck it in his powels.

In this fery way
    Tied ta faliant Fhairshon,
Who was always thought
    A superior person.
Fhairshon had a son,
    Who married Noah's daughter,
And nearly spoiled ta Flood,
    By trinking up ta water:

Which he would have done,
    I at least pelieve it,
Had ta mixture peen
    Only half Glenlivet.
This is all my tale:
    Sirs, I hope 'tis new t'ye!
Here's your fery good healths,
    And tamn ta whusky duty!

                                    W. E. Aytoun

IDLE FYNO

A ha ha ha! this world doth pass
Most merrily, most merrily, I'll be sworn,
For many an honest Indian ass
Goes for a unicorn.
   Farra diddle diddle dyno,
   This is idle idle fyno.

Tygh hygh, tygh hygh! O sweet delight,
He tickles this age that can
Call Tullia's ape a marmosyte
And Leda's goose a swan.
   Farra diddle diddle dyno,
   This is idle idle fyno.

So so, so so! fine English days,
For false play is no reproach,
For he that doth the coachman praise,
May safely use the coach.
   Farra diddle diddle dyno,
   This is idle idle fyno.

2. NEVER STEW YOUR SISTER

Never Stew Your Sister

In the woodcut two soldiers and a housewife are attacking a snail, or defending themselves from a snail; which is nonsense (and old nonsense from the Middle Ages). So here are more game or nonsense poems. A snail, of course, could be attacked with a spear and a sword and whatever it is (I think a distaff) that the housewife is wielding. And nonsense poems are not entire nonsense. Often they are a kind of snail-battle between nonsense and the opposite. Or nonsense, rather, will introduce its own sense. A Dong — supposing a Dong existed, as it does in Edward Lear's poem on page 24, and supposing it had the habit of walking over plains at night — might very sensibly, in such a nonsensical existence, have developed a luminous nose.

In Shakespeare's time they had a song which remarked

With hey trixy terlery whiskin
The world it runs on wheels.

Well, it does — and it doesn't. That is the truth of the matter, as well as quite a bit of the truth about poems of all kinds, not only nonsense ones. Also *Never stew your sister* is, when all is said and done, the most sound moral advice, as you will agree after reading the poem on page 26.

TO THE CUCKOO

O Cuckoo! shall I call thee Bird,
Or but a wandering voice?
State the alternative preferred
With reasons for your choice.

F. H. Townsend

HEXAMETER AND PENTAMETER

Down in a deep dark ditch sat an old cow munching a bean-
stalk.
Out of her mouth came forth strawberry, strawberry froth.

THE COMMON CORMORANT OR SHAG

The common cormorant or shag
Lays eggs inside a paper bag.
The reason you will see, no doubt,
It is to keep the lightning out.
But what these unobservant birds
Have never noticed is that herds
Of wandering bears may come with buns
And steal the bags to hold the crumbs.

THE DODO

The Dodo used to walk around,
And take the sun and air.
The Sun yet warms his native ground —
The Dodo is not there!

The voice which used to squawk and squeak
Is now for ever dumb —
Yet may you see his bones and beak
All in the Mu-se-um.

Hilaire Belloc

21

THE SHADES OF NIGHT

The shades of night were falling fast
And the rain was falling faster
When through an Alpine village passed
An Alpine village pastor.

A. E. Housman

THE RHINOCEROS

Rhinoceros, your hide looks all undone,
You do not take my fancy in the least:
You have a horn where other brutes have none:
Rhinoceros, you are an ugly beast.

Hilaire Belloc

JIM

Who ran away from his Nurse, and was eaten by a Lion

There was a Boy whose name was Jim;
His Friends were very good to him.
They gave him Tea, and Cakes, and Jam,
And slices of delicious Ham,
And Chocolate with pink inside,
And little Tricycles to ride,
And read him Stories through and through,
And even took him to the Zoo —
But there it was the dreadful Fate
Befel him, which I now relate.

You know — at least you ought to know,
For I have often told you so —
That Children never are allowed
To leave their Nurses in a Crowd;
Now this was Jim's especial Foible,
He ran away when he was able,
And on this inauspicious day
He slipped his hand and ran away!
He hadn't gone a yard when — Bang!
With open Jaws, a Lion sprang,
And hungrily began to eat
The Boy: beginning at his feet.

Now, just imagine how it feels
When first your toes and then your heels,
And then by gradual degrees,
Your shins and ankles, calves and knees,
Are slowly eaten, bit by bit.
No wonder Jim detested it!
No wonder that he shouted 'Hi!'
The Honest Keeper heard his cry,
Though very fat he almost ran
To help the little gentleman.
'Ponto!' he ordered as he came
(For Ponto was the Lion's name),
'Ponto!' he cried, with angry Frown.
'Let go, Sir! Down, Sir! Put it down!'

The Lion made a sudden Stop,
He let the Dainty Morsel drop,
And slunk reluctant to his Cage,
Snarling with Disappointed Rage.
But when he bent him over Jim,
The Honest Keeper's Eyes were dim.
The Lion having reached his Head,
The Miserable Boy was dead!
When Nurse informed his Parents, they
Were more Concerned than I can say —
His Mother, as she dried her eyes,
Said, 'Well — it gives me no surprise,
He would not do as he was told!'
His Father, who was self-controlled,
Bade all the children round attend
To James's miserable end,
And always keep a-hold of Nurse
For fear of finding something worse.

Hilaire Belloc

INFANT INNOCENCE

The Grizzly Bear is huge and wild;
He has devoured the infant child.
The infant child is not aware
He has been eaten by the bear.

A. E. Housman

23

THE DONG WITH A LUMINOUS NOSE

When awful darkness and silence reign
Over the great Gromboolian plain,
  Through the long, long wintry nights; –
When the angry breakers roar
As they beat on the rocky shore; –
  When Storm-clouds brood on the towering heights
Of the Hills of the Chankly Bore: –

Then, through the vast and gloomy dark,
There moves what seems a fiery spark,
  A lonely spark with silvery rays
  Piercing the coal-black night, –
  A Meteor strange and bright: –
Hither and thither the vision strays,
  A single lurid light.

Slowly it wanders, – pauses, – creeps, –
Anon it sparkles, – flashes and leaps;
And ever as onward it gleaming goes
A light on the Bong-tree stems it throws.
And those who watch at that midnight hour
From Hall or Terrace, or lofty Tower,
Cry, as the wild light passes along, –
  'The Dong! – the Dong!
  The wandering Dong through the forest goes!
    The Dong! the Dong!
  The Dong with a luminous Nose!'

    Long years ago
  The Dong was happy and gay,
Till he fell in love with a Jumbly Girl
  Who came to those shores one day,
For the Jumblies came in a sieve, they did, –
Landing at eve near the Zemmery Fidd
  Where the Oblong Oysters grow,
  And the rocks are smooth and gray.
And all the woods and the valleys rang
With the Chorus they daily and nightly sang, –
  'Far and few, far and few,
  Are the lands where the Jumblies live;
  Their heads are green, and their hands are blue
  And they went to sea in a sieve.'

Happily, happily passed those days!
  While the cheerful Jumblies staid;
  They danced in circlets all night long,
  To the plaintive pipe of the lively Dong,
    In moonlight, shine, or shade.
For day and night he was always there
By the side of the Jumbly Girl so fair,
With her sky-blue hands, and her sea-green hair.
Till the morning came of that hateful day
When the Jumblies sailed in their sieve away,
And the Dong was left on the cruel shore
Gazing — gazing for evermore, —
Ever keeping his weary eyes on
That pea-green sail on the far horizon, —
Singing the Jumbly Chorus still
As he sate all day on the grassy hill, —
  'Far and few, far and few,
  Are the lands where the Jumblies live;
  Their heads are green, and their hands are blue,
  And they went to sea in a sieve.'

But when the sun was low in the West,
  The Dong arose and said; —
— 'What little sense I once possessed
  Has quite gone out of my head!' —
And since that day he wanders still
By lake and forest, marsh and hill,
Singing — 'O somewhere, in valley or plain
Might I find my Jumbly Girl again!
For ever I'll seek by lake and shore
Till I find my Jumbly Girl once more!'

    Playing a pipe with silvery squeaks,
    Since then his Jumbly Girl he seeks,
    And because by night he could not see,
    He gathered the bark of the Twangum Tree
      On the flowery plain that grows.
      And he wove him a wondrous Nose, —
    A Nose as strange as a Nose could be!
Of vast proportions and painted red,
And tied with cords to the back of his head.

In a hollow rounded space it ended
With a luminous Lamp within suspended,
　All fenced about
　With a bandage stout
　To prevent the wind from blowing it out; –
And with holes all round to send the light,
In gleaming rays on the dismal night.

And now each night, and all night long,
Over those plains still roams the Dong;
And above the wail of the Chimp and Snipe
You may hear the squeak of his plaintive pipe
While ever he seeks, but seeks in vain
To meet with his Jumbly Girl again;
Lonely and wild – all night he goes,—
The Dong with the luminous Nose!
And all who watch at the midnight hour,
From Hall or Terrace, or lofty Tower,
Cry, as they trace the Meteor bright,
Moving along through the dreary night, –
　'This is the hour when forth he goes,
　The Dong with a luminous Nose!
　Yonder – over the plain he goes;
　　He goes!
　　He goes;
　The Dong with a luminous Nose!'

Edward Lear

BROTHER AND SISTER

'Sister, sister, go to bed!
Go and rest your weary head.'
Thus the prudent brother said.

'Do you want a battered hide,
Or scratches to your face applied?'
Thus his sister calm replied.

'Sister, do not raise my wrath.
I'd make you into mutton broth
As easily as kill a moth!'

The sister raised her beaming eye
And looked on him indignantly
And sternly answered, 'Only try!'

Off to the cook he quickly ran.
'Dear Cook, please lend a frying-pan
To me as quickly as you can.'

'And wherefore should I lend it you?'
'The reason, Cook, is plain to view.
I wish to make an Irish stew.'

'What meat is in that stew to go?'
'My sister'll be the contents!'
                      'Oh!'
'You'll lend the pan to me, Cook?'
                      'No!'
Moral: Never stew your sister.

Lewis Carroll

PUDDEN TAME

What's your name?
   Pudden Tame.
What's your other?
   Bread and Butter.
Where do you live?
   In a sieve.
What's your number?
   Cucumber.

THE YOUNG LADY OF LYNN

There was a young lady of Lynn
Who was so excessively thin
  That when she essayed
  To drink lemonade
She slipped through the straw and fell in.

THE PLAYING CARDS

Behold, four Kings in majesty rever'd,
With hoary whiskers and a forky beard;
And four fair Queens whose hands sustain a flow'r,
Th'expressive emblem of their softer pow'r;
Four Knaves in garbs succinct, a trusty band,
Caps on their heads, and halberts in their hand;
And particolour'd troops, a shining train,
Draw forth to combat on the velvet plain . . .

Alexander Pope

FIVE LIMERICKS

i

There was an Old Man with a beard,
Who said, 'It is just as I feared! —
Two owls and a Hen, four Larks and a Wren,
Have all built their nests in my beard!'

ii

There was an old person of Skye,
Who waltz'd with a Bluebottle fly:
They buzz'd a sweet tune, to the light of the moon,
And entranced all the people of Skye.

iii

There was a young lady of Corsica,
Who purchased a little brown saucy-cur;
Which she fed upon ham, and hot raspberry jam,
That expensive young lady of Corsica.

iv

There was an old man of the Dargle
Who purchased six barrels of Gargle;
For he said, 'I'll sit still, and will roll them down hill.
For the fish in the depths of the Dargle.'

v

There was an Old Person of Gretna,
Who rushed down the crater of Etna;
When they said, 'Is it hot?' he replied, 'No, it's not!'
That mendacious Old Person of Gretna.

Edward Lear

THE MOCK TURTLE'S SONG

'Will you walk a little faster?' said a whiting to a snail.
'There's a porpoise close behind us, and he's treading on my
tail.
See how eagerly the lobsters and the turtles all advance!
They are waiting on the shingle – will you come and join the
dance?
  Will you, won't you, will you, won't you, will you join the
  dance?
  Will you, won't you, will you, won't you, won't you join
  the dance?

'You can really have no notion how delightful it will be,
When they take us up and throw us, with the lobsters, out to
sea!'
But the snail replied 'Too far, too far!' and gave a look
askance –
Said he thanked the whiting kindly, but he would not join the
dance.
  Would not, could not, would not, could not, would not
  join the dance.
  Would not, could not, would not, could not, could not
  join the dance.

'What matters it how far we go?' his scaly friend replied.
'There is another shore, you know, upon the other side.
The further off from England the nearer is to France –
Then turn not pale, beloved snail, but come and join the
dance.
  Will you, won't you, will you, won't you, will you join
  the dance?
  Will you, won't you, will you, won't you, won't you join
  the dance?'

Lewis Carroll

HUMPTY DUMPTY'S RECITATION

In winter, when the fields are white,
I sing this song for your delight –

In spring, when woods are getting green,
I'll try and tell you what I mean.

In summer, when the days are long,
Perhaps you'll understand the song:

In autumn, when the leaves are brown,
Take pen and ink, and write it down.

I sent a message to the fish:
I told them 'This is what I wish.'

The little fishes of the sea,
They sent an answer back to me.

The little fishes' answer was
'We cannot do it, Sir, because —'

I sent to them again to say
'It will be better to obey.'

The fishes answered with a grin,
'Why, what a temper you are in!'

I told them once, I told them twice:
They would not listen to advice.

I took a kettle large and new,
Fit for the deed I had to do.

My heart went hop, my heart went thump;
I filled the kettle at the pump.

Then someone came to me and said
'The little fishes are in bed.'

I said to him, I said it plain,
'Then you must wake them up again.'

I said it very loud and clear;
I went and shouted in his ear.

But he was very stiff and proud;
He said 'You needn't shout so loud!'

And he was very proud and stiff;
He said 'I'd go and wake them, if —'

I took a corkscrew from the shelf;
I went to wake them up myself.

And when I found the door was locked,
I pulled and pushed and kicked and knocked

And when I found the door was shut,
I tried to turn the handle, but —

Lewis Carroll

THREE YOUNG RATS

Three young rats with black felt hats,
Three young ducks with white straw flats,
Three young dogs with curling tails,
Three young cats with demi-veils,
Went out to walk with three young pigs
In satin vests and sorrel wigs.
    But suddenly it chanced to rain
    And so they all went home again.

ONE OLD OX

One old ox opening oysters,
Two toads totally tired
Trying to trot to Tewkesbury,
Three tame tigers taking tea,
Four fat friars fishing for frogs,
Five fairies finding fire-flies,
Six soldiers shooting snipe,
Seven salmon sailing in Solway,
Eight elegant engineers eating excellent eggs;
Nine nimble noblemen nibbling non-pareils,
Ten tall tinkers tasting tamarinds,
Eleven electors eating early endive,
Twelve tremendous tale-bearers telling truth.

ARCHBISHOP TAIT

There was an Archbishop named Tait
Who dined with a friend at 8.8.
    I regret to relate
    I'm unable to state
What Tait's tête-à-tête ate at 8.8.

HENRY WARD BEECHER

The Reverend Henry Ward Beecher
Called a hen 'a most elegant creature'.
    The hen, proud of that,
    Laid an egg in his hat,
And thus did the hen reward Beecher.

TO MINERVA
(from the Greek)

My temples throb, my pulses boil,
    I'm sick of Song and Ode, and Ballad –
So, Thyrsis, take the Midnight Oil
    And pour it on a lobster salad.

My brain is dull, my sight is foul,
    I cannot write a verse, or read –
Then, Pallas, take away thine Owl,
    And let us have a lark instead.

Thomas Hood

THE RATCATCHER'S DAUGHTER

In Westminster not long ago,
There lived a Ratcatcher's Daughter.
She was not born at Westminster,
But on the t'other side of the water.
Her father killed rats and she sold sprats
All round and over the water,
And the gentlefolks, they all bought sprats
Of the pretty Ratcatcher's daughter.

She wore no hat upon her head,
Nor cap nor dandy bonnet,
Her hair of her head it hung down her neck
Like a bunch of carrots upon it.
When she cried sprats in Westminster,
She had such a sweet loud voice, Sir,
You could hear her all down Parliament Street,
And as far as Charing Cross, Sir.

The rich and poor both far and near
In matrimony sought her,
But at friends and foes she cocked her nose,
Did this pretty Ratcatcher's daughter.
For there was a man cried 'Lily white Sand',
Who in Cupid's net had caught her,
And over head and ears in love,
Was the pretty Ratcatcher's daughter.

Now 'Lily white Sand' so ran in her head,
When coming down the Strand, oh,
She forgot that she'd got sprats on her head,
And cried, 'Buy my Lily white Sand, oh!'
The folks, amazed, all thought her crazed
All along the Strand, oh,
To hear a girl with sprats on her head,
Cry, 'Buy my Lily white Sand, oh!'

The Ratcatcher's Daughter so ran in his head,
He didn't know what he was arter,
Instead of crying 'Lily white Sand',
He cried 'Do you want any Ratcatcher's daughter?'
His donkey cocked his ears and brayed,
Folks couldn't tell what he was arter,
To hear a lily white sand man cry,
'Do you want any Ratcatcher's daughter?'

Now they both agreed to married be
Upon next Easter Sunday,
But the Ratcatcher's daughter had a dream
· That she shouldn't be alive next Monday.
To buy some sprats once more she went,
And tumbled into the water,
Went down to the bottom all covered with mud,
Did the pretty Ratcatcher's daughter.

When Lily white Sand he heard the news,
His eyes ran down with water,
Says he in love I'll constant prove,
And, blow me if I live long arter,
So he cut his throat with a piece of glass,
And stabbed his donkey arter,
So there was an end of Lily white Sand,
His ass, and the Ratcatcher's daughter.

THE BELLS OF SHANDON

With deep affection
And recollection
I often think of
   Those Shandon bells,
Whose sound so wild would
In the days of childhood
Fling round my cradle
   Their magic spells.
On this I ponder
Where'er I wander,
And thus grow fonder,
   Sweet Cork, of thee;
With thy bells of Shandon,
That sound so grand on
The pleasant waters
   Of the river Lee.

I've heard bells chiming
Full many a clime in,
Tolling sublime in
   Cathedral shrine,
While at a glib rate
Brass tongues would vibrate –
But all their music
   Spoke naught like thine;
For memory dwelling
On each proud swelling
Of the belfry knelling
   Its bold notes free,
Made the bells of Shandon
Sound far more grand on
The pleasant waters
   Of the river Lee.

I've heard bells tolling
Old Adrian's Mole in,
Their thunder rolling
   From the Vatican,
And cymbals glorious
Swinging uproarious
In the gorgeous turrets
   Of Notre Dame

But thy sounds were sweeter
Than the dome of Peter
Flings o'er the Tiber,
   Pealing solemnly; –
O! the bells of Shandon
Sound far more grand on
The pleasant waters
   Of the river Lee.

There's a bell in Moscow,
While on tower and kiosk, O!
In Saint Sophia
   The Turkman gets,
And loud in air
Calls men to prayer
From the tapering summit
   Of tall minarets.
Such empty phantom
I freely grant them;
But there is an anthem
   More dear to me –
'Tis the bells of Shandon
That sound so grand on
The pleasant waters
   Of the river Lee.

Francis Sylvester Mahony

BUTTERED PIPPIN-PIES

*The Author loving these homely meats specially, viz.: cream, pan-
cakes, butter'd pippin-pies (laugh, good people) and tobacco, writ to
that worthy and virtuous gentlewoman whom he calls mistress, as
followeth:*

If there were, oh! an Hellespont of cream
Between us (milk-white mistress), I would swim
To you, to show to both my love's extreme,
Leander-like – yea, dive from brim to brim.
But met I with a buttered pippin-pie
Floating upon 't, that would I make my boat
To waft me to you without jeopardy,
Though sea-sick I might be while it did float.

Yet if a storm should rise (by night or day)
Of sugar-snows and hail of care-a-ways,
Then, if I found a pancake in my way,
It (like a plank) should bring me to your kays;
   Which having found, if they tobacco kept,
   The smoke should dry me well before I slept.

John Davies of Hereford

A RIDDLE

'Twas in heaven pronounced, and 'twas muttered in hell,
And echo caught faintly the sound as it fell;
On the confines of earth 'twas permitted to rest,
And the depths of the ocean its presence confest.
'Twill be found in the sphere, when 'tis riven asunder,
Be seen in the lightning, and heard in the thunder.
'Twas allotted to man with his earliest breath,
Attends at his birth, and awaits him in death,
Presides o'er his happiness, honour, and health,
Is the prop of his house, and the end of his wealth.
In the heaps of the miser 'tis hoarded with care,
But is sure to be lost on the prodigal heir.
It begins every hope, every wish it must bound,
With the husbandman toils, and with monarchs is crown'd.
Without it the soldier, the seaman may roam,
But woe to the wretch who expels it from home!
In the whispers of conscience its voice will be found,
Not e'en in the whirlpool of passion be drown'd.
'Twill not soften the heart; but though deaf be the ear,
It will make it acutely and instantly hear.
Yet in shade let it rest like a delicate flower,
Ah, breathe on it softly — it dies in an hour.

(The letter H)

Catherine Maria Fanshawe

3. APRIL AND MAY

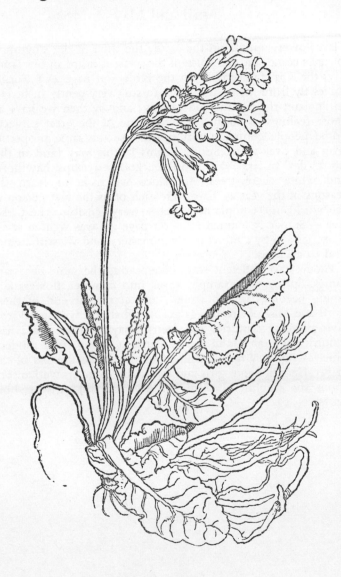

April and May

'The flowers appear on the earth; the time of the singing of birds is come, and the voice of the turtle is heard in our land,' says the *Song of Solomon*, from the Bible (on page 43). Turtle-doves fly from Africa and begin to sing very gently in hedges in England right at the end of May; and by then we have all those feelings of Spring, which is one of the great subjects. Some people complain that poems use the same properties over and over again. Spring poems in this way (and in this book) deal in larks, dew, April, cuckoos, cowslips, hawthorn, and white cherry-trees. But since we have to learn the seasons of the year as if we were each of us the first person in the world, the complaint is not so very sensible. The *Cuckoo Song* — 'Sumer is icumen in' — on page 48 was written seven centuries ago by a monk in his monastery, and we still are not deaf to cuckoos.

Poems have different ways of repeating the same necessary things. Spring, for example, turns into summer, flowers fail, young becomes not so young; and at the far end of these April and May poems this is exactly what you will find Virgil saying twenty centuries ago, Herrick saying three and a half centuries ago, and John Crowe Ransom saying from modern America. Only Virgil says it about the white flowers of the privet, Herrick about girls and roses, and John Crowe Ransom about the singing bluebirds of America and girls in blue skirts.

HAIL, BISHOP VALENTINE

(On St Valentine's Day, February 14th, the birds choose their mates)

Hail, Bishop Valentine, whose day this is,
    All the air is thy diocese,
    And all the chirping choristers
And other birds are thy parishioners;
      Thou marriest every year
The lyric Lark, and the grave whispering Dove,
The sparrow that neglects his life for love,
The household Bird, with the red stomacher;
    Thou mak'st the Blackbird speed as soon
As doth the Goldfinch, or the Halcyon;
The husband cock looks out, and straight is sped,
And meets his wife, which brings her feather-bed.
This day more cheerfully than ever shine,
This day, which might enflame thy self, Old Valentine . .

John Donne

SPRING

Pleasure it is
    To hear, iwis,
    The birdës sing.
The deer in the dale,
The sheep in the vale,
    The corn springing;
God's purveyance
For sustenance
    It is for man.
Then we always
To give him praise,
    And thank him than,
    And thank him than.

William Cornish

iwis: *indeed*; than: *then*

THE MAIDEN MAKELES

I syng of a myden   that is makeles,
Kyng of alle kynges   to here sone che ches.

He cam also stylle   ther his moder was
As dew in aprylle,   that fallyt on the gras.

He cam also stylle   to his moderes bowr
As dew in aprille,   that fallyt on the flour.

He cam also stylle   ther his moder lay
As dew in aprille,   that fallyt on the spray.

Moder and mayden   was never non but che —
Wel may swych a lady   godès moder be

makeles: *matchless*; che ches: *she chose*; also: *as*

HOW DO YOU DO?

Misty-moisty was the morn,
   Chilly was the weather;
There I met an old man
   Dressed all in leather,

Dressed all in leather
   Against the wind and rain,
With 'how do you do?' and 'how do you do?'
   And 'how do you do?' again.

THE MILL

Two leaps the water from its race
   Made to the brook below,
The first leap it was curving glass,
   The second bounding snow.

William Allingham

LO! HERE THE GENTLE LARK

Lo! here the gentle lark, weary of rest,
   From his moist cabinet mounts up on high,
And wakes the morning, from whose silver breast

40

The sun ariseth in his majesty;
  Who doth the world so gloriously behold,
  That cedar-tops and hills seem burnished gold . . .

William Shakespeare

THE LARK IN THE MORNING

As I was a-walking
One morning in spring,
I heard a pretty ploughboy,
And so sweetly he did sing:
And as he was a-singing O
These words I heard him say:
'There's no life like the ploughboy's
In the sweet month of May.'

There's the lark in the morning
She will rise up from her nest,
And she'll mount the white air
With the dew on all her breast,
And with this pretty ploughboy O,
She'll whistle and she'll sain,
And at night she'll return
To her nest back again.

she'll sain: she'll sing

THE LARK NOW LEAVES HIS WAT'RY NEST

The lark now leaves his wat'ry nest
  And climbing, shakes his dewy wings;
He takes this window for the east;
  And to implore your light, he sings:
Awake, awake, the morn will never rise,
Till she can dress her beauty at your eyes.

The merchant bows unto the seaman's star,
  The ploughman from the sun his season takes;
But still the lover wonders what they are,
  Who look for day before his mistress wakes.
Awake, awake, break through your veils of lawn!
Then draw your curtains, and begin the dawn.

Sir William Davenant

WHEN DAFFODILS BEGIN TO PEER

When daffodils begin to peer,
  With heigh! the doxy, over the dale,
Why, then comes in the sweet o' the year;
  For the red blood reigns in the winter's pale.

The white sheet bleaching on the hedge,
  With heigh! the sweet birds, O, how they sing!
Doth set my pugging tooth on edge,
  For a quart of ale is a dish for a king.

The lark, that tirra-lirra chants,
  With heigh! with heigh! the thrush and the jay,
Are summer songs for me and my aunts,
  While we lie tumbling in the hay.

William Shakespeare

ON A BIRTHDAY

Friend of Ronsard, Nashe, and Beaumont,
Lark of Ulster, Meath, and Thomond,
Heard from Smyrna and Sahara
To the surf of Connemara,
Lark of April, June, and May,
Sing loudly this my Lady-day.

J. M. Synge

I AM THE ROSE OF SHARON

I am the rose of Sharon, and the lily of the valleys. As the lily among thorns, so is my love among the daughters.

As the apple tree among the trees of the wood, so is my beloved among the sons. I sat down under his shadow with great delight, and his fruit was sweet to my taste. He brought me to the banqueting house, and his banner over me was love.

Stay me with flagons, comfort me with apples, for I am sick of love. His left hand is under my head, and his right hand doth embrace me. I charge you, O ye daughters of Jerusalem, by the roes, and by the hinds of the field, that ye stir not up, nor awake my love, till he please.

The voice of my beloved! behold, he cometh leaping upon the mountains, skipping upon the hills. My beloved is like a roe or a young hart: behold, he standeth behind our wall, he looketh forth at the windows, shewing himself through the lattice.

My beloved spake, and said unto me, Rise up, my love, my fair one, and come away. For, lo, the winter is past, the rain is over and gone. The flowers appear on the earth; the time of the singing of birds is come, and the voice of the turtle is heard in our land. The fig tree putteth forth her green figs, and the vines with the tender grape give a good smell. Arise, my love, my fair one, and come away.

O my dove that art in the clefts of the rock, in the secret places of the stairs, let me see thy countenance, let me hear thy voice; for sweet is thy voice, and thy countenance is comely. Take us the foxes, the little foxes, that spoil the vines: for our vines have tender grapes.

My beloved is mine, and I am his: he feedeth among the lilies. Until the day break, and the shadows flee away, turn, my beloved, and be thou like a roe or a young hart upon the mountains of Bether . . .

The Song of Solomon

BY A CHAPEL AS I CAME

Merry it is in May morning
Merry ways for to gonne

And by a chapel as I came
Met I white Jesu to churchward gone,
Peter and Paul, Thomas and John,
And his disciples everyone.
            Merry it is.

Saint Thomas the bells gane ring,
And Saint Collas the mass gane sing,
Saint John took that sweet offering,
And by a chapel as I came.
            Merry it is.

Our Lord offered what he wolde,
A chalice all of rich red golde;
Our Lady the crown off her mowld,
The son out of her bosom shone.
            Merry it is.

Saint George that is our Lady knight,
He tended the tapers fair and bright,
To mine eye a seemly sight,
And by a chapel as I came.
                    Merry it is.

        mowld: *head*

THE PADSTOW NIGHT SONG
(for *May Day*)

Unite, unite, let us all unite,
For Summer is a-come unto day
And whither we are going we will all unite
  On the merry morning of May.

The young men of Padstow, they might if they would,
For Summer is a-come unto day.
They might have built a ship and gilded her with gold,
  On the merry morning of May.

The maidens of Padstow, they might if they would,
For Summer is a-come unto day.
They might have made a garland of the white rose and the red
  On the merry morning of May.

Up Merry Spring, and up the merry ring,
For Summer is a-come unto day!
How happy are those little birds that merrily do sing
  On the merry morning of May!

THE MONTH OF MAY

London, to thee I do present the merry Month of May,
Let each true subject be content to hear me what I say:
For from the top of conduit head, as plainly may appear,
I will both tell my name to you, and wherefore I came here.
My name is Rafe, by due descent, though not ignoble I,
Yet far inferior to the stock of gracious Grocery.
And by the Common Council of my fellows in the Strand,
With gilded staff, and crossed scarf, the May Lord here I stand.

Rejoice, O English hearts! Rejoice, rejoice, O lovers dear!
Rejoice, O City, Town, and Country, rejoice eke every Shire!
For now the fragrant flowers do spring and sprout in seemly sort,
The little birds do sit and sing, the lambs do make fine sport,

44

And now the birchen tree doth bud that makes the schoolboy
    cry,
The morris rings while hobby-horse doth foot it featuously:
The lords and ladies now abroad for their disport and play,
Do kiss sometimes upon the grass, and sometimes in the hay,
Now butter with a leaf of sage is good to purge the blood,
Fly Venus and Phlebotomy, for they are neither good.
Now little fish on tender stone, begin to cast their bellies,
And sluggish snails, that erst were mute, do creep out of their
    shellies,
The rumbling rivers now do warm for little boys to paddle,
The sturdy steed now goes to grass, and up they hang his
    saddle.
The heavy hart, the blowing buck, the rascal and the pricket,
Are now among the yeoman's peas, and leave the fearful
    thicket.
And be like them, O you, I say, of this same noble town,
And lift aloft your velvet heads, and slipping off your gown,
With bells on legs, and napkins clean unto your shoulders tied,
With scarfs and garters as you please, and Hey for our town
    cried:
March out and shew your willing minds, by twenty, and by
    twenty,
To Hogdon or to Newington, where ale and cakes are plenty.
And let it ne'er be said for shame, that we the youths of London
Lay thrumming of our caps at home, and left our custom
    undone.

Up then, I say, both young and old, both man and maid a-
    maying
With drums and guns that bounce aloud, and merry tabor
    playing;
Which to prolong, God save our King, and send his country
    peace,
And root out treason from the land, and so, my friends, I
    cease . . .

                        John Fletcher and Francis Beaumont

FROM YOU HAVE I BEEN ABSENT
IN THE SPRING

From you have I been absent in the spring,
   When proud pied April, dressed in all his trim,
Hath put a spirit of youth in every thing,
   That heavy Saturn laughed and leaped with him.
Yet nor the lays of birds, nor the sweet smell
   Of different flowers in odour and in hue,
Could make me any summer's story tell,
   Or from their proud lap pluck them where they grew:
Nor did I wonder at the lily's white,
   Nor praise the deep vermilion in the rose;
They were but sweet, but figures of delight,
   Drawn after you, you pattern of all those.
     Yet seemed it winter still, and, you away,
     As with your shadow I with these did play.

William Shakespeare

THE HAWTHORN

Of everykunė tre –
  Of everykunė tre –
The hawethorn blowet suotes
  Of everykunė tre.

My lemmon she shal be –
  My lemmon she shal be –
The fairest of erthkinne
  My lemmon she shal be.

everykune: *every kind of*; suotes: *sweetest*; lemmon: *lover*

O WERE MY LOVE YON LILAC FAIR

O were my love yon lilac fair,
  Wi' purple blossoms to the spring;
And I, a bird to shelter there,
  When wearied on my little wing!

How I wad mourn, when it was torn
  By autumn wild, and winter rude!
But I wad sing on wanton wing,
  When youthfu' May its bloom renew'd.

O gin my love were yon red rose
  That grows upon the castle wa',
And I mysel' a drap o' dew,
  Into her bonnie breast to fa'!

O there, beyond expression blest,
  I'd feast on beauty a' the night;
Seal'd on her silk-saft faulds to rest,
  Till fley'd awa' by Phoebus light.

Robert Burns

SPRING GOETH ALL IN WHITE

Spring goeth all in white,
Crowned with milk-white may:
In fleecy flocks of light
O'er heaven the white clouds stray:

  White butterflies in the air;
White daisies prank the ground:
The cherry and hoary pear
Scatter their snow around.

Robert Bridges

LOVELIEST OF TREES, THE CHERRY NOW

Loveliest of trees, the cherry now
Is hung with bloom along the bough,
And stands about the woodland ride
Wearing white for Eastertide.

Now, of my threescore years and ten,
Twenty will not come again,
And take from seventy springs a score,
It only leaves me fifty more.

And since to look at things in bloom
Fifty springs are little room,
About the woodlands I will go
To see the cherry hung with snow.

A. E. Housman

THE HOLLOW LAND

Christ keep the Hollow Land
  Through the sweet spring-tide,
When the apple-blossoms bless
  The lowly bent hill side.

Christ keep the Hollow Land
  All the summer-tide;
Still we cannot understand
  Where the waters glide;

Only dimly seeing them
  Coldly slipping through
Many green-lipp'd cavern mouths,
  Where the hills are blue.

William Morris

THE CUCKOO SONG

Sumer is icumen in,
Lhudė sing cuccu!
Groweth sed and bloweth med
And springeth the wodė nu.
Sing cuccu!

Awė bleteth after lomb,
Lhouth after calve cu,
Bulluc sterteth, bucke verteth.
Murie sing cuccu!
Cuccu, cuccu,
Wel singės thu cuccu.
Ne swik thu naver nu!

Sing cuccu nu, Sing cuccu!
Sing cuccu,
Sing cuccu nu!

nu: now; ne swik thu naver nu: *never cease now*

MAY

Mother o'blossoms, and ov all
That's feäir a-vield vrom Spring till Fall,
The gookoo over white-weäv'd seas
Do come to zing in thy green trees . . .

William Barnes

JOG ON, JOG ON

Jog on, jog on, the footpath way,
   And merrily hent the stile-a;
A merry heart goes all the day,
   And your sad heart tires in a mile-a.

Your paltry money-bags of gold
   What need have we to stare for?
When little or nothing soon is told,
   And we have the less to care for.

Cast away care, let sorrow cease,
   A fig for melancholy;
Let's laugh and sing, or, if you please,
   We'll frolic with sweet Dolly.

hent: *take*

THE CUCKOO

The cuckoo's a bonny bird,
   He sings as he flies;
He brings us good tidings;
   He tells us no lies.

He drinks the cold water,
   To keep his voice clear;
And he'll come again
   In the spring of the year.

CUCKOO

Cuckoo, cuckoo!
Is it thy double note I hear
Now far away, now near,
   Now soft, now clear,
     Cuckoo?

Cuckoo, cuckoo!
Laughs now through the spring's misty wood
And leaf-winged sap in flood
   Thy mocking mood,
     Cuckoo?

Cuckoo, cuckoo!
So sits among sky-tangling trees
Our Mephistopheles
Singing at ease,
Cuckoo.

Begone, cuckoo!
For soon thy bubble-note twin-born,
Pricked by the June rose-thorn,
Shall burst in scorn,
Cuckoo.

Andrew Young

CUCKOOS

When coltsfoot withers and begins to wear
Long silver locks instead of golden hair,
And fat red catkins from black poplars fall
And on the ground like caterpillars crawl,
And bracken lifts up slender arms and wrists
And stretches them, unfolding sleepy fists,
The cuckoos in a few well-chosen words
Tell they give Easter eggs to the small birds.

Andrew Young

WHITE PRIMIT FALLS

Trust not too much, fair youth, unto thy feature,
Be not enamoured of thy blushing hue;
Be gamesome whilst thou art a goodly creature,
The flowers will fade that in thy garden grew:
Sweet violets are gathered in their spring,
White primit falls withouten pitying.

(After Virgil)

primit: primprint or privet

I CALL AND I CALL

I call, I call. Who do ye call?
The maids to catch this cowslip-ball:
But since these cowslips fading be,
Troth, leave the flowers, and maids, take me.
Yet, if that neither you will do,
Speak but the word, and I'll take you.

Robert Herrick

Gather ye rose-buds while ye may,
  Old Time is still a-flying:
And this same flower that smiles to-day,
  To-morrow will be dying.

The glorious lamp of heaven, the Sun,
  The higher he's a-getting,
The sooner will his race be run,
  And nearer he's to setting.

That age is best, which is the first,
  When youth and blood are warmer;
But being spent, the worse, and worst
  Times, still succeed the former.

Then be not coy, but use your time;
  And while ye may, go marry:
For having lost but once your prime,
  You may for ever tarry.

Robert Herrick

BLUE GIRLS

Twirling your blue skirts, travelling the sward
Under the towers of your seminary,
Go listen to your teachers old and contrary
Without believing a word.

Tie the white fillets then about your hair
And think no more of what will come to pass
Than bluebirds that go walking on the grass
And chattering on the air.

Practise your beauty, blue girls, before it fail;
And I will cry with my loud lips and publish
Beauty which all our power shall never establish,
It is so frail.

For I could tell you a story which is true;
I know a lady with a terrible tongue,
Blear eyes fallen from blue,
All her perfections tarnished — yet it is not long
Since she was lovelier than any of you.

John Crowe Ransom

FRESH SPRING, THE HERALD OF LOVE'S
MIGHTY KING

Fresh Spring, the herald of love's mighty king,
In whose coat-armour richly are displayed
All sorts of flowers the which on earth do spring,
In goodly colours gloriously arrayed;
Go to my love, where she is careless laid,
Yet in her winter's bower not well awake;
Tell her the joyous time will not be stayed,
Unless she do him by the forelock take;
Bid her therefore her self soon ready make,
To wait on Love amongst his lovely crew;
Where every one, that misseth then her make,
Shall be by him amearst with penance due.
   Make haste, therefore, sweet love, whilst it is prime;
   For none can call again the passèd time.

Edmund Spenser

make: *mate*; amearst: *punished with a fine*

4. AMO, AMAS

Amo, Amas

The rather worldly young prince in Perrault's fairy-tales pushes aside the brambles and finds his Sleeping Beauty very fast asleep inside them, yet extremely beautiful and young – since Love is always freshness, though the scene is always old (if you come to think about it).

Then he kisses her. She wakes up, and is so lovely (which really means, or used to mean, 'fit to be loved') that the prince does not tell her about the clothes she is wearing, that they remind him of his grandmother, as you might expect, since they are a hundred years out of fashion. Words change as well, and even more our fashions of using them; but the waking beauties you encounter inside the love poems don't change at all.

Love goes far beyond A loving B (read Sir Walter Ralegh on the next page, or John Clare on the page after); but all the same, in all its transformations and elaborations, it is still young, it is still like April and May most of all months of the year, and is still rightly described as joy in excess. Here is what John Clare has to say of love and a spring morning:

> Among the mossy oaks now coos the dove
> And the hoarse crow finds softer notes for love.
> The foxes play around their dens, and bark
> In joy's excess, 'mid woodland shadows dark.
> The flowers join lips below, the leaves above;
> And every sound that meets the air is Love.

THIS SPRING OF LOVE

O, how this spring of love resembleth
  The uncertain glory of an April day,
Which now shows all the beauty of the sun,
  And by and by a cloud takes all away! . . .

William Shakespeare

AS YOU CAME FROM THE HOLY LAND

As you came from the holy land
    Of Walsinghame,
Met you not with my true love,
    By the way as you came?

How shall I know your true love
    That have met many one
As I went to the holy land,
    That have come, that have gone?

She is neither white nor brown,
    But as the heavens fair,
There is none hath a form so divine
    In the earth or the air.

Such an one did I meet, good Sir,
    Such an angelic face,
Who like a queen, like a nymph, did appear
    By her gait, by her grace.

She hath left me here all alone,
    All alone as unknown,
Who sometimes did me lead with herself,
    And me loved as her own.

What's the cause that she leaves you alone
    And a new way doth take,
Who loved you once as her own
    And her joy did you make?

I have loved her all my youth,
  But now old, as you see,
Love likes not the falling fruit
  From the withered tree.

Know that love is a careless child
  And forgets promise past,
He is blind, he is deaf when he list,
  And in faith never fast.

His desire is a dureless content
  And a trustless joy,
He is won with a world of despair
  And is lost with a toy.

Of womenkind such indeed is the love,
  Or the word Love abused,
Under which many childish desires
  And conceits are excused.

But true Love is a durable fire
  In the mind ever burning;
Never sick, never old, never dead,
  From itself never turning.

Sir Walter Ralegh

LOVE

Connection largely conjecture - "In some form it certainly existed before Ralegh"

  Love lives beyond
The tomb, the earth, which fades like dew —
  I love the fond,
The faithful, and the true.

  Loves lies in sleep,
The happiness of healthy dreams,
  Eve's dews may weep,
But love delightful seems.

  'Tis seen in flowers,
And in the even's pearly dew,
  On earth's green hours,
And in the heaven's eternal blue.

  'Tis heard in spring
When light and sunbeams, warm and kind,
  On angel's wing
Brings love and music to the wind.

56

And where is voice
So young and beautifully sweet
As nature's choice,
When spring and lovers meet?

Love lives beyond
The tomb, the earth, the flowers, and dew.
I love the fond,
The faithful, young, and true.

John Clare

TRUE LOVE

My true love hath my heart and I have his,
By just exchange one for another given;
I hold his dear, and mine he cannot miss,
There never was a better bargain driven.
My true love hath my heart and I have his.

His heart in me keeps him and me in one,
My heart in him his thoughts and senses guides;
He loves my heart, for once it was his own,
I cherish his, because in me it bides.
My true love hath my heart and I have his.

Sir Philip Sidney

EVE SPEAKS TO ADAM

With thee conversing I forget all time,
All seasons and their change, all please alike.
Sweet is the breath of morn, her rising sweet,
With charm of earliest birds; pleasant the sun
When first on this delightful land he spreads
His orient beams, on herb, tree, fruit, and flower,
Glistring with dew; fragrant the fertile earth
After soft showers; and sweet the coming on
Of grateful evening mild, then silent night
With this her solemn bird and this fair moon,
And these the gems of heav'n, her starry train:
But neither breath of morn when she ascends
With charm of earliest birds, nor rising sun

On this delightful land, nor herb, fruit, flower,
Glistring with dew, nor fragrance after showers,
Nor grateful evening mild, nor silent night
With this her solemn bird, nor walk by moon,
Or glittering starlight without thee is sweet . . .

John Milton

BALADE

Hyd, Absolon, thy giltè tresses clere;
Ester, ley thou thy meknesse al a-doun;
Hyd, Jonathas, al thy frendly manere;
Penalopee, and Marcia Catoun,
Mak of your wyfhod no comparisoun;
Hyde ye your beautes, Isoude and Eleyne,
Alceste is here, that al that may desteyne.

Thy fairè bodye, lat hit nat appere,
Lavyne; and thou, Lucresse of Rome toun,
And Polixene, that boghtè love so dere,
Eek Cleopatre, with al thy passioun,
Hyde ye your trouthe in love and your renoun;
And thou, Tisbe, that hast for love swich peyne:
Alceste is here, that al that may desteyne.

Herro, Dido, Laudomia, alle in-fere,
Eek Phyllis, hanging for thy Demophoun,
And Canace, espyed by thy chere,
Ysiphile, betrayed with Jasoun,
Mak of your trouthe in love no bost ne soun;
Nor Ypermistre or Adriane, ne pleyne;
Alceste is here, that al that may desteyne.

Geoffrey Chaucer

desteyne: *disdain, look down upon*; in-fere: *together, in company*

QUEENS

Seven dog-days we let pass
Naming Queens in Glenmacnass,
All the rare and royal names
Wormy sheepskin yet retains:
Etain, Helen, Maeve, Fand,
Golden Deirdre's tender hand;
Bert, the big-foot, sung by Villon,

Cassandra, Ronsard found in Lyon,
Queens of Sheba, Meath, and Connaught,
Coifed with crown, or gaudy bonnet;
Queens whose finger once did stir men,
Queens were eaten of fleas and vermin,
Queens men drew like Monna Lisa,
Or slew with drugs in Rome and Pisa.
We named Lucrezia Crivelli,
And Titian's lady with amber belly,
Queens acquainted in learned sin,
Jane of Jewry's slender shin;
Queens who cut the bogs of Glanna,
Judith of Scripture, and Gloriana,
Queens who wasted the East by proxy,
Or drove the ass-cart, a tinker's doxy.
Yet these are rotten — I ask their pardon —
And we've the sun on rock and garden;
These are rotten, so you're the Queen
Of all are living, or have been.

J. M. Synge

CONFESSION

My ghostly fadir, I me confess,
  First to God and then to you
  That at a window (wot ye how)
I stole a kiss of great sweetness,
Which done was out avisiness;
  But it is done, not undone, now —
My ghostly fadir, I me confess,
  First to God and then to you.
But I restore it shall, doubtless,
  Again, if so be that I mow;
  And that, God, I make a vow,
And else I ask forgiveness —
My ghostly fadir, I me confess
  First to God and then to you.

Charles d'Orléans

out: without; avisiness: thought; mow: may

AMO, AMAS

Amo, Amas, I love a lass
As a cedar tall and slender;
Sweet cowslip's grace is her nominative case,
And she's of the feminine gender.

Rorum, Corum, sunt divorum,
Harum, Scarum divo;
Tag-rag, merry-derry, periwig and hat-band
Hic hoc horum genitivo.

Can I decline a Nymph divine?
Her voice as a flute is dulcis.
Her oculus bright, her manus white,
And soft, when I tacto, her pulse is.

Rorum, Corum, sunt divorum,
Harum, Scarum divo;
Tag-rag, merry-derry, periwig and hat-band
Hic hic horum genitivo.

Oh, how bella my puella,
I'll kiss secula seculorum.
If I've luck, sir, she's my uxor,
O dies benedictorum.

Rorum, Corum, sunt divorum,
Harum, Scarum divo;
Tag-rag, merry-derry, periwig and hat-band
Hic hoc horum genitivo.

John O'Keefe

FIRST LOVE

I ne'er was struck before that hour
    With love so sudden and so sweet,
Her face it bloomed like a sweet flower
    And stole my heart away complete.
My face turned pale as deadly pale,
    My legs refused to walk away,
And when she looked, what could I ail?
    My life and all seemed turned to clay.

And then my blood rushed to my face
　　And took my eyesight quite away,
The trees and bushes round the place
　　Seemed midnight at noonday.
I could not see a single thing,
　　Words from my eyes did start —
They spoke as chords do from the string,
　　And blood burnt round my heart.

Are flowers the winter's choice?
　　Is love's bed always snow?
She seemed to hear my silent voice,
　　Not love's appeals to know.
I never saw so sweet a face
　　As that I stood before.
My heart has left its dwelling-place
　　And can return no more.

John Clare

IN YOUTH IS PLEASURE

In a herber green, asleep where as I lay,
The birds sang sweet in the middes of the day;
I dreamed fast of mirth and play:
　　In youth is pleasure, in youth is pleasure.

Methought as I walked still to and fro,
And from her company I could not go;
But when I waked it was not so:
　　In youth is pleasure, in youth is pleasure.

Therefore my heart is surely pight
Of her alone to have a sight,
Which is my joy and heart's delight:
　　In youth is pleasure, in youth is pleasure.

Robert Wever

herber: *arbour*; pight: *determined*

DEVOURING TIME, BLUNT THOU THE LION'S PAWS

Devouring Time, blunt thou the lion's paws,
　　And make the earth devour her own sweet brood;
Pluck the keen teeth from the fierce tiger's jaws,
　　And burn the long-lived phoenix in her blood;

Make glad and sorry seasons as thou fleets,
    And do whate'er thou wilt, swift-footed Time,
To the wide world and all her fading sweets;
    But I forbid thee one most heinous crime:
O! carve not with thy hours my Love's fair brow,
    Nor draw no lines there with thine antique pen;
Him in thy course untainted do allow
    For beauty's pattern to succeeding men.
        Yet, do thy worst, old Time: despite thy wrong,
        My Love shall in my verse ever live young.

                                    William Shakespeare

UPON JULIA'S CLOTHES

When as in silks my Julia goes,
Then, then (me thinks) how sweetly flows
That liquefaction of her clothes!

Next, when I cast mine eyes and see
That brave vibration each way free;
O how that glittering taketh me!

                                    Robert Herrick

GIRLS ON THE YUEH RIVER

Girls on the Yueh river have jade faces,
And dark-skinned foreheads. They wear
Red skirts, and sandals spiked
With gold. And O, as white
As frost their feet!

                                    Li Po

BEAUTY EXTOLLED

Gaze not on swans, in whose soft breast
A full-hatched beauty seems to nest,
Nor snow, which falling from the sky,
Hovers in its virginity.

Gaze not on roses, though new-blown,
Graced with a fresh complexion,
Nor lilies, which no subtle bee
Hath robbed by kissing-chemistry.

Gaze not on that pure Milky Way,
Where night vies splendour with the day,
Nor pearl, whose silver walls confine
The riches of an Indian mine.

For if my Emperess appears,
Swans moulting die, snow melts to tears,
Roses do blush and hang their heads,
Pale lilies shrink into their beds,

The Milky Way rides post to shroud
Its baffled glories in a cloud,
And pearls do climb into her ear,
To hang themselves for envy there.

So have I seen stars big with light
Prove lanterns to the moon-eyed night,
Which when Sol's rays were once displayed,
Sunk in their sockets, and decayed.

Henry Noel (?)

NOW SLEEPS THE CRIMSON PETAL

Now sleeps the crimson petal, now the white;
Nor waves the cypress in the palace walk;
Nor winks the gold fin in the porphyry font:
The fire-fly wakens; waken thou with me.

Now droops the milkwhite peacock like a ghost
And like a ghost she glimmers on to me.

Now lies the Earth all Danaë to the stars,
And all thy heart lies open unto me.

Now slides the silent meteor on, and leaves
A shining furrow, as thy thoughts in me.

Now folds the lily all her sweetness up,
And slips into the bosom of the lake:
So fold thyself, my dearest, thou, and slip
Into my bosom and be lost in me.

Alfred, Lord Tennyson

A RED, RED ROSE

O, my luve is like a red, red rose,
   That's newly sprung in June;
O, my luve is like the melodie
   That's sweetly play'd in tune.

As fair art thou, my bonnie lass,
   So deep in luve am I;
And I will luve thee still, my dear,
   Till a' the seas gang dry.

Till a' the seas gang dry, my dear,
   And the rocks melt wi' the sun:
And I will love thee still, my dear,
   While the sands o' life shall run.

And fare thee weel, my only luve,
   And fare thee weel a while!
And I will come again, my luve,
   Tho' it were ten thousand mile!

Robert Burns

THE SEAMAN'S HAPPY RETURN

When Sol did cast no light,
   Being darkened over,
And the dark time of night
   Did the skies cover,
Running a river by,
   There were ships sailing,
A maid most fair I spied,
   Crying and wailing.

Unto this maid I stept,
   Asking what grieved her,
She answered me and wept,
   Fates had deceived her:
'My love is prest', quoth she,
   'To cross the ocean,
Proud waves do make the ship
   Ever in motion.

'We lov'd seven years and more,
  Both being sure,
But I am left on shore,
  Grief to endure.
He promised back to turn,
  If life was spared him,
With grief I daily mourn,
  Death hath debarred him.'

Straight a brisk lad she spied,
  Made her admire,
A present she received
  Pleased her desire.
'Is my love safe', quoth she,
  'Will he come near me?'
The young man answer made,
  'Virgin, pray hear me:

'Under one banner bright,
  For England's glory,
Your love and I did fight —
  Mark well my story:
By an unhappy shot
  We two were parted;
His death's wound then he got
  Though valiant-hearted.

'All this I witness can,
  For I stood by him,
For courage, I must say,
  None did outvie him:
He still would foremost be,
  Striving for honour;
But Fortune is a whore, —
  Vengeance upon her.

'But ere he was quite dead,
  Or his heart broken,
To me these words he said,
  "Pray give this token
To my love, for there is
  Than she no fairer;
Tell her she must be kind
  And love the bearer."

65

'Entombed he now doth lie,
    In stately manner,
'Cause he fought valiantly
    For love and honour.
The right he had in you,
    To me he gave it:
Now, since it is my due,
    Pray let me have it.'

She raging, fled away,
    Like one distracted,
Not knowing what to say,
    Nor what she acted.
So last she curst her fate,
    And showed her anger,
Saying, 'Friend, you come too late,
    I'll have no stranger.

'To your own house return,
    I am best pleased,
Here for my love to mourn,
    Since he's deceased.
In sable weeds I'll go,
    Let who will jeer me;
Since Death has served me so,
    None shall come near me

'The chaste Penelope
    Mourned for Ulysses.
I have more grief than she,
    Robbed of my blisses.
I'll ne'er love man again,
    Therefore, pray hear me;
I'll slight you with disdain
    If you come near me.

'I know he loved me well,
    For when we parted,
None did in grief excel, —
    Both were true-hearted.
Those promises we made
    Ne'er shall be broken;
Those words that then he said
    Ne'er shall be spoken.'

He, hearing what she said,
  Made his love stronger.
Off his disguise he laid,
  And staid no longer.
When her dear love she knew,
  In wanton fashion
Into his arms she flew, —
  Such is love's passion.

He asked her how she liked
  His counterfeiting,
Whether she was well pleased
  With such like greeting?
'You are well versed,' quoth she,
  'In several speeches:
Could you coin money so,
  You might get riches.

'O happy gale of wind
  That waft thee over,
May heaven preserve that ship
  That brought my lover.'
'Come kiss me now, my sweet,
  True love's no slander;
Thou shalt my Hero be,
  I thy Leander.'

'Dido of Carthage queen
  Loved stout Eneas,
But my true love is found
  More true than he was.
Venus ne'er fonder was
  Of young Adonis,
Than I will be of thee,
  Since thy love her own is.'

Then hand in hand they walk,
  With mirth and pleasure,
They laugh, they kiss, they talk —
  Love knows no measure.
Now both do sit and sing —
  But she sings clearest;
Like nightingale in Spring,
  Welcome my dearest.

O she looked out of the window,
   As white as any milk;
But he looked into the window,
   As black as any silk,

Hulloa, hulloa, hulloa, hulloa, you coal black smith!
   O what is your silly song?
You never shall change my maiden name
   That I have kept so long;
I'd rather die a maid, yes, but then she said,
And be buried all in my grave,
Than I'd have such a nasty, husky, dusky, musty, fusky,
   Coal black smith
      A maiden I will die.

Then she became a duck,
   A duck all on the stream;
And he became a water dog,
   And fetched her back again.
      Hulloa, etc.

Then she became a hare,
   A hare all on the plain;
And he became a greyhound dog,
   And fetched her back again.
      Hulloa, etc.

Then she became a fly,
   A fly all in the air;
And he became a spider,
   And fetched her to his lair.

Hulloa, hulloa, hulloa, hulloa, you coal black smith!
   O what is your silly song?
You never shall change my maiden name
   That I have kept so long;
I'd rather die a maid, yes, but then she said,
And be buried all in my grave,
Than I'd have such a nasty, husky, dusky, musty, fusky,
   Coal black smith
      A maiden I will die.

5. THE GRIEF OF LOVE

The Grief of Love

Then the Grief of Love; for which the image I have chosen is not, for example, the moon by itself in the sky (page 71) –

With how sad steps, O Moon, thou climb'st the skies

– but the proud cold girl in a head-dress, with jewels around her neck. Her likeness was engraved in Florence, one of the five most beautiful cities in the world, about 1450, a time of great delight in women and in flowers. Why have most poems about Love and about the Grief of Love been written by men about girls? Men have written all the poems, at any rate, in this fifth part of *The Cherry-Tree*, except perhaps the Irish ballad of *The Grief of a Girl's Heart*, translated from the Irish by Lady Gregory. Even that may have been written by a man imagining the girl's grief, just as Shakespeare imagined words of grief for Ophelia (page 77) and William Morris for the grief of Jehane du Castel Beau (page 74). Of course, men pursue, women reject. But the real reason for so few love poems by women, is that in past centuries women were given too little education, and escaped too little from home, and could not train themselves into poets. In a thousand English years I think there has been only one great woman poet, Christina Rossetti (who never married and wrote the saddest of love poems, on the corner of her wash-stand, in her bedroom –

> I go alone to my bed,
> Dug deep at the foot and deep at the head,
> Roofed in with a load of lead.)

Things should be different during the next thousand years.

LOVE WITHOUT HOPE

Love without hope, as when the young bird-catcher
Swept off his tall hat to the Squire's own daughter,
So let the imprisoned larks escape and fly
Singing about her head, as she rode by.

Robert Graves

THE ROCK

By a flat rock on the shore of the sea
My dear one spoke to me. Wild thyme
Now grows by the rock,
And a sprig of the rosemary.

From the Welsh of the seventeenth century

WITH HOW SAD STEPS, O MOON

With how sad steps, O Moon, thou climb'st the skies!
How silently, and with how wan a face!
What, may it be that even in heav'nly place
That busy archer his sharp arrows tries!
Sure, if that long-with-love-acquainted eyes
Can judge of love, thou feel'st a lover's case,
I read it in thy looks; thy languisht grace,
To me, that feel the like, thy state descries.
Then, ev'n of fellowship, O Moon, tell me,
Is constant love deem'd there but want of wit?
Are beauties there as proud as here they be?
Do they above love to be lov'd, and yet
Those lovers scorn whom that love doth possess?
Do they call virtue there ungratefulness?

Sir Philip Sidney

THE CAP AND BELLS

The jester walked in the garden:
The garden had fallen still;
He bade his soul rise upward
And stand on her window-sill.

It rose in a straight blue garment,
When owls began to call:
It had grown wise-tongued by thinking
Of a quiet and light footfall;

But the young queen would not listen;
She rose in her pale night-gown;
She drew in the heavy casement
And pushed the latches down.

He bade his heart go out to her,
When the owls called out no more;
In a red and quivering garment
It sang to her through the door.

It had grown sweet-tongued by dreaming
Of a flutter of flower-like hair;
But she took up her fan from the table
And waved it off on the air.

'I have cap and bells', he pondered,
'I will send them to her and die';
And when the morning whitened
He left them where she went by.

She laid them upon her bosom,
Under a cloud of her hair,
And her red lips sang them a love-song
Till the stars grew out of the air.

She opened her door and her window,
And the heart and the soul came through,
To her right hand came the red one,
To her left hand came the blue.

They set up a noise like crickets,
A chattering wise and sweet,
And her hair was a folded flower
And the quiet of love in her feet.

W. B. Yeats

SO SHUTS THE MARIGOLD HER LEAVES

Marina's gone, and now sit I,
  As Philomela (on a thorn,
Turn'd out of nature's livery),
  Mirthless, alone, and all forlorn:

Only she sings not, while my sorrows can
Breathe forth such notes as fit a dying swan.

   So shuts the marigold her leaves
     At the departure of the sun;
   So from the honeysuckle sheaves
     The bee goes when the day is done;
So sits the turtle when she is but one,
And so all woe, as I, since she is gone . . .

William Browne

livery: company

SONG

   How sweet I roam'd from field to field,
     And tasted all the summer's pride,
   Till I the prince of love beheld,
     Who in the sunny beams did glide!

   He shew'd me lilies for my hair,
     And blushing roses for my brow;
   He led me through his gardens fair,
     Where all his golden pleasures grow.

   With sweet May dews my wings were wet,
     And Phoebus fir'd my vocal rage;
   He caught me in his silken net,
     And shut me in his golden cage.

   He loves to sit and hear me sing,
     Then laughing, sports and plays with me;
   Then stretches out my golden wing,
     And mocks my loss of liberty.

William Blake

TO SHADES OF UNDERGROUND

When thou must home to shades of underground,
   And there arrived, a new admired guest,
The beauteous spirits do engirt thee round,
   White Iope, blithe Helen and the rest,
To hear the story of thy finished love
From that smooth tongue, whose music hell can move:

Then wilt thou speak of banqueting delights,
  Of masks and revels which sweet youth did make,
Of tourneys and great challenges of knights,
  And all these triumphs for thy beauty's sake.
When thou hast told these honours done to thee,
Then tell, O! tell, how thou didst murder me.

Thomas Campion

EARLY ONE MORNING

Early one morning, just as the sun was rising,
I heard a maid sing in the valley below:
'Oh, don't deceive me! Oh, never leave me!
How could you use a poor maiden so?

'Remember the vows you made to your Mary,
Remember the bower where you vowed to be true;
Oh, don't deceive me! Oh, never leave me!
How could you use a poor maiden so?

'Oh, gay is the garland, and fresh are the roses
I've culled from the garden to bind on your brow;
Oh, don't deceive me! Oh, never leave me!
How could you use a poor maiden so?'

Thus sang the poor maid, her sorrows bewailing,
Thus sang the poor maiden in the valley below:
'Oh, don't deceive me! Oh, never leave me!
How could you use a poor maiden so?'

THE SONG OF JEHANE DU CASTEL BEAU

Gold wings across the sea!
Grey light from tree to tree,
Gold hair beside my knee,
I pray thee come to me,
Gold wings!
      The water slips,
The red-bill'd moorhen dips.
Sweet kisses on red lips;

74

Alas! the red rust grips,
And the blood-red dagger rips,
Yet, O knight, come to me!

Are not my blue eyes sweet?
The west wind from the wheat
Blows cold across my feet;
Is it not time to meet
Gold wings across the sea?

White swans on the green moat,
Small feathers left afloat
By the blue-painted boat;
Swift running of the stoat;
Sweet gurgling note by note
Of sweet music.
               O gold wings,
Listen how gold hair sings,
And the Ladies' Castle rings,
Gold wings across the sea.

I sit on a purple bed,
Outside, the wall is red,
Thereby the apple hangs,
And the wasp, caught by the fangs,

Dies in the autumn night,
And the bat flits till light,
And the love-crazed knight

Kisses the long wet grass:
The weary days pass, —
Gold wings across the sea!

Gold wings across the sea!
Moonlight from tree to tree,
Sweet hair laid on my knee,
O, sweet knight, come to me!

Gold wings, the short night slips,
The white swan's long neck drips,
I pray thee, kiss my lips,
Gold wings across the sea . . .

William Morris

THE GRIEF OF A GIRL'S HEART

(A West Irish Ballad)

It is late last night the dog was speaking of you; the snipe was speaking of you in her deep marsh. It is you are the lonely bird through the woods; and that you may be without a mate till you find me.

You promised me, and you said a lie to me, that you would be before me where the sheep are flocked; I gave a whistle and three hundred cries to you, and I found nothing there but a bleating lamb.

You promised me a thing that was hard for you, a ship of gold under a silver mast; twelve towns with a market in all of them, and a fine white court by the side of the sea.

You promised me a thing that is not possible, that you would give me gloves of the skin of a fish; that you would give me shoes of the skin of a bird; and a suit of the dearest silk in Ireland . . .

It is early in the morning that I saw him coming, going along the road on the back of a horse; he did not come to me; he made nothing of me; and it is on my way home that I cried my fill.

When I go by myself to the Well of Loneliness, I sit down and I go through my trouble; when I see the world and do not see my boy, he that has an amber shade in his hair.

It was on that Sunday I gave my love to you; the Sunday that is last before Easter Sunday. And myself on my knees reading the Passion; and my two eyes giving love to you for ever . .

My mother said to me not to be talking with you to-day, or to-morrow, or on the Sunday; it was a bad time she took for telling me that; it was shutting the door after the house was robbed.

My heart is as black as the blackness of the sloe, or as the black coal that is on the smith's forge; or as the sole of a shoe left in white halls; it was you that put that darkness over my life.

You have taken the east from me; you have taken the west from me; you have taken what is before me and what is behind me; you have taken the moon, you have taken the sun from me; and my fear is great that you have taken God from me!

(Translated by Lady Gregory)

OPHELIA'S SONG

How should I your true love know
  From another one?
By his cockle hat and staff,
  And his sandal shoon.

He is dead and gone, lady,
  He is dead and gone;
At his head a grass-green turf,
  At his heels a stone.

White his shroud as the mountains snow,
  Larded with sweet flowers;
Which bewept to the grave did go
  With true-love showers.

William Shakespeare

OPHELIA'S DEATH

There is a willow grows aslant a brook,
That shows his hoar leaves in the glassy stream.
There with fantastic garlands did she come
Of crow-flowers, nettles, daisies, and long purples
That liberal shepherds give a grosser name,
But our cold maids do dead men's fingers call them;
There, on the pendent boughs her coronet weeds
Clamb'ring to hang, an envious sliver broke,
When down her weedy trophies and herself
Fell in the weeping brook. Her clothes spread wide,
And, mermaid-like, a while they bore her up;
Which time she chanted snatches of old tunes,
As one incapable of her own distress,
Or like a creature native and indued
Unto that element. But long it could not be
Till that her garments, heavy with their drink,
Pull'd the poor wretch from her melodious lay
To muddy death . . .

William Shakespeare

OPHELIA

i

On still black waters where the stars lie sleeping
  Moves a tall lily – Ophelia floating by;
Slowly she floats couched in her trailing gauzes;
  From woods afar echoes the hind's death-cry.

For more than a thousand years has sad Ophelia
  Passed, a white ghost, on the black river's bier;
For more than a thousand years has her sweet madness
  Murmured her love song in the night-wind's ear.

Fondling her limbs the breeze unfolds long petals
  Of her apparel rocked in its gentle bed;
Over her dreaming brow stoop low the rushes,
  The willows mourn and tremble overhead.

Bruised in her passing, nenuphars sigh round her;
  Sometimes, where leafy boughs on nodding trees
Conceal a nest, she wakes a brief wing-flutter;
  From golden stars drift down strange harmonies.

ii

O pale Ophelia, lovely as the snowflake!
  Child, when you perished in your river-tomb,
It was because bleak winds from Norway's mountains
  Whispered of liberty and its harsh doom.

Because an unknown breath, stirring your tresses,
  Brought tidings to your soul of curious things;
Because your heart heard Nature round you speaking
  In leaves of trees and night's soft murmurings.

Because your breast, too sweetly kind, too youthful,
  Was bruised by the mighty heaving of the sea;
Because a handsome prince one April mutely
  Rested his pale crazed head against your knee.

Heaven, love, liberty! Witless, unhappy fancies!
  You sank into them as snow in the fire's red blaze;
Your speech was strangled by your majestic visions,
  And the dread Infinite lured your innocent gaze.

And the poet sings how you seek by night your garlands,
The flowers you plucked under the starry sky;
How he has seen, couched in her trailing gauzes,
A tall white lily — Ophelia floating by.

Arthur Rimbaud (translated by Brian Hill)

BALLAD OF ANOTHER OPHELIA

O the green glimmer of apples in the orchard,
Lamps in a wash of rain!
O the wet walk of my brown hen through the stackyard!
O tears on the window-pane!

Nothing now will ripen the bright green apples
Full of disappointment and of rain;
Blackish they will taste, of tears, when the yellow dapples
Of autumn tell the withered tale again.

All round the yard it is cluck! my brown hen.
Cluck! and the rain-wet wings;
Cluck! my marigold bird, and again
Cluck! for your yellow darlings.

For a grey cat found the gold thirteen
Huddled away in the dark.
Flutter for a moment, oh, the beast is quick and keen,
Extinct one yellow-fluffy spark!

Once I had a lover bright like running water,
Once his face was open like the sky,
Once like the sky looking down in all its laughter
On the buttercups, and the buttercups was I.

What then is there hidden in the skirts of all the blossom?
What is peeping from your skirts, O mother hen?
'Tis the sun that asks the question, in a lovely haste for
    wisdom;
What a lovely haste for wisdom is in men!

Yea, but it is cruel when undressed is all the blossom
And her shift is lying white upon the floor,
That a grey one, like a shadow, like a rat, a thief, a rainstorm
Creeps upon her then and ravishes her store!

O the grey garner that is full of half-grown apples!
O the golden sparkles laid extinct!
And O, behind the cloud-leaves, like yellow autumn dapples,
Did you see the wicked sun that winked?

D. H. Lawrence

THE YEW-TREE

What happiness you gave to me
Underneath this graveyard tree
When in my embraces wound,
Dear heart, you lay above the ground.

From the seventeenth-century Welsh

MY SILKS AND FINE ARRAY

My silks and fine array,
  My smiles and languish'd air,
By love are driv'n away;
  And mournful lean Despair
Brings me yew to deck my grave:
Such end true lovers have.

His face is fair and heav'n,
  When springing buds unfold;
O why to him was't giv'n,
  Whose heart is wintry cold?
His breast is love's all worship'd tomb,
Where all love's pilgrims come.

Bring me an axe and spade,
  Bring me a winding sheet;
When I my grave have made,
  Let winds and tempests beat:
Then down I'll lie, as cold as clay.
True love doth pass away!

William Blake

STAND CLOSE AROUND

Stand close around, ye Stygian set,
  With Dirce in one boat convey'd,
Or Charon, seeing, may forget
  That he is old, and she a shade.

Walter Savage Landor

6. A BUNCH OF SONGS

A Bunch of Songs

Orpheus made songs and sang them to his own music, as you see him doing in the woodcut for this section. The Muses taught him, and the animals forgot their wild nature and listened to him, the birds flew to hear him, waterfalls stopped, forests and rocks came up to him, and storms died down.

> Orpheus with his lute made trees,
> And the mountain tops that freeze,
> Bow themselves when he did sing.
> To his music plants and flowers
> Ever sprung; as sun and showers
> There had made a lasting spring.
> Everything that heard him play,
> Even the billows of the sea,
> Hung their heads, and then lay by.
> In sweet music is such art,
> Killing care and grief of heart
> Fall asleep, or hearing die.
>
> (John Fletcher)

For music and poems, or for songs, only death is at last too powerful, and that is what Orpheus discovered when he sang and played his way into Hell in search of his dead wife Eurydice. He played such exquisite tunes that even the King and Queen of Hell wept and allowed Eurydice to leave again for the pleasures of Earth, but on condition that he did not look back at her on the upward journey. But he did, and Eurydice, still drowsy with death, had to go back down the twilit cave.

When Orpheus himself died, torn to pieces by the savage women of Dionysus, the Muses collected the scraps of his body and buried them, and nightingales sang over them at night; and the Muses turned his lyre (in the woodcut, which was made for a book of poems in Florence about 1500, it is not a lyre but a viol, which he is playing to the animals) into a constellation. This is the constellation Lyra, which is overhead in the summer and which you can tell by its very bright and clear star, Vega.

For John Milton on the murder of Orpheus, turn to page 464.

ADAM LAY I-BOWNDYN

Adam lay i-bowndyn, bowndyn in a bond,
Fowre thowsand wynter thowt he not to long;
And al was for an appil, an appil that he tok,
As clerkis fyndyn wretyn in here book.

Ne hadde the appil take ben, the appil taken ben,
Ne hadde never our Lady a ben hevene qwen;
Blyssid be the tyme that appil take was,
Ther-fore we mown syngyn *Deo Gratias*!

clerkis: *clergy*; here: *their*; ne hadde: *had not*; mown: *may*

HEY NONNY NO!

Hey nonny no!
Men are fools that wish to die!
Is't not fine to dance and sing
When the bells of death do ring?
Is't not fine to swim in wine,
And turn upon the toe
And sing hey nonny no,
When the winds do blow,
And the seas do flow?
Hey nonny no!

A HEALTH UNTO HIS MAJESTY

Here's a health unto His Majesty,
With a fa, la, la, la, la, la, la,
Confusion to his enemies,
With a fa, la, la, la, la, la, la;
And he that will not drink his health,
I wish him neither wit nor wealth,
Nor yet a rope to hang himself,
With a fa, la, la, la, la, la, la, la, la, la,
With a fa, la, la, la, la, la, la.

Jeremy Savile

'Her savour is neither warm nor sweet;
It's close for two in a winding-sheet,
And lice are too good for worms to eat;
So here's no place for me.'

The louse made off unhappy and wet –
Ahumm, Ahumm, Ahee; –
He's looking for us, the little pet;
So haste, for her chin's to tie up yet,
And let us be gone with what we can get –
Her ring for thee, her gown for Bet,
Her pocket turned out for me.

Gordon Bottomley

CRAIGBILLY FAIR

As I went up to Craigbilly Fair,
Who did I meet but a jolly beggar,
And the name of this beggar they callèd him Rover,
And the name of his wife it was Kitty-lie-over;
There was Rover and Rover and Kitty-lie-over,
There was Rooney and Mooney,
And Nancy and Francey,
And Lily and Billy,
And Jamie and Joe;
And away went the beggar-men all in a row.

Again I went up to Craigbilly Fair,
And who should I meet but another beggar,
And this beggar's name they callèd him Rallax,
And the name of his wife it was Ould Madam Ball-o'-Wax;
There was Rallax and Rallax and Ould Madam Ball-o'-Wax,
There was Rover and Rover and Kitty-lie-over,
There was Rooney and Mooney,
And Nancy and Francey,
And Lily and Billy,
And Jamie and Joe;
And away went the beggar-men all in a row.

Again I went up to Craigbilly Fair,
And who should I meet but another beggar,
And the name of this beggar they callèd him Dick,
And the name of his wife it was Ould Lady Splooterstick,
There was Dick and Dick and Ould Lady Splooterstick,

There was Rallax and Rallax and Ould Madam Ball-o'-Wax,
There was Rover and Rover and Kitty-lie-over,
There was Rooney and Mooney,
And Nancy and Francey,
And Lily and Billy,
And Jamie and Joe;
And away went the beggar-men all in a row.

YANKEE DOODLE

Yankee Doodle went to town,
He rode a little pony,
He stuck a feather in his hat
And called it macaroni.

Yankee Doodle fa, so, la,
Yankee Doodle dandy.
Yankee Doodle fa, so, la,
Buttermilk and brandy,

Yankee Doodle went to town
To buy a pair of trousers,
He swore he could not see the town
For so many houses.

Yankee Doodle fa, so, la,
Yankee Doodle dandy.
Yankee Doodle fa, so, la,
Buttermilk and brandy.

WE BE SOLDIERS THREE

We be soldiers three,
Pardona moy, je vous an pree,
Lately come forth of the Low Country,
With never a penny of money.

Here, good fellow, I drink to thee,
Pardona moy, je vous an pree,
To all good fellows, wherever they be,
With never a penny of money.

And he that will not pledge me thus,
Pardona moy, je vous an pree,
Pays for the shot, whatever it is,
With never a penny of money.

Charge it again, boy, charge it again,
Pardona moy, je vous an pree,
As long as there is any ink in thy pen,
With never a penny of money.

OH LUCKY JIM!

Jim and I as children played together,
Best of friends for many years were we
I, alas! had no luck, was a Jonah,
Jim, my chum, was lucky as could be.
Oh lucky Jim, how I envy him!

Years passed by, still Jim and I were comrades.
He and I both loved the same sweet maid.
She loved Jim, and married him one evening.
Jim was lucky, I unlucky stayed.
Oh lucky Jim, how I envy him!

Years rolled on, and death took Jim away, boys,
Left his widow, and she married me.
Now we're married, oft I think of Jim, boys,
Sleeping in the churchyard, peacefully.
Oh lucky Jim, how I envy him!

JACK THE PIPER

As I was going up the hill
I met with Jack the Piper,
And all the tunes that he could play
Was 'Tie up your petticoats tighter.'

I tied them once, I tied them twice,
I tied them three times over,
And all the songs that he could sing
Was 'Carry me safe to Dover.'

MAZILLA AND MAZURA

Have you any gooseberry wine,
Gooseberry wine, gooseberry wine,
Have you any gooseberry wine,
Mazilla and Mazura?

Yes, we have some gooseberry wine,
Gooseberry wine, gooseberry wine,
Yes, we have some gooseberry wine,
Mazilla and Mazura.

Will you lend me a quart of it,
Quart of it, quart of it,
Will you lend me a quart of it,
Mazilla and Mazura?

POURQUOI YOU GREASED

O Jean Baptiste, pourquoi,
O Jean Baptiste, pourquoi,
O Jean Baptiste,
Pourquoi you greased
My little dog's nose with tar?

Your little dog had catarrh,
Your little dog had catarrh,
And that was the reason
Why I have greasen
Your little dog's nose with tar.

O Jean Baptiste, I'm glad,
O Jean Baptiste, I'm glad,
O Jean Baptiste,
I'm glad you greased
My little dog's nose with tar.

GOLDENHAIR

Lean out of the window,
    Goldenhair,
I heard you singing
    A merry air.

My book is closed,
    I read no more,
Watching the fire dance
    On the floor.

I have left my book:
   I have left my room:
For I heard you singing
   Through the gloom,

Singing and singing
   A merry air.
Lean out of the window,
   Goldenhair.

James Joyce

AH FADING JOY!

Ah fading Joy! how quickly art thou past!
   Yet we thy ruin haste.
As if the cares of human life were few,
   We seek out new:
And follow fate, which would too fast pursue.

See how on every bough the birds express,
   In their sweet notes, their happiness.
   They all enjoy, and nothing spare;
   But on their Mother Nature lay their care:
Why then should Man, the lord of all below,
   Such troubles choose to know,
As none of all his subjects undergo?

Hark, hark, the waters fall, fall, fall,
And with a murmuring sound
Dash, dash upon the ground,
   To gentle slumbers call.

John Dryden

7. CREATURES OF THE AIR

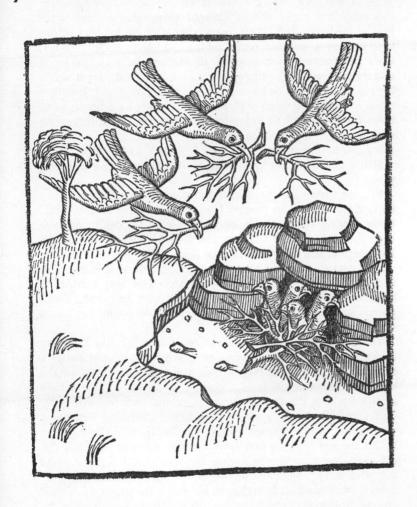

Creatures of the Air

When I was five or six, I was taken out by men who went shooting in a deep valley. One of them shot a bird with bright feathers. Years and years after (when he was more than eighty) he told me that the bird had been a cock pheasant. Cock pheasants are wonderful birds, but he was wrong. I remember green and yellow and scarlet, and I am sure it was a Hewel or Rainbird or Green Woodpecker (page 96). It might equally well have been a Phoenix, the best of all birds, who lived for five hundred years in the wastes of India, then flew with spices to a temple in Egypt's City of the Sun, where in a spicy fire or burning nest he burnt himself to the ashes from which a new Phoenix was born, to live another five hundred years.

We may have imagined this hundred-sunned Phoenix, but he is quite as real in poems (pages 99 to 101) as the 'real' birds, among which the poetical favourites for centuries have been the Lark and the Cuckoo, the Owl, the Swallow and the Nightingale, and the Swan, bird of Apollo, the god of poets, for which reason it sang, said the Greeks, before it died. The Lark and Cuckoo poems are in the April and May section of this book. Owl poems come on pages 107 and 108, Swan poems on pages 97 and 98, and Nightingale poems on pages 102 to 106.

The best Nightingale poems can be wonderful (like listening to nightingales by moonlight), even when we do not know a thing about the ancient Nightingale and Swallow stories which come into them. But it is a good idea to look these savage stories up in a classical dictionary, which will tell you why Philomela, the Nightingale of the night, is sad, and sings and throbs, and why her sister Procne, the Swallow of the day, has blood on her feathers and only twitters (it will also tell the different story that Queen Aedon was turned into a nightingale for grief at killing her child Itylus). What the American poet John Crowe Ransom is saying in his poem on page 106, about Procne, Philomela, and Itylus, is that nightingales can never be properly translated from European life to American life, from earlier to modern life.

> Unto more beautiful, persistently more young,
> Thy fabulous provinces belong,

he says to Philomela.

FOUR BIRDS

The robin and the wren
Are God Almighty's cock and hen:
The martin and the swallow
Are God Almighty's bow and arrow.

A CHARM AGAINST A MAGPIE

Clean birds by sevens,
Unclean by twos,
The dove in the heavens
Is the one I choose.

GO NOW, MY SONG

Go now, my song,
Let your wing be strong;
Fly and dart and dip
With a chip-chip,
A wren among the thorn
Of the world's scorn.

Never have a fear
Of thorn that would tear
Or the cold stare of men:
O my chitty-wren,
Let not courage fail
Your upturned tail.

Andrew Young

THE ANIMALS IN THE ARK

Noe   Have done, you men and women all!
Hie you lest this water fall,
That each beast were in his stall,
And into the ship brought.

Of clean beastes seven shall be,
Of unclean two, this God bade me;
This flood is nigh, well may we see,
Therefore tarry you nought.

Sem   Sir, here are lions, libards in,
Horses, mares, oxen, and swine,
Geates, calves, sheep and kine
Here sitten thou may see.

Ham   Camels, asses, men may find,
Buck, doe, hart, and hind,
And beastes of all manner kind
Here been, as thinkes me.

Japhet   Take here cattes and dogs too,
Otter, fox, fulmart also,
Hares hopping gaylie can go
Have cowl here for to eat.

Noe's Wife   And here are beares, wolfes sett,
Apes, owles, marmoset,
Weesells, squirrels, and firret;
Here they eaten their meat.

Sem's Wife   Yet more beastes are in this house:
Here cattis maken it full crowse,
Here a rotten, here a mowse,
They stand nigh together.

Ham's Wife   And here are fowles, less and more:
Hearnes, cranes and byttour,
Swans, peacocks, and them before
Meat for this wedder.

Japhet's Wife   Here are cockes, kites, crows,
Rookes, ravens, many rows,
Ducks, curlews, who ever knows
Each one in his kind?

And here are doves, diggs, drakes,
Redshanks running through the lakes;
And each fowl that ledden makes
In this ship men may find . . .

From the Chester Play of 'The Deluge'

geates: *goats;* cowl: *cabbage, kale;* crowse: *cheerful;* rotten: *rat;* hearnes: *herons;* byttour: *bitterns;* diggs: *ducks;* ledden: *song, language*

94

The Duck, and Mallard first, the falconers' only sport
(Of river-flights the chief, so that all other sort
They only green-fowl term) in every mere abound,
That you would think they sat upon the very ground,
Their numbers be so great, the waters covering quite,
That rais'd, the spacious air is darkened with their flight;
Yet still the dangerous dykes from shot do them secure,
Where they from flash to flash like the full epicure
Waft, as they lov'd to change their diet every meal;
And near to them ye see the lesser dibbling Teal
In bunches, with the first that fly from mere to mere,
As they above the rest were lords of earth and air.
The Gossander with them my goodly fens do show,
His head as ebon black, the rest as white as snow,
With whom the Widgeon goes, the Golden-Eye, the Smeath;
And in odd scattered pits, the flags and reeds beneath,
The Coot; bald, else clean black, that whiteness it doth bear
Upon the forehead starred, the Water-Hen doth wear
Upon her little tail in one small feather set.
The Water-woosel next, all over black as jet.
With various colours, black, green, blue, red, russet, white,
Do yield the gazing eye as variable delight
As do those sundry fowls whose several plumes they be.
The diving Dob-chick here among the rest you see,
Now up, now down again, that hard it is to prove,
Whether under water most it liveth, or above:
With which last little fowl (that water may not lack
More than the Dob-chick doth, and more doth love the brack)
The Puffin we compare, which coming to the dish
Nice palates hardly judge if it be flesh or fish.
   But wherefore should I stand upon such toys as these,
That have so goodly fowls the wandring eye to please?
Here in my vaster pools, as white as snow or milk
(In water black as Styx) swims the wild Swan, the Ilke,
Of Hollanders so term'd, no niggard of his breath
(As poets say of Swans, which only sing in death)
But oft as other birds, is heard his tunes to rote,
Which like a trumpet comes, from his long arched throat;
And tow'rds this wat'ry kind, about the flashes' brim,
Some cloven-footed are, by nature not to swim.
There stalks the stately Crane, as though he march'd in war,

By him that hath the Herne, which (by the fishy carr)
Can fetch with their long necks, out of the rush and reed,
Snigs, fry, and yellow frogs, whereon they often feed:
And under them again (that water never take,
But by some ditch's side or little shallow lake
Lie dabbling night and day) the palate-pleasing Snite,
The Bidcock, and like them the Redshank, that delight
Together still to be, in some small reedy bed
In which these little fowls in summer time were bred.
The buzzing Bitter sits, which through his hollow bill
A sudden bellowing sends, which many times doth fill
The neighbouring marsh with noise, as though a bull did roar;
But scarcely have I yet recited half my store:
And with my wondrous flocks of Wild-Geese come I then,
Which look as though alone they peopled all the fen,
Which here in winter time, when all is overflow'd
And want of solid sward inforceth them abroad,
Th'abundance then is seen, that my full fens do yield,
That almost through the isle do pester every field . . .

Michael Drayton

smeath: *smew*; snigs: *elvers*; snite: *snipe*; bidcock: *water-rail*;
bitter: *bittern*; flash: *water from sluice or weir*; carr: *shallow pool*

THE KINGFISHER

The viscous air, wheres'ere she fly,
Follows and sucks her azure dye;
The jellying stream compacts below,
If it might fix her shadow so;
The stupid fishes hang, as plain
As flies in crystal overta'en;
And men the silent scene assist,
Charm'd with the sapphire-wingèd mist . . .

Andrew Marvell

THE HEWEL, OR WOODPECKER

He walks still upright from the root,
Meas'ring the timber with his foot;
And all the way, to keep it clean,
Doth from the bark the wood-moths glean,
He, with his beak, examines well
Which fit to stand and which to fell.

The good he numbers up, and hacks,
As if he mark'd them with the axe.
But where he tinkling with his beak,
Does find the hollow oak to speak,
That for his building he designs,
And through the tainted side he mines . . .

Andrew Marvell

A RIDDLE FROM THE OLD ENGLISH

Clothes make no sound when I tread ground,
Or dwell in dwellings or disturb the flow.
And lofty air and gear at times
Above men's towns will lift me:
Brisk breezes bear me far, and then
My frettings loudly rush and ring
Above the folk and clearly sing
When I forth-fare on air
And feel and know
No fold or flow.

(*A swan*)

THE WILD SWANS AT COOLE

The trees are in their autumn beauty,
The woodland paths are dry,
Under the October twilight the water
Mirrors a still sky;
Upon the brimming water among the stones
Are nine-and-fifty swans.

The nineteenth autumn has come upon me
Since first I made my count;
I saw, before I had well finished,
All suddenly mount
And scatter wheeling in great broken rings
Upon their clamorous wings.

I have looked upon those brilliant creatures,
And now my heart is sore.
All's changed since I, hearing at twilight,
The first time on this shore,
The bell-beat of their wings above my head,
Trod with a lighter tread.

Unwearied still, lover by lover,
They paddle in the cold
Companionable streams or climb the air;
Passion or conquest, wander where they will,
Attend upon them still.

But now they drift on the still water,
Mysterious, beautiful;
Among what rushes will they build,
By what lake's edge or pool
Delight men's eyes when I awake some day
To find they have flown away?

W. B. Yeats

THE SILVER SWAN

The silver swan, who living had no note,
When death approach'd unlockt her silent throat,
Leaning her breast against the reedy shore,
Thus sung her first and last, and sung no more:
Farewell all joys, O death come close mine eyes,
More geese than swans now live, more fools than wise.

THE DYING SWAN

The white delightful swan
Sweet singing dieth, and I lamenting
Feel both sense and life relenting:
Strange and unlike proceeding,
   That he should die distressed
   And I die most blessed.
Death which in all thy wronging,
Fill'st me with gladness, and with sweet love-longing,
If in thy pangs no greater grief do seize me,
A thousand deaths a day should not displease me.

THE RED COCKATOO

Sent as a present from Annam —
A red cockatoo.
Coloured like the peach-tree blossom,
Speaking with the speech of men.

And they did to it what is always done
To the learned and eloquent.
They took a cage with stout bars
And shut it up inside.

Po Chǔ-i (translated by Arthur Waley)

I SAW A PHOENIX IN THE WOOD ALONE

I saw a Phoenix in the wood alone,
With purple wings, and crest of golden hue;
Strange bird he was, whereby I thought anone,
That of some heavenly wight I had the view;
Until he came unto the broken tree,
And to the spring, that late devourèd was.
What say I more? each thing at last we see
Doth pass away: the Phoenix there alas,
Spying the tree destroyed, the water dried,
Himself smote with his beak, as in disdain,
And so forthwith in great despite he died,
That yet my heart burns in exceeding pain,
  For ruth and pity of so hapless plight:
  O let mine eyes no more see such a sight! . . .

Edmund Spenser

THE PHOENIX

O blest unfabled Incense Tree,
That burns in glorious Araby,
With red scent chalicing the air,
Till earth-life grow Elysian there!

Half buried to her flaming breast
In this bright tree she makes her nest,
Hundred-sunned Phoenix! when she must
Crumble at length to hoary dust!

Her gorgeous death-bed! her rich pyre
Burnt up with aromatic fire!
Her urn, sight high from spoiler men!
Her birthplace when self-born again!

99

The mountainless green wilds among,
Here ends she her unechoing song!
With amber tears and odorous sighs
Mourned by the desert where she dies! . . .

George Darley

THE PHOENIX SELF-BORN

The cubs of bears a living lump appear,
When whelped, and no determin'd figure wear.
Their mother licks 'em into shape, and gives
As much of form, as she herself receives.
The grubs from their sexangular abode
Crawl out unfinish'd, like the maggot's brood:
Trunks without limbs; till time at leisure brings
The thighs they wanted, and their tardy wings.
The bird who draws the car of Juno, vain
Of her crown'd head, and of her starry train,
And he that bears th'artillery of Jove,
The strong-pounc'd Eagle, and the billing Dove,
And all the feather'd kind, who could suppose
(But that from sight the surest sense he knows)
They from th'included yolk, not ambient white, arose?
There are who think the marrow of a man,
Which in the spine, while he was living, ran,
When dead, the pith corrupted, will become
A snake, and hiss within the hollow tomb.

All these receive their birth from other things;
But from himself the Phoenix only springs:
Self-born, begotten by the parent flame
In which he burn'd, another and the same:
Who not by corn or herbs his life sustains,
But the sweet essence of amomum drains
And watches the rich gums Arabia bears,
While yet in tender dew they drop their tears.
He (his five centuries of life fulfill'd)
His nest on oaken boughs begins to build,
Or trembling tops of palm: and first he draws
The plan with his broad bill, and crooked claws,
Nature's artificers; on this the pile
Is form'd, and rises round. Then with the spoil

Of cassia, cinnamon, and stems of nard
(For softness strew'd beneath) his funeral bed is rear'd:
Fun'ral and bridal both; and all around
The borders with corruptless myrrh are crown'd:
On this incumbent; till aetherial flame
First catches, then consumes the costly frame;
Consumes him too, as on the pile he lies;
He liv'd on odours, and in odours dies.

An infant Phoenix from the former springs,
His father's heir, and from his tender wings
Shakes off his parent dust; his method he pursues,
And the same lease of life on the same terms renews:
When grown to manhood he begins his reign,
And with stiff pinions can his flight sustain,
He lightens of its load the tree that bore
His father's royal sepulchre before,
And his own cradle: This (with pious care)
Plac'd on his back, he cuts the buxom air,
Seeks the Sun's city, and his sacred church,
And decently lays down his burden in the porch.

A wonder more amazing would we find?
Th'Hyaena shows it, of a double kind,
Varying the sexes in alternate years,
In one begets, and in another bears.
The thin Cameleon, fed with air, receives
The colour of the thing to which he cleaves.

India when conquer'd, on the conqu'ring god
For planted vines, the sharp-ey'd Lynx bestow'd,
Whose urine shed, before it touches earth,
Congeals in air, and gives to gems their birth.
So coral soft and white in ocean's bed,
Comes harden'd up in air, and glows with red . . .

John Dryden (after Ovid)

THE PHOENIX

Some say the Phoenix dwells in Aethiopia,
In Turkey, Syria, Tartary or Utopia:
Others assume the continuance of the creature
In unexplored cosmographies of Nature:
One styles it Bird of Paradise; and one
Swears that its nest is built of cinnamon:

While sceptic Eastern Travellers would arraign
The existence of this paragon; and feign
That, since it seemed so rare and unprolific,
The bird's a Pseudomorphous Hieroglyphic.

Siegfried Sassoon

NIGHTINGALES

On moonlight bushes,
Whose dewy leaflets are but half disclosed,
You may perchance behold them on the twigs,
Their bright, bright eyes, their eyes both bright and full,
Glistening, while many a glow-worm in the shade
Lights up her love-torch . . .

S. T. Coleridge

TO A NIGHTINGALE

My heart aches, and a drowsy numbness pains
    My sense, as though of hemlock I had drunk,
Or emptied some dull opiate to the drains
    One minute past, and Lethe-wards had sunk:
'Tis not through envy of thy happy lot,
    But being too happy in thy happiness, —
        That thou, light-winged Dryad of the trees,
            In some melodious plot
Of beechen green, and shadows numberless,
    Singest of summer in full-throated ease.

O for a draught of vintage, that hath been
    Cool'd a long age in the deep-delved earth,
Tasting of Flora and the country-green,
    Dance, and Provençal song, and sun-burnt mirth!
O for a beaker full of the warm South,
    Full of the true, the blushful Hippocrene,
        With beaded bubbles winking at the brim,
            And purple-stained mouth;
That I might drink, and leave the world unseen,
    And with thee fade away into the forest dim:

Fade far away, dissolve, and quite forget
    What thou among the leaves hast never known,
The weariness, the fever, and the fret
    Here, where men sit and hear each other groan;

Where palsy shakes a few, sad, last grey hairs,
  Where youth grows pale, and spectre-thin, and dies;
    Where but to think is to be full of sorrow
    And leaden-eyed despairs;
  Where beauty cannot keep her lustrous eyes,
    Or new Love pine at them beyond to-morrow.

Away! Away! for I will fly to thee,
  Not charioted by Bacchus and his pards,
But on the viewless wings of Poesy,
  Though the dull brain perplexes and retards:
Already with thee! tender is the night,
  And haply the Queen-Moon is on her throne,
    Cluster'd around by all her starry Fays;
      But here there is no light,
  Save what from heaven is with the breezes blown
    Through verdurous glooms and winding mossy ways.

I cannot see what flowers are at my feet,
  Nor what soft incense hangs upon the boughs,
But, in embalmed darkness, guess each sweet
  Wherewith the seasonable month endows
The grass, the thicket, and the fruit-tree wild;
  White hawthorn, and the pastoral eglantine;
    Fast-fading violets cover'd up in leaves;
      And mid-May's eldest child,
  The coming musk-rose, full of dewy wine,
    The murmurous haunt of flies on summer eves.

Darkling I listen; and for many a time
  I have been half in love with easeful Death,
Call'd him soft names in many a mused rhyme,
  To take into the air my quiet breath;
Now more than ever seems it rich to die,
  To cease upon the midnight with no pain,
    While thou art pouring forth thy soul abroad
      In such an ecstasy!
  Still wouldst thou sing, and I have ears in vain —
    To thy high requiem become a sod.

Thou wast not born for death, immortal Bird!
  No hungry generations tread thee down;
The voice I hear this passing night was heard
  In ancient days by emperor and clown:

103

Perhaps the selfsame song that found a path
  Through the sad heart of Ruth, when sick for home,
  She stood in tears amid the alien corn;
    The same that oft-times hath
  Charm'd magic casements, opening on the foam
  Of perilous seas, in faery lands forlorn.

Forlorn! the very word is like a bell
  To toll me back from thee to my sole self.
Adieu! the fancy cannot cheat so well
  As she is famed to do, deceiving elf.
Adieu! adieu! thy plaintive anthem fades
  Past the near meadows, over the still stream,
    Up the hill-side; and now 'tis buried deep
    In the next valley-glades:
  Was it a vision, or a waking dream?
  Fled is that music: — do I wake or sleep?

John Keats

ITYLUS

Swallow, my sister, O sister swallow,
  How can thine heart be full of the spring?
  A thousand summers are over and dead.
What hast thou found in the spring to follow?
  What hast thou found in thine heart to sing?
  What wilt thou do when the summer is shed?

O swallow, sister, O fair swift swallow,
  Why wilt thou fly after spring to the south,
  The soft south whither thine heart is set?
Shall not the grief of the old time follow?
  Shall not the song thereof cleave to thy mouth?
  Hast thou forgotten ere I forget?

Sister, my sister, O fleet sweet swallow,
  Thy way is long to the sun and the south;
  But I, fulfilled of my heart's desire,
Shedding my song upon height, upon hollow,
  From tawny body and sweet small mouth
  Feed the heart of the night with fire.

I the nightingale all spring through,
  O swallow, sister, O changing swallow,
  All spring through till the spring be done,

Clothed with the light of the night on the dew,
  Sing, while the hours and the wild birds follow,
    Take flight and follow and find the sun.

Sister, my sister, O soft light swallow,
  Though all things feast in the spring's guest-chamber
    How hast thou heart to be glad thereof yet?
For where thou fliest I shall not follow,
  Till life forget and death remember,
    Till thou remember and I forget.

Swallow, my sister, O singing swallow,
  I know not how thou hast heart to sing.
    Hast thou the heart? Is it all past over?
Thy lord the summer is good to follow,
  And fair the feet of thy lover the spring:
    But what wilt thou say to the spring thy lover?

O swallow, sister, O fleeting swallow,
  My heart in me is a molten ember
    And over my head the waves have met.
But thou wouldst tarry or I would follow,
  Could I forget or thou remember,
    Couldst thou remember and I forget.

O sweet stray sister, O shifting swallow,
  The heart's division divideth us.
    Thy heart is as light as a leaf of a tree;
But mine goes forth among sea-gulfs hollow
  To the place of the slaying of Itylus,
    The feast of Daulis, the Thracian sea.

O swallow, sister, O rapid swallow,
  I pray thee sing not a little space.
    Are not the roofs and the lintels wet?
The woven web that was plain to follow,
  The small slain body, the flower-like face,
    Can I remember if thou forget?

O sister, sister, thy first-begotten!
  The hands that cling and the feet that follow,
    The voice of the child's blood crying yet
Who hath remembered me? Who hath forgotten?
  Thou hast forgotten, O summer swallow,
    But the world shall end when I forget.

                                        A. C. Swinburne

THE FIELDS ABROAD WITH SPANGLED
FLOWERS

The fields abroad with spangled flowers are gilded,
    The meads are mantled and the closes,
    In May each bush arrayed with sweet wild roses.

The nightingale her bower hath gaily builded:
    And full of kindly lust and love's inspiring,
    I love, I love (she sings) — hark — her mate inspiring.

PHILOMELA

Procne, Philomela, and Itylus,
Your names are liquid, your improbable tale
Is recited in the classic numbers of the nightingale.
Ah, but our numbers are not felicitous,
It goes not liquidly for us.

Perched on a Roman ilex, and duly apostrophized,
The nightingale descanted unto Ovid;
She has even appeared to the Teutons, the swilled and gravid;
At Fontainebleu it may be the bird was gallicized;
Never was she baptized.

To England came Philomela with her pain,
Fleeing the hawk her husband; querulous ghost,
She wanders when he sits heavy on his roost,
Utters herself in the original again,
The untranslatable refrain.

Not to these shores she came! this other Thrace,
Environ barbarous to the royal Attic;
How could her delicate dirge run democratic,
Delivered in a cloudless boundless public place
To an inordinate race?

I pernoctated with the Oxford students once,
And in the quadrangles, in the cloisters, on the Cher,
Precociously knocked at antique door ajar,
Fatuously touched the hems of the hierophants,
Sick of my dissonance.

I went out to Bagley Wood, I climbed the hill;
Even the moon had slanted off in a twinkling,
I heard the sepulchral owl and a few bells tinkling,
There was no more villainous day to unfulfil,
The diuturnity was still.

Up from the darkest wood where Philomela sat,
Her fairy numbers issued. What then ailed me?
My ears are called capacious but they failed me,
Her classics registered a little flat!
I rose, and venomously spat.

Philomela, Philomela, lover of song,
I am in despair if we may make us worthy,
A bantering breed sophistical and swarthy;
Unto more beautiful, persistently more young,
Thy fabulous provinces belong.

John Crowe Ransom

SWEET SUFFOLK OWL

Sweet Suffolk owl, so trimly dight
With feathers like a lady bright,
Thou sing'st alone sitting by night,
Te whit, te whoo! Te whit, te whoo!

Thy note that forth so freely rolls,
With shrill command the mouse controls;
And sings a dirge for dying souls,
Te whit, te whoo! Te whit, te whoo!

THE OWL

Downhill I came, hungry, and yet not starved;
Cold, yet had heat within me that was proof
Against the North wind; tired, yet so that rest
Had seemed the sweetest thing under a roof.

Then at the inn I had food, fire, and rest,
Knowing how hungry, cold, and tired was I.
All of the night quite barred out except
An owl's cry, a most melancholy cry

Shaken out long and clear upon the hill,
No merry note, nor cause of merriment,
But one telling me plain what I escaped
And others could not, that night, as in I went.

And salted was my food, and my repose,
Salted and sobered, too, by the bird's voice
Speaking for all who lay under the stars,
Soldiers and poor, unable to rejoice.

Edward Thomas

THE WHITE OWL

Lovely are curves of the white owl sweeping
Wavy in the dusk lit by one large star . . .

George Meredith

O LAPWING!

O Lapwing, thou fliest around the heath,
Nor seest the net that is spread beneath.
Why dost thou not fly among the corn fields?
They cannot spread nets where a harvest yields.

William Blake

THE OLD GREY GOOSE

Go and tell Aunt Nancy,
Go and tell Aunt Nancy,
Go and tell Aunt Nancy
The old grey goose is dead:

The one that she'd been saving,
The one that she'd been saving,
The one that she'd been saving
To make her feather bed.

She died last Friday,
She died last Friday,
She died last Friday,
Behind the old barn shed.

She left nine little goslings,
She left nine little goslings,
She left nine little goslings
To scratch for their own bread.

Go and tell Aunt Nancy,
Go and tell Aunt Nancy,
Go and tell Aunt Nancy
The old grey goose is dead.

EPITAPH ON LADY OSSORY'S BULLFINCH

All flesh is grass and so are feathers too:
Finches must die as well as I or you.
Beneath a damask rose in good old age
Here lies the tenant of a noble cage.
For forty moons he charmed his lady's ear
And piped obedient oft as she drew near,
Though now stretched out upon a clay-cold bier.
But when the last shrill flageolet shall sound
And raise all dicky-birds from holy ground
This little corpse again its wings shall prune
And sing eternally the selfsame tune
From everlasting night to everlasting noon.

Horace Walpole

THE AMBER BEAD

I saw a fly within a bead
Of amber cleanly burièd:
The urn was little, but the room
More rich than Cleopatra's tomb.

Robert Herrick

8. CREATURES
OF THE FIELD

Creatures of the Field

As with birds, so with beasts. The 'unreal' ones are more real than the real ones, the unicorns are more real than the rabbits. Or a poet's animal may be more real than the same animal in 'real life'. For instance, William Blake's tiger, furious-eyed and strong in those forests of the night which we may see with our eyes shut, in dreams, is more splendidly real than the rather baggy smelly cats in cages which are the tigers most of us know. Blake's tiger on page 115 is a little different, by the way, from the Tiger Burning Bright as you will find him in most books. I have printed an earlier version, and I suspect it is nearer the original tiger which came to Blake in a vision of fire and darkness and surprise, and words.

While I have a unicorn – two unicorns – in this part of *The Cherry-Tree*, I realize I haven't a lion, who is the King of Beasts, except for the royal one in the woodcut. Lions occur, though, in one poem and another in other parts of the book. There is a very splendid one to be found, in misfortune, on page 204.

'Real' and 'unreal' is a problem on which the greatest of modern poets had something to say. Two people (two sides of himself) argue in one of his poems. One asks if there are not poets who make their art out of love of life or the world? The other says, no, lovers of the world do not sing, but serve the world by action, and that if they write, it is still action, not singing: 'the struggle of the fly in the marmalade'; whereas poetry is 'a vision of reality'.

The woodcut comes from a book of fables printed at Ulm in Germany in 1483.

THE FALSE FOX

The false fox came unto our croft,
And so our geese full fast he sought.
With how, fox, how, with hey, fox, hey!
Come no more unto our house to bear our geese away!

The false fox came unto our sty,
And took our geese there by and by.

The false fox came into our yerd,
And there he made the geese aferd.

The false fox came unto our gate,
And took our geese there where they sate.

The false fox came to our hall door,
And shrove our geese there in the floor.

The false fox came into our hall,
And assoiled our geese both great and small.

The false fox came unto our coop,
And there he made our geese to stoop.

He took a goose fast by the neck,
And the goose thoo began to queck.

The goodwife came out in her smock,
And at the goose she threw her rok.

The goodman came out with his flail,
And smote the fox upon the tail.

He threw a goose upon his back,
And furth he went thoo with his pack.

The goodman swore if that he might,
He would him slee or it were night.

The false fox went into his den,
And there he was full merry then.

He came ayen yet the next week,
And took away both hen and cheke.

The goodman said unto his wife,
'This false fox liveth a merry life.'

The false fox came upon a day,
And with our geese he made affray.

He took a goose fast by the neck,
And made her to say 'wheccumquek.'

'I pray thee, fox', said the goose thoo,
'Take of my feders but not of my toe.'

thoo: then; rok: distaff

I HAVE TWELVE OXEN

I have twelve oxen that be fair and brown,
And they go a-grazing down by the town.
    With hay, with how, with hay!
Sawest thou not mine oxen, thou little pretty boy?

I have twelve oxen, and they be fair and white,
And they go a-grazing down by the dyke.
    With hay, with how, with hay!
Sawest not thou mine oxen, thou little pretty boy?

I have twelve oxen and they be fair and blak,
And they go a-grazing down by the lak.
    With hay, with how, with hay!
Sawest not thou mine oxen, thou little pretty boy?

I have twelve oxen, and they be fair and rede,
And they go a-grazing down by the mede.
    With hay, with how, with hay!
Sawest not thou mine oxen, thou little pretty boy?

THE HERD BOY

In the southern village the boy who minds the ox
With his naked feet stands on the ox's back.
Through the hole in his coat the river wind blows;
Through his broken hat the mountain rain pours.
On the long dyke he seemed to be far away;
In the narrow lane suddenly we were face to face.

The boy is home and the ox is back in its stall;
And a dark smoke oozes through the thatched roof.

Lu Yu (translated by Arthur Waley)

THE TIGER

Tiger, tiger, burning bright
In the forests of the night,
What immortal hand or eye
Dare frame thy fearful symmetry?

Burnt in distant deeps or skies
The cruel fire of thine eyes?
On what wings dare he aspire?
What the hand dare seize the fire?

And what shoulder and what art
Could twist the sinews of thy heart?
And when thy heart began to beat
What dread hand and what dread feet

Could fetch it from the furnace deep
And in thy horrid ribs dare steep
In the well of sanguine woe?
In what clay and in what mould
Were thy eyes of fury roll'd?

Where the hammer? Where the chain?
In what furnace was thy brain?
What the anvil? What dread grasp
Dare its deadly terrors clasp?

When the stars threw down their spears
And water'd heaven with their tears
Dare he laugh his work to see?
Dare he who made the lamb make thee?

Tiger, tiger, burning bright
In the forests of the night,
What immortal hand and eye
Dare frame thy fearful symmetry?

William Blake

GAZELLES AND UNICORN

Fleet and fair
Gazelles by hippogriffins torn,
A wild curvetting unicorn
Across a cherry-coloured morn . . .

John Gray

THE UNICORN

Lo! in the mute, mid wilderness,
What wondrous Creature? – of no kind! –
His burning lair doth largely press, –
Gaze fixt, and feeding on the wind?
His fell is of the desert dye,
And tissue adust, dun-yellow and dry,
Compact of living sands; his eye
Black luminary, soft and mild,
With its dark lustre cools the wild;
From his stately forehead springs,
Piercing to heaven, a radiant horn, –
Lo! the compeer of lion-kings!
The steed self-armed, the Unicorn!
Ever heard of, never seen,
With a main of sands between
Him and approach; his lonely pride
To course his arid arena wide,
Free as the hurricane, or lie here,
Lord of his couch as his career! . . .

George Darley

UPON THE SNAIL

She goes but softly, but she goeth sure,
She stumbles not as stronger creatures do;
Her journey's shorter, so she may endure
Better than they which do much further go.

She makes no noise, but stilly seizeth on
The flower or herb appointed for her food,
The which she quietly doth feed upon,
While others range and gare but find no good.

And though she doth but very softly go,
However 'tis not fast, nor slow, but sure;
And certainly they that do travel so,
The prize they do aim at, they do procure.

John Bunyan

gare: *busy themselves*

THE FAIRY RING

Here the horse-mushrooms make a fairy ring,
  Some standing upright and some overthrown,
A small Stonehenge, where heavy black snails cling
  And bite away, like Time, the tender stone.

                                    Andrew Young

SUMMER IMAGES

I love at early morn, from new-mown swath,
  To see the startled frog his route pursue,
And mark, while leaping o'er the dripping path,
  His bright sides scatter dew;
And early lark that from its bustle flies
  To hail his matin new;
    And watch him to the skies:

And note on hedgerow baulks, in moisture sprent,
  The jetty snail creep from the mossy thorn,
With earnest heed and tremulous intent,
  Frail brother of the morn,
That from the tiny bents and misted leaves
  Withdraws his timid horn,
    And fearful vision weaves;

Or swallow heed on smoke-tanned chimney-top,
  Wont to be first unsealing Morning's eye,
Ere yet the bee hath gleaned one wayward drop
  Of honey on his thigh;
To see him seek morn's airy couch to sing,
  Until the golden sky
    Bepaint his russet wing . . .

                                    John Clare

LAT TAKE A CAT

Lat take a cat, and fostre him well with milk,
And tendre flesh, and make his couche of silk,
And lat him seen a mous go by the wall;
Anon he weyveth milk, and flesh, and al,
And every deyntee that is in that hous,
Swich appetyt hath he to ete a mous . . .

                                    Geoffrey Chaucer

117

THE CAT

They call me cruel. Do I know if mouse or songbird feels?
I only know they make me light and salutary meals:
And if, as 'tis my nature to, ere I devour I tease 'em,
Why should a low-bred gardener's boy pursue me with a
    besom? . . .

C. S. Calverley

THE CAT AND THE BIRD

Tell me, tell me, gentle Robin,
What is it sets thy heart a-throbbing?
Is it that Grimalkin fell
Hath killed thy father or thy mother,
Thy sister or thy brother,
Or any other?
Tell me but that,
And I'll kill the Cat.

But stay, little Robin, did you ever spare
A grub on the ground or a fly in the air?
No, that you never did, I'll swear;
So I won't kill the Cat,
That's flat.

George Canning

O CAT OF CARLISH KIND

That vengeaunce I ask and cry,
By way of exclamation,
On all the whole cat nation
Of cattes wild and tame:
God send them sorrow and shame!
That cat specially
That slew so cruelly
My litell pretty sparrow
That I brought up at Carow.
    O cat of carlish kind,
The finde was in thy mind
Whan thou my bird untwined!
I would thou haddest ben blind!
The leopardes savage,
The lions in their rage,

Might catch thee in their paws,
And gnaw thee in their jaws!
The serpentes of Lybany
Might stinge thee venimously!
The dragons with their tongues
Might poison thy liver and lungs!
The manticors of the montains
Might feed them on thy brains! . . .
    Of Inde the greedy gripes
Might tear out all thy tripes!
Of Arcady the bears
Might pluck away thine ears!
The wild wolf Lycaon
Bite asonder thy back bone!
Of Ethna the brenning hill,
That day and night brenneth still,
Set in thy tail a blaze,
That all the world may gaze
And wonder upon thee,
From Ocean the great sea
Unto the Isles of Orchady,
From Tillbery ferry
To the plain of Salisbery!
So traitorously my bird to kill
That never ought thee evil will! . . .

John Skelton

finde: *fiend*; gripes: *griffins*; ought: *bore*

THE MYSTERIOUS CAT

I saw a proud, mysterious cat,
I saw a proud mysterious cat,
Too proud to catch a mouse or rat —
Mew, mew, mew.

But catnip she would eat, and purr,
But catnip she would eat, and purr.
And goldfish she did much prefer —
Mew, mew, mew.

I saw a cat — 'twas but a dream,
I saw a cat — 'twas but a dream,
Who scorned the slave that brought her cream —
Mew, mew, mew,

Unless the slave were dressed in style,
Unless the slave were dressed in style,
And knelt before her all the while –
Mew, mew, mew.

Did you ever hear of a thing like that?
Did you ever hear of a thing like that?
Did you ever hear of a thing like that?
Oh, what a proud mysterious cat.
Oh, what a proud mysterious cat.
Oh, what a proud mysterious cat.
Mew . . . mew . . . mew.

Vachel Lindsay

MY CAT JEOFFRY

For I will consider my Cat Jeoffry.

For he is the servant of the Living God duly and daily serving him.

For at the first glance of the glory of God in the East he worships in his way.

For is this done by wreathing his body seven times round with elegant quickness.

For then he leaps up to catch the musk, which is the blessing of God upon his prayer.

For he rolls upon prank to work it in.

For having done duty and received blessing he begins to consider himself.

For this he performs in ten degrees.

For first he looks upon his fore-paws to see if they are clean.

For secondly he kicks up behind to clear away there.

For thirdly he works it upon stretch with the fore-paws extended.

For fourthly he sharpens his paws by wood.

For fifthly he washes himself.

For sixthly he rolls upon wash.

For seventhly he fleas himself, that he may not be interrupted upon the beat.

For eighthly he rubs himself against a post.

For ninthly he looks up for his instructions.

For tenthly he goes in quest of food.

For having consider'd God and himself he will consider his neighbour.

For if he meets another cat he will kiss her in kindness.

For when he takes his prey he plays with it to give it a chance.

For one mouse in seven escapes by his dallying.

For when his day's work is done his business more properly begins.

For he keeps the Lord's watch in the night against the adversary.

For he counteracts the powers of darkness by his electrical skin and glaring eyes.

For he counteracts the Devil, who is death, by brisking about the life.

For in his morning orisons he loves the sun and the sun loves him.

For he is of the tribe of Tiger.

For the Cherub Cat is a term of the Angel Tiger.

For he has the subtlety and hissing of a serpent, which in goodness he suppresses.

For he will not do destruction if he is well fed, neither will he spit without provocation.

For he purrs in thankfulness, when God tells him he's a good Cat.

For he is an instrument for the children to learn benevolence upon.

For every house is incomplete without him and a blessing is lacking in the spirit . . .

Christopher Smart

GARDEN-LION

O Michael, you are at once the enemy
And the chief ornament of our garden,
Scrambling up rose-posts, nibbling at nepeta,
Making your lair where tender plants should flourish,
Or proudly couchant on a sun-warmed stone.

What do you do all night there,
When we seek our soft beds,
And you go off, old roisterer,
Away into the dark?

I think you play at leopards and panthers;
I think you wander on to foreign properties;
But on winter mornings you are a lost orphan
Pitifully wailing underneath our windows;

And in summer, by the open doorway,
You come in pad, pad, lazily to breakfast,
Plumy tail waving, with a fine swagger,
Like a drum-major, or a parish beadle,
Or a rich rajah, or the Grand Mogul.

Evelyn Hayes

》

CRUEL CLEVER CAT

Sally, having swallowed cheese,
Directs down holes the scented breeze,
Enticing thus with bated breath,
Nice mice to an untimely death.

Geoffrey Taylor

ENGRAVED ON THE COLLAR OF A DOG,
WHICH I GAVE TO HIS ROYAL HIGHNESS

I am his Highness' dog at Kew;
Pray tell me, sir, whose dog are you?

Alexander Pope

I'd often seen before
That sheaf of corn hung from the bough –
Strange in a wood a sheaf of corn
Though by the winds half torn
And thrashed by rain to empty straw.
And then to-day I saw
A small pink twitching snout
And eyes like black beads sewn in fur
Peep from a hole in doubt,
And heard on dry leaves go tat-tat
The stiff tail of the other rat.
And now as the short day grows dim
And here and there farms in the dark
Turn to a spark,
I on my stumbling way think how
With indistinguishable limb
And tight tail round each other's head
They'll make to-night one ball in bed,
Those long-tailed lovers who have come
To share the pheasants' harvest-home.

Andrew Young

MOUSE'S NEST

I found a ball of grass among the hay
And progged it as I passed and went away;
And when I looked I fancied something stirred,
And turned agen, and hoped to catch the bird—
When out an old mouse bolted in the wheats
With all her young ones hanging at her teats;
She looked so odd and so grotesque to me,
I ran and wondered what the thing could be,
And pushed the knapweed bunches where I stood.
Then the mouse hurried from the craking brood,
The young ones squeaked, and as I went away,
She found her nest again among the hay.
The water o'er the pebbles scarce could run,
And broad old cesspools glittered in the sun.

John Clare

Hast thou given the horse strength? Hast thou clothed his neck with thunder?

Canst thou make him afraid as a grasshopper? The glory of his nostrils is terrible. He paweth in the valley, and rejoiceth in his strength: he goeth on to meet the armed men.

He mocketh at fear, and is not affrighted; neither turneth he back from the sword. The quiver rattleth against him, the glittering spear and the shield. He swalloweth the ground with fierceness and rage: neither believeth he that it is the sound of the trumpet.

He saith among the trumpets, Ha, ha; and he smelleth the battle afar off, the thunder of the captains, and the shouting . . .

The Book of Job

THE FLOWER-FED BUFFALOES

The flower-fed buffaloes of the spring
In the days of long ago,
Ranged where the locomotives sing
And the prairie flowers lie low;
The tossing, blooming, perfumed grass
Is swept away by wheat,
Wheat and wheels and wheels spin by
In the spring that still is sweet.
But the flower-fed buffaloes of the spring
Left us long ago.
They gore no more, they bellow no more,
They trundle around the hills no more: —
With the Blackfeet lying low,
With the Pawnees lying low.

Vachel Lindsay

9. TALES
AND BALLADS

Tales and Ballads

The woodcut for Tales and Ballads (by the artist Hans Weiditz, and again from a German book, an Old Testament of 1524) tells the hero-tale of Samson carrying off the gates of Gaza. Tales are not so often told now in poems (or pictures); though when few people could read or write, there was no better way of remembering a good story and making it enjoyable than by telling it in the shape and the beat and the regularity of a poem. The telling was done to music.

The old tales might be ones about more than human power, like the ballad of the Laily Worm (page 135), the boy whose stepmother had turned him into the loathsome dragon at the foot of the tree (dragons are worse when you think of them as enormous worms), or the ballad (page 134) of the sons who come back from the dead and wear birchen hats made from trees which grow outside Paradise, or (in another section, page 206) the ballad of the silkie or seal which turned into a man. The tales might be about heroes or murders. Again they might be retellings of stories out of the wonder gospels, which were made up in other countries when Christianity was young. Two of this kind are the *Cherry Tree Carol* on page 127 (really a ballad, and not a carol) and *The Bitter Withy* on page 145, which explains why old willow-trees are hollow.

Sometimes it is suggested that ballads were made and told to music only in the wild border country, with the added suggestion that the poor English in the south were never 'poetical' enough. But ballads were made and sung everywhere. In Scotland and on the border they remembered them when most of the English had forgotten them (just as in Scotland they still play the bagpipes, which the English and most other Europeans also used to play). Sir Philip Sidney the poet said his heart was 'moved more than with a trumpet' when he heard (perhaps in Sussex, Shropshire, or Wiltshire) an old blind minstrel singing *Chevy Chace*, accompanying himself on a small fiddle, or 'crowd'. That ballads were sung, or told to music, often explains why, when you are merely reading them, the metre goes wrong in some of the lines. The lines would have fitted the music perfectly.

More of the old ballads are on pages 162, 175, 185, 206.

THE CHERRY-TREE CAROL

Joseph was an old man,
  And an old man was he,
And he married Mary,
  The Queen of Galilee.

Joseph and Mary walked
  Through an orchard good,
Where was cherries and berries,
  So red as any blood.

Joseph and Mary walked
  Through an orchard green,
Where was berries and cherries,
  As thick as might be seen.

O then bespoke Mary,
  So meek and so mild:
'Pluck me one cherry, Joseph,
  For I am with child.'

O then bespoke Joseph,
  With words most unkind:
'Let him pluck thee a cherry
  That brought thee with child.'

O then bespoke the babe,
  Within his mother's womb:
'Bow down then the tallest tree,
  For my mother to have some.'

Then bowed down the highest tree
  Unto his mother's hand;
Then she cried: 'See, Joseph,
  I have cherries at command.'

O then bespake Joseph:
  'I have done Mary wrong;
But cheer up, my dearest,
  And be not cast down.'

Then Mary plucked a cherry,
  As red as the blood,
Then Mary went home
  With her heavy load.

Then Mary took her babe,
  And sat him on her knee,
Saying: 'My dear son, tell me
  What this world will be.'

'Oh I shall be as dead, mother,
  As the stones in the wall;
O the stones in the streets, mother,
  Shall mourn for me all.

'Upon Easter-day, mother,
  My uprising shall be;
O the sun and the moon, mother,
  Shall both rise with me.'

THE ROYAL FISHERMAN

One morning in the month of June
  Down by the riverside,
There she beheld a bold fisherman,
  Come rowing on the tide.

'Morning to you, bold fisherman,
  How come you fishing here?'
'I've come a-fishing for your sweet sake
  All on the river clear.'

He lashed his boat up by the stem,
  And to this lady went.
He took her by the milkwhite hand
  For she was his intent.

He then took off his morning robe
  And laid it on the ground,
So she beheld three chains of gold,
  All on his neck around.

Straightway she fell upon her knees
  And loud for mercy called.
'I thought you were a bold fisherman,
  I see you are some lord.'

'Stand up, stand up, unto my father's hall.
  There I'll make you my bride,
And you shall have a Royal Fisherman
  To row you on the tide.'

There were four of us about that bed;
   The mass-priest knelt at the side,
I and his mother stood at the head,
   Over his feet lay the bride;
We were quite sure that he was dead,
   Though his eyes were open wide.

He did not die in the night,
   He did not die in the day,
But in the morning twilight
   His spirit pass'd away,
When neither sun nor moon was bright,
   And the trees were merely grey.

He was not slain with the sword,
   Knight's axe, or the knightly spear,
Yet spoke he never a word
   After he came in here;
I cut away the cord
   From the neck of my brother dear.

He did not strike one blow,
   For the recreants came behind,
In a place where the hornbeams grow,
   A path right hard to find,
For the hornbeam boughs swing so,
   That the twilight makes it blind.

They lighted a great torch then,
   When his arms were pinion'd fast,
Sir John the knight of the Fen,
   Sir Guy of the Dolorous Blast,
With knights threescore and ten,
   Hung brave Lord Hugh at last.

I am threescore and ten,
   And my hair is all turn'd grey,
But I met Sir John of the Fen
   Long ago on a summer day,
And am glad to think of the moment when
   I took his life away.

I am threescore and ten,
    And my strength is mostly pass'd,
But long ago I and my men,
    When the sky was overcast,
And the smoke roll'd over the reeds of the fen,
    Slew Guy of the Dolorous Blast.

And now, knights all of you,
    I pray you pray for Sir Hugh,
A good knight and a true,
    And for Alice, his wife, pray too.

                            William Morris

BISHOP HATTO

The summer and autumn had been so wet,
That in winter the corn was growing yet,
'Twas a piteous sight to see all around
The grain lie rotting on the ground.

Every day the starving poor,
Crowded around Bishop Hatto's door,
For he had a plentiful last year's store,
And all the neighbourhood could tell
His granaries were furnish'd well.

At last Bishop Hatto appointed a day
To quiet the poor without delay;
He bade them to his great Barn repair,
And they should have food for the winter there.

Rejoiced such tidings good to hear,
The poor folk flock'd from far and near;
The great Barn was full as it could hold
Of women and children, and young and old.

Then when he saw it could hold no more,
Bishop Hatto he made fast the door;
And while for mercy on Christ they call,
He set fire to the Barn and burnt them all.

'I'faith 'tis an excellent bonfire!' quoth he,
'And the country is greatly obliged to me,
For ridding it in these times forlorn
Of Rats that only consume the corn.'

So then to his palace returned he,
And he sat down to supper merrily,
And he slept that night like an innocent man;
But Bishop Hatto never slept again.

In the morning as he enter'd the hall
Where his picture hung against the wall,
A sweat like death all over him came,
For the Rats had eaten it out of the frame.

As he look'd there came a man from his farm,
He had a countenance white with alarm;
'My Lord, I open'd your granaries this morn,
And the Rats had eaten all your corn.'

Another came running presently,
And he was pale as pale could be.
'Fly! my Lord Bishop, fly', quoth he,
'Ten thousand Rats are coming this way, . . .
The Lord forgive you for yesterday!'

'I'll go to my tower on the Rhine', replied he,
'Tis the safest place in Germany;
The walls are high and the shores are steep,
And the stream is strong and the water deep.'

Bishop Hatto fearfully hasten'd away,
And he crost the Rhine without delay,
And reach'd his tower, and barr'd with care
All the windows, doors, and loop-holes there.

He laid him down and closed his eyes; . . .
But soon a scream made him arise.
He started and saw two eyes of flame
On his pillow from whence the screaming came.

He listen'd and look'd; . . . it was only the Cat;
But the Bishop he grew more fearful for that,
For she sat screaming, mad with fear,
At the Army of Rats that were drawing near.

For they have swam over the river so deep,
And they have climb'd the shores so steep,
And up the Tower their way is bent,
To do the work for which they were sent.

They are not to be told by the dozen or score,
By thousands they come, and by myriads and more,
Such numbers had never been heard of before,
Such a judgement had never been witness'd of yore.

Down on his knees the Bishop fell,
And faster and faster his beads did he tell,
As louder and louder drawing near
The gnawing of their teeth he could hear.

And in at the windows and in at the door,
And through the walls helter-skelter they pour,
And down from the ceiling and up through the floor,
From the right and the left, from behind and before,
From within and without, from above and below,
And all at once to the Bishop they go.

They have whetted their teeth against the stones,
And now they pick the Bishop's bones;
They gnaw'd the flesh from every limb,
For they were sent to do judgement on him!

Robert Southey

THE STRANGE VISITOR

A wife was sitting at her reel ae night;
  And aye she sat, and aye she reeled, and aye she wished for
  company.

In came a pair o' braid braid shoes, and sat down at the fireside;
  And aye she sat, and aye she reeled, and aye she wished for
  company.

In came a pair o' sma' sma' legs, and sat down on the braid
  braid soles;
  And aye she sat, and aye she reeled, and aye she wished for
  company.

In came a pair o' muckle muckle knees, and sat down on the
  sma' sma' legs;
  And aye she sat, and aye she reeled, and aye she wished for
  company.

In came a pair o' sma' sma' thees, and sat down on the muckle
  muckle knees;
  And aye she sat, and aye she reeled, and aye she wished for
  company.

In came a pair o' muckle muckle hips, and sat down on the
    sma' sma' thees;
  And aye she sat, and aye she reeled, and aye she wished for
    company.

In came a sma' sma' waist, and sat down on the muckle muckle
    hips;
  And aye she sat, and aye she reeled, and aye she wished for
    company.

In came a pair o' braid braid shouthers, and sat down on the
    sma' sma' waist;
  And aye she sat, and aye she reeled, and aye she wished for
    company.

In came a pair o' sma' sma' arms, and sat down on the braid
    braid shouthers;
  And aye she sat, and aye she reeled, and aye she wished for
    company.

In came a pair o' muckle muckle hands, and sat down on the
    sma' sma' arms;
  And aye she sat, and aye she reeled, and aye she wished for
    company.

In came a sma' sma' neck, and sat down on the braid braid
    shouthers;
  And aye she sat, and aye she reeled, and aye she wished for
    company.

In came a great big head, and sat down on the sma' sma' neck;
  And aye she sat, and aye she reeled, and aye she wished for
    company.

'What way hae ye sic braid braid feet?' quo' the wife.
  'Muckle ganging, muckle ganging.'
'What way hae ye sic sma' sma' legs?'
  'Aih-h-h — late — and wee-e-e moul.'
'What way hae ye sic muckle muckle knees?'
  'Muckle praying, muckle praying.'
'What way hae ye sic sma' sma' thees?'
  'Aih-h-h — late — and wee-e-e — moul.'
'What way hae ye sic big big hips?'
  'Muckle sitting, muckle sitting.'
'What way hae ye sic a sma' sma' waist?'
  'Aih-h-h — late — and wee-e-e moul.'

'What way hae ye sic braid braid shouthers?'
    'Wi' carrying broom, wi' carrying broom.'
'What way hae ye sic sma' sma' arms?'
    '*Aih-h-h* — late — and *wee-e-e* — moul.'
'What way hae ye sic muckle muckle hands?'
    'Threshing wi' an iron flail, threshing wi' an iron flail.'
'What way hae ye sic a sma' sma' neck?'
    '*Aih-h-h* — late — and *wee-e-e* — moul.'
'What way hae ye sic a muckle muckle head?'
    'Muckle wit, muckle wit.'
'What do you come for?'
    'FOR YOU.'

reel: *spinning-wheel*

THE WIFE OF USHER'S WELL

There lived a wife at Usher's Well,
    And a wealthy wife was she;
She had three stout and stalwart sons,
    And sent them o'er the sea.

They hadna been a week from her,
    A week but barely ane,
But word came to the carlin wife
    That her three sons were gane.

They hadna been a week from her,
    A week but barely three,
Whan word came to the carlin wife
    That her sons she'd never see.

'I wish the wind may never cease,
    Nor fashes in the flood,
Till my three sons come hame to me,
    In earthly flesh and blood.'

It fell about the Martinmass,
    When nights are lang and mirk,
The carlin wife's three sons came hame,
    And their hats were o the birk.

It neither grew in syke nor ditch,
    Nor yet in ony sheugh;
But at the gates o Paradise
    That birk grew fair eneugh.

'Blow up the fire, my maidens,
    Bring water from the well;
For a' my house shall feast this night,
    Since my three sons are well.'

And she has made to them a bed,
    She's made it large and wide,
And she's taen her mantle her about,
    Sat down at the bed-side.

Up then crew the red, red cock,
    And up and crew the gray;
The eldest to the youngest said,
    ''Tis time we were away.'

The cock he hadna crawd but once,
    And clappd his wings at a',
When the youngest to the eldest said,
    'Brother, we must awa.'

'The cock doth craw, the day doth daw,
    The channerin worm doth chide;
Gin we be mist out o our place,
    A sair pain we maun bide.'

'Fare ye weel, my mother dear!
    Farewell to barn and byre!
And fare ye weel, the bonny lass
    That kindles my mother's fire!'

carlin: old; fashes in the flood: *sorrows on the sea*; syke: *dell*;
sheugh: *gulley*; channerin: *muttering*; maun bide: *must
await*

THE LAILY WORM AND THE MACHREL
OF THE SEA

'I was bat seven year alld
    Fan my mider she did dee,
My father marred the ae warst woman
    The wardle did ever see.

'For she has made me the laily worm
    That lays at the fitt of the tree,
An o my sister Messry
    The machrel of the sea.

135

'An every Saturday at noon
     The machrel comes to me,
An she takes my laily head,
     An lays it on her knee,
An kames it we a silver kame,
     An washes it in the sea.

'Seven knights ha I slain
     San I lay at the fitt of the tree;
An ye war na my ain father,
     The eight an ye sud be.'

'Sing on your song, ye laily worm,
     That ye sung to me';
'I never sung that song
     But fatt I wad sing to ye.

'I was but seven year alld
     Fan my mider she did dee,
My father marred the ae warst woman
     The wardle did ever see.

'She changed me to the laily worm
     That lays at the fitt of the tree,
An my sister Messry
     To the machrel of the sea.

'And every Saturday at noon
     The machrel comes to me
An she takes my laily head
     An lays it on her knee,
An kames it weth a silver kame,
     An washes it in the sea.

'Seven knights ha I slain
     San I lay at the fitt of the tree;
An ye war na my ain father,
     The eight an ye sud be.'

He sent for his lady
     As fast as sen cod he:
'Far is my son,
     That ye sent fra me,
And my daughter,
     Lady Messry?'

'Yer son is at our king's court,
   Sarving for meat and fee,
And yer daughter is at our quin's court,
   A mary suit an free.'

'Ye lee, ye ill woman,
   Sa loud as I hear ye lee,
For my son is the laily worm
   That lays at the fitt of the tree,
An my daughter Messry
   The machrel of the sea.'

She has tain a silver wan
   An gine him stroks three,
An he started up the bravest knight
   Your eyes did ever see.

She has tain a small horn
   An loud an shill blew she,
An a' the fish came her tell but the proud machrel,
   An she stood by the sea;
'Ye shaped me ance an unshemly shape,
   An ye's never mare shape me.'

He has sent to the wood
   For hathorn and fune,
An he has tain that gay lady,
   An ther he did her burn.

laily: *loathsome*; far: *where*; a mary: *a maid-of-honour*; suit:
sweet; came her tell: *came to her*; fune: *furze*

THE COWBOY'S LAMENT

As I walked out in the streets of Laredo,
As I walked out in Laredo one day,
I spied a poor cowboy wrapped up in white linen,
Wrapped up in white linen as cold as the clay.

'Oh beat the drum slowly and play the fife lowly,
Play the Dead March as you carry me along;
Take me to the green valley, there lay the sod o'er me,
For I'm a young cowboy and I know I've done wrong.

'I see by your outfit that you are a cowboy' –
These words he did say as I boldly stepped by.
'Come sit down beside me and hear my sad story,
I am shot in the breast and I know I must die.

137

'Let sixteen gamblers come handle my coffin,
Let sixteen cowboys come sing me a song.
Take me to the graveyard and lay the sod o'er me,
For I'm a poor cowboy and I know I've done wrong.

'My friends and relations they live in the Nation,
They know not where their boy has gone.
I first came to Texas and hired to a ranchman.
Oh I'm a young cowboy and I know I've done wrong.

'It was once in the saddle I used to go dashing,
It was once in the saddle I used to go gay
First to the dram-house and then to the card-house,
Got shot in the breast and I am dying to-day.

'Get six jolly cowboys to carry my coffin,
Get six pretty maidens to bear up my pall.
Put bunches of roses all over my coffin,
Put roses to deaden the sods as they fall.

'Then swing your rope slowly and rattle your spurs lowly,
And give a wild whoop as you carry me along,
And in the grave throw me and roll the sod o'er me,
For I'm a young cowboy and I know I've done wrong.

'Oh bury beside me my knife and six-shooter,
My spurs on my heel, as you sing me a song,
And over my coffin put a bottle of brandy
That the cowboys may drink as they carry me along.

'Go bring me a cup, a cup of cold water
To cool my parched lips,' the cowboy then said;
Before I returned his soul had departed,
And gone to the round-up, the cowboy was dead.

We beat the drum slowly and played the fife lowly,
And bitterly wept as we bore him along;
For we all loved our comrade, so brave, young, and handsome,
We all loved our comrade although he'd done wrong.

WALTZING MATILDA

Once a jolly swagman camped by a billabong
Under the shade of a coolibah tree,
And he sang as he watched and waited till his billy boiled,
'You'll come a-waltzing, Matilda, with me!'

Waltzing Matilda, waltzing Matilda,
You'll come a-waltzing, Matilda, with me!
And he sang as he watched and waited till his billy boiled,
'You'll come a-waltzing, Matilda, with me!'

Down come a jumbuck to drink at the billabong,
Up jumped the swagman and grabbed him with glee,
And he sang as he stowed that jumbuck in his tucker-bag,
'You'll come a-waltzing, Matilda, with me!'
Waltzing Matilda, waltzing Matilda,
You'll come a-waltzing, Matilda, with me!
And he sang as he stowed that jumbuck in his tucker-bag,
'You'll come a-waltzing, Matilda, with me!'

Up rode the squatter mounted on his thoroughbred,
Up rode the troopers, one, two, three.
'Where's that jolly jumbuck you've got in your tucker-bag?
You'll come a-waltzing, Matilda, with me!'
Waltzing Matilda, waltzing Matilda,
You'll come a-waltzing, Matilda, with me!
'Where's that jolly jumbuck you've got in your tucker-bag?
You'll come a-waltzing, Matilda, with me!'

Up jumped the swagman and sprang into the billabong.
'You'll never take me alive!' said he.
And his ghost may be heard as you pass by that billabong.
'You'll never take me alive!' said he.
Waltzing Matilda, waltzing Matilda,
You'll come a-waltzing, Matilda, with me!
And his ghost may be heard as you pass by that billabong,
'You'll come a-waltzing, Matilda, with me!'

A. B. Paterson

billabong: *a blind channel of a river*; jumbuck: *sheep*

THE DROWNED LADY

Oh, it was not a pheasant cock,
    Nor yet a pheasant hen,
But oh it was a lady fair
    Came swimming down the stream.

An ancient harper passing by
    Found this poor lady's body,
To which his pains he did apply
    To make a sweet melòdy.

To catgut dried he her inside,
  He drew out her backbone,
And made thereof a fiddle
  All for to play upon.

And all her hair so long and fair,
  That down her back did flow,
Oh he did lay it up with care,
  To string his fiddle bow.

And what did he do with her fingers
  Which were so straight and small?
Oh, he did cut them into pegs
  To screw up his fid-dòll.

Then forth went he, as it might be,
  Upon a summer's day,
And met a goodly company,
  Which asked him in to play.

Then from her bones he drew such tones
  As made their bones to ache,
They sounded so like human groans,
  Their hearts began to quake.

They ordered him in ale to swim,
  For sorrow's mighty dry,
And he to share their wassail fare
  Essayed right willingly.

He laid his fiddle on a shelf
  In that old manor-hall,
It played and sung all by itself
  And thus sung this fid-dòll:

'There sits the squire, my worthy sire,
  A-drinking his-self drunk,
And so did he, ah woe is me!
  The day my body sunk.

'There sits my mother, half asleep,
  A-taking of her ease,
Her mind is deep, if one might peep,
  In her preserves and keys.

'There sits my sister, cruel Joan,
    Who last week drownded me;
And there's my love, with heart of stone,
    Sits making love to she.

'There sits the Crowner, Uncle Joe,
    Which comforteth poor me;
He'll hold his Crowner's quest, I know,
    To get his Crowner's fee.'

Now when this fiddle thus had spoke,
    It fell upon the floor,
And into little pieces broke
    No word spoke never more.

THE INCHCAPE ROCK

No stir in the air, no stir in the sea,
The ship was still as she could be,
Her sails from heaven received no motion,
Her keel was steady in the ocean.

Without either sign or sound of their shock
The waves flow'd over the Inchcape Rock;
So little they rose, so little they fell,
They did not move the Inchcape Bell.

The Abbot of Aberbrothok
Had placed that bell on the Inchcape Rock;
On a buoy in the storm it floated and swung,
And over the waves its warning rung.

When the Rock was hid by the surge's swell,
The mariners heard the warning bell;
And then they knew the perilous Rock,
And blest the Abbot of Aberbrothok.

The Sun in heaven was shining gay,
All things were joyful on that day;
The sea-birds scream'd as they wheel'd round,
And there was joyaunce in their sound.

The buoy of the Inchcape Bell was seen
A darker speck on the ocean green;
Sir Ralph the Rover walk'd his deck,
And he fixed his eye on the darker speck.

He felt the cheering power of spring,
It made him whistle, it made him sing;
His heart was mirthful to excess,
But the Rover's mirth was wickedness.

His eye was on the Inchcape float;
Quoth he, 'My men, put out the boat,
And row me to the Inchcape Rock,
And I'll plague the Abbot of Aberbrothok.'

The boat is lower'd, the boatmen row,
And to the Inchcape Rock they go;
Sir Ralph bent over from the boat,
And he cut the Bell from the Inchcape float.

Down sunk the Bell with a gurgling sound,
The bubbles rose and burst around;
Quoth Sir Ralph, 'The next who comes to the Rock
Wo'n't bless the Abbot of Aberbrothok.'

Sir Ralph the Rover sail'd away,
He scour'd the seas for many a day;
And now grown rich with plunder'd store,
He steers his course for Scotland's shore.

So thick a haze o'erspreads the sky
They cannot see the Sun on high;
The wind hath blown a gale all day,
At evening it hath died away.

On the deck the Rover takes his stand,
So dark it is they see no land,
Quoth Sir Ralph, 'It will be lighter soon,
For there is the dawn of the rising Moon.'

'Canst hear,' said one, 'the breakers roar?
For methinks we should be near the shore.'
'Now where we are I cannot tell,
But I wish I could hear the Inchcape Bell.'

They hear no sound, the swell is strong;
Though the wind hath fallen they drift along,
Till the vessel strikes with a shivering shock, –
'Oh Christ! it is the Inchcape Rock!'

Sir Ralph the Rover tore his hair;
He curst himself in his despair;
The waves rush in on every side,
The ship is sinking beneath the tide.

But even in his dying fear
One dreadful sound could the Rover hear,
A sound as if with the Inchcape Bell,
The Devil below was ringing his knell.

Robert Southey

DANIEL

Darius the Mede was a king and a wonder.
His eye was proud, and his voice was thunder.
He kept bad lions in a monstrous den.
He fed up the lions on Christian men.

Daniel was the chief hired man of the land.
He stirred up the music in the palace band.
He whitewashed the cellar. He shovelled in the coal.
And Daniel kept a-praying: — 'Lord save my soul.'
Daniel kept a-praying: — 'Lord save my soul.'
Daniel kept a-praying: — 'Lord save my soul.'

Daniel was the butler, swagger and swell.
He ran upstairs. He answered the bell.
And *he* would let in whoever came a-calling: —
Saints so holy, scamps so appalling.
'Old man Ahab leaves his card.
Elisha and the bears are a-waiting in the yard.
Here comes Pharaoh and his snakes a-calling.
Here comes Cain and his wife a-calling.
Shadrach, Meshach and Abednego for tea.
Here comes Jonah and the whale,
And the *Sea*!
Here comes St Peter and his fishing pole.
Here comes Judas and his silver a-calling.
Here comes old Beelzebub a-calling.'
And Daniel kept a-praying: — 'Lord save my soul.'
Daniel kept a-praying: — 'Lord save my soul.'
Daniel kept a-praying: — 'Lord save my soul.'

His sweetheart and his mother were Christian and meek.
They washed and ironed for Darius every week.
One Thursday he met them at the door: —
Paid them as usual, but acted sore.

He said: — 'Your Daniel is a dead little pigeon.
He's a good hard worker, but he talks religion.'
And he showed them Daniel in the lions' cage.
Daniel standing quietly, the lions in a rage.
His good old mother cried: —
'Lord save him.'
And Daniel's tender sweetheart cried: —
'Lord save him.'

And she was a golden lily in the dew.
And she was as sweet as an apple on the tree,
And she was as fine as a melon in the corn-field,
Gliding and lovely as a ship on the sea,
Gliding and lovely as a ship on the sea.

And she prayed to the Lord: —
'Send Gabriel. Send Gabriel.'

King Darius said to the lions: —
'Bite Daniel. Bite Daniel.
Bite him. Bite him. Bite him!'

Thus roared the lions: —
'We want Daniel, Daniel, Daniel,
We want Daniel, Daniel, Daniel.'

And Daniel did not frown,
Daniel did not cry.
He kept looking at the sky.
And the Lord said to Gabriel: —
'Go chain the lions down,
Go chain the lions down.
Go chain the lions down.
Go chain the lions down.'

And *Gabriel* chained the lions,
And *Gabriel* chained the lions,
And *Gabriel* chained the lions,
And Daniel got out of the den,
And Daniel got out of the den,
And Daniel got out of the den.

And Darius said: — 'You're a Christian child,'
Darius said: — 'You're a Christian child,'
Darius said: — 'You're a Christian child,'
And gave him his job again,
And gave him his job again,
And gave him his job again.

Vachel Lindsay

THE BITTER WITHY

As it befell on a bright holiday
   Small hail from the sky did fall.
Our Saviour asked his mother dear
   If he might go and play at ball.

'At ball, at ball, my own dear son,
   It is time that you were gone.
But don't let me hear of any doings
   At night when you come home.'

So up the hill and down the hill
   Our sweet young Saviour run,
Until he met three rich young lords
   A-walking in the sun.

'Good morn, good morn, good morn', said they.
   'Good morning all', said he.
'And which of you three rich young lords
   Will play at ball with me?'

'We are all lords' and ladies' sons
   Born in our bower and hall,
And you are nothing but a Jewess's child
   Born in an ox's stall.'

'If you're all lords' and ladies' sons
   Born in your bower and hall,
I'll make you believe in your latter end
   I'm an angel above you all.'

So he made him a bridge of the beams of the sun
   And over the river danced he.
The rich young lords danced after him
   And drowned they were all three.

F

145

Then up the hill and down the hill
  Three rich young mothers run,
Crying: 'Mary mild, fetch home your child,
  For ours he's drowned each one.'

So Mary mild fetched home her child,
  And laid him across her knee,
And with a handful of withy twigs
  She gave him slashes three.

'Ay, bitter withy! Ay, bitter withy!
You've causèd me to smart.
And the withy shall be the very first tree
  To perish at the heart.'

THE DEATH OF CUCHULAIN

A man came slowly from the setting sun,
To Forgail's daughter, Emer, in her dun,
And found her dyeing cloth with subtle care,
And said, casting aside his draggled hair:
'I am Aleel, the swineherd, whom you bid
Go dwell upon the sea cliffs, vapour hid;
But now my years of watching are no more.'

Then Emer cast her web upon the floor,
And stretching her arms, red with the dye,
Parted her lips with a loud sudden cry.

Looking on her, Aleel, the swineherd, said:
'Not any god alive, nor mortal dead,
Has slain so mighty armies, so great kings,
Nor won the gold that now Cuchulain brings.'

'Why do you tremble thus from feet to crown?'

Aleel, the swineherd, wept and cast him down
Upon the web-heaped floor, and thus his word:
'With him is one sweet-throated like a bird.'

'Who bade you tell these things?' and then she cried
To those about, 'Beat him with thongs of hide
And drive him from the door.'
                              And thus it was:
And where her son, Finmole, on the smooth grass
Was driving cattle, came she with swift feet,
And called out to him, 'Son, it is not meet
That you stay idling here with flocks and herds.'

'I long have waited, mother, for those words:
But wherefore now?'
                          'There is a man to die;
You have the heaviest arm under the sky.'

'My father dwells among the sea-worn bands
And breaks the ridge of battle with his hands.'

'Nay, you are taller than Cuchulain, son.'

'He is the mightiest man in ship or dun.'

'Nay, he is old and sad with many wars,
And weary of the crash of battle cars.'

'I only ask what way my journey lies,
For God, who made you bitter, made you wise.'

'The Red Branch kings a tireless banquet keep,
Where the sun falls into the Western deep.
Go there, and dwell on the green forest rim;
But tell alone your name and house to him
Whose blade compels, and bid them send you one
Who has a like vow from their triple dun.'

Between the lavish shelter of a wood
And the gray tide, the Red Branch multitude
Feasted, and with them old Cuchulain dwelt,
And his young dear one close beside him knelt,
And gazed upon the wisdom of his eyes,
More mournful than the depth of starry skies,
And pondered on the wonder of his days;
And all around the harp-string told his praise,
And Concobar, the Red Branch king of kings,
With his own fingers touched the brazen strings.
At last Cuchulain spake: 'A young man strays
Driving the deer along the woody ways.
I often hear him singing to and fro,
I often hear the sweet sound of his bow.
Seek out what man he is.'
                          One went and came.
'He bade me let all know he gives his name
At the sword point, and bade me bring him one
Who had a like vow from our triple dun.'

'I only of the Red Branch hosted now,'
Cuchulain cried, 'have made and keep that vow.'

After short fighting in the leafy shade,
He spake to the young man, 'Is there no maid
Who loves you, no white arms to wrap you round,
Or do you long for the dim sleepy ground,
That you come here to meet this ancient sword?'

'The dooms of men are in God's hidden hoard.'

'Your head a while seemed like a woman's head
That I loved once.'
                    Again the fighting sped,
But now the war rage in Cuchulain woke,
And through the other's shield his long blade broke,
And pierced him.
                    'Speak before your breath is done.'

'I am Finmole, mighty Cuchulain's son.'

'I put you from your pain. I can no more.'

While day its burden on to evening bore,
With head bowed on his knees Cuchulain stayed;
Then Concobar sent that sweet-throated maid,
And she, to win him, his gray hair caressed;
In vain her arms, in vain her soft white breast.
Then Concobar, the subtlest of all men,
Ranking his Druids round him ten by ten,
Spake thus: 'Cuchulain will dwell there and brood,
For three days more in dreadful quietude,
And then arise, and raving slay us all.
Go, cast on him delusions magical,
That he may fight the waves of the loud sea.'
And ten by ten under a quicken tree,
The Druids chaunted, swaying in their hands
Tall wands of alder, and white quicken wands.

In three days' time, Cuchulain with a moan
Stood up, and came to the long sands alone:
For four days warred he with the bitter tide;
And the waves flowed above him, and he died.

                                      W. B. Yeats

10.
CHARMS AND SPELLS

Where is it now? 'tis gone: and see, where God
Stretcheth out his arm, and bends his ireful brows:
Mountains and hills, come, come, and fall on me,
And hide me from the heavy wrath of God!
No, no!
Then will I headlong run into the earth:
Earth, gape! O no, it will not harbour me.
You stars that reign'd at my nativity,
Whose influence hath allotted death and hell,
Now draw up Faustus like a foggy mist,
Into the entrails of yon lab'ring cloud,
That when you vomit forth into the air,
My limbs may issue from your smoky mouths,
So that my soul may but ascend to heaven!
                                    [The clock strikes the half-hour.
Ah, half the hour is past:
'Twill all be past anon:
Oh God,
If thou wilt not have mercy on my soul,
Yet for Christ's sake, whose blood hath ransom'd me,
Impose some end to my incessant pain!
Let Faustus live in hell a thousand years,
A hundred thousand, and at last be saved!
O no end is limited to damnèd souls,
Why wert thou not a creature wanting soul?
Or, why is this immortal that thou hast?
Ah, Pythagoras' *metemsucosis*, were that true,
This soul should fly from me, and I be chang'd
Unto some brutish beast! all beasts are happy,
For when they die,
Their souls are soon dissolv'd in elements,
But mine must live still to be plagued in hell:
Curst be the parents that ingend'red me:
No, Faustus, curse thyself, curse Lucifer,
That hath depriv'd thee of the joys of heaven:
                                    [The clock strikes twelve.
O it strikes, it strikes! Now, body, turn to air,
Or Lucifer will bear thee quick to hell!
                                    [Thunder and lightning.
O soul, be chang'd into little water drops,
And fall into the ocean, ne'er be found!
My God, my God, look not so fierce on me!
                                    [Enter devils.

152

Adders and serpents, let me breathe a while!
Ugly hell, gape not, come not, Lucifer!
I'll burn my books! — Ah, Mephastophilis!

[*Exeunt devils with Faustus.*

Chorus   Cut is the branch that might have grown full straight,
And burnèd is Apollo's laurel-bough,
That sometime grew within this learnèd man.
Faustus is gone: regard his hellish fall,
Whose fiendful fortune may exhort the wise,
Only to wonder at unlawful things,
Whose deepness doth entice such forward wits
To practise more than heavenly power permits.

Christopher Marlowe

A SPELL

Be not afraid of every stranger,
Start not aside at every danger:
Things that seem are not the same,
Blow a blast at every flame:
For when one flame of fire goes out,
Then comes your wishes well about:
If any ask who told you this good,
Say the white Bear of England's wood.

George Peele

I SAW A FISH-POND ALL ON FIRE

I saw a fish-pond all on fire,
I saw a house bow to a squire,
I saw a parson twelve feet high,
I saw a cottage in the sky,
I saw a balloon made of lead,
I saw a coffin drop down dead,
I saw two sparrows run a race,
I saw two horses making lace,
I saw a girl just like a cat,
I saw a kitten wear a hat,
I saw a man who saw these too,
And said though strange they all were true.

(*In each line move the comma back behind the first
noun, and read it again*)

I SAW A PEACOCK

I saw a peacock with a fiery tail,
I saw a blazing comet drop down hail,
I saw a cloud wrapped with ivy round,
I saw an oak creep along the ground,
I saw a pismire swallow up a whale,
I saw the sea brimful of ale,
I saw a Venice glass full fifteen fathom deep,
I saw a well full of men's tears that weep,
I saw red eyes all of a flaming fire,
I saw a house bigger than the moon and higher,
I saw the sun at twelve o'clock at night,
I saw the man that saw this wondrous sight.

(In each line move the comma back as before)

A SPELL OF INVISIBILITY

Whilst on thy head I lay my hand,
And charm thee with this magic wand,
First wear this girdle, then appear
Invisible to all are here:
The Planets seven, the gloomy air,
Hell, and the Furies' forkèd hair,
Pluto's blue fire, and Hecat's tree
With magic spells so compass thee,
That no eye may thy body see.

Christopher Marlowe (?)

THE VILLAGE OF ERITH

There are men in the village of Erith
Whom nobody seeth or heareth,
And there looms, on the marge
Of the river, a barge
That nobody roweth or steereth.

NOW THE HUNGRY LION ROARS

Now the hungry lion roars,
And the wolf behowls the moon;
Whilst the heavy ploughman snores,
All with weary task fordone.

Now the wasted brands do glow,
  Whilst the screech-owl, screeching loud,
Puts the wretch that lies in woe
  In remembrance of a shroud.
Now it is the time of night,
  That the graves, all gaping wide,
Every one lets forth his sprite,
  In the church-way paths to glide . . .

William Shakespeare

THE CAULD LAD'S SONG

Wae's me, wae's me,
The acorn's not yet
Fallen from the tree
That's to grow the wood
That's to make the cradle
That's to rock the bairn.
That's to grow a man,
That's to lay me.

LOLLOCKS

By sloth on sorrow fathered,
These dusty-featured Lollocks
Have their nativity in all disordered
Backs of cupboard drawers.

They play hide and seek
Among collars and novels
And empty medicine bottles,
And letters from abroad
That never will be answered.

Every sultry night
They plague little children,
Gurgling from the cistern,
Humming from the air,
Skewing up the bed-clothes,
Twitching the blind.

When the imbecile agèd
Are over-long in dying
And the nurse drowses,

Lollocks come skipping
Up the tattered stairs
And are nasty together
In the bed's shadow.

The signs of their presence
Are boils on the neck,
Dreams of vexation suddenly recalled
In the middle of the morning,
Languor after food.

Men cannot see them,
Men cannot hear them,
Do not believe in them —
But suffer the more,
Both in neck and belly.

Women can see them —
O those naughty wives
Who sit by the fireside
Munching bread and honey,
Watching them in mischief
From corners of their eyes,
Slily allowing them to lick
Honey-sticky fingers.

Sovereign against Lollocks
Are hard broom and soft broom,
To well comb the hair,
To well brush the shoe,
And to pay every debt
As it falls due.

Robert Graves

THE GOBLIN'S SONG

O where is tiny Hewe?
  O where is little Lenne?
An' where is bonnie Lu?
  An' Menie o' the Glen?
An' where's the place o' rest?
  The ever-changin' hame —
Is't in the gowan's breast
  Or 'neath the bells o' faem?
    Ay lu lan, lan dil y'u.

156

The fairest rose you'll find
  May have a taint within —
The flower o' womankind
  May ope her breast to sin.
The fox-glove cupp you'll bring,
  The tayle o' shootin' sterne,
An' at the grassy ringe
  We'll pledge the bluid o' ferne.
    Ay lu lan, lan dil y'u.

And when the blushing moon
  Glides down the western skye,
By streamers wing, we soone
  Upon her top will lye:
Her hiest horne we'll ride
  An' quaffe her yellow dewe,
An' frae her skaddowy side
  The burnin' daie we'll view.
    Ay lu lan, lan dil y'u.

James Telfer

THE FAIRIES

Up the airy mountain,
  Down the rushy glen,
We daren't go a-hunting
  For fear of little men;
Wee folk, good folk,
  Trooping all together;
Green jacket, red cap,
  And white owl's feather!

Down along the rocky shore
  Some make their home,
They live on crispy pancakes
  Of yellow tide-foam;
Some in the reeds
  Of the black mountain lake,
With frogs for their watch-dogs,
  All night awake.

High on the hill-top
  The old King sits;

157

He is now so old and gray
  He's nigh lost his wits.
With a bridge of white mist
  Columbkill he crosses,
On his stately journeys
  From Slieveleague to Rosses;
Or going up with music
  On cold starry nights,
To sup with the Queen
  Of the gay Northern Lights.

They stole little Bridget
  For seven years long;
When she came down again
  Her friends were all gone.
They took her lightly back,
  Between the night and morrow,
They thought that she was fast asleep,
  But she was dead with sorrow.
They have kept her ever since
  Deep within the lake,
On a bed of flag-leaves,
  Watching till she wake.

By the craggy hill-side,
  Through the mosses bare,
They have planted thorn-trees
  For pleasure here and there.
If any man so daring
  As dig them up in spite,
He shall find their sharpest thorns
  In his bed at night.

Up the airy mountain,
  Down the rushy glen,
We daren't go a-hunting
  For fear of little men;
Wee folk, good folk,
  Trooping all together;
Green jacket, red cap,
  And white owl's feather!

William Allingham

ALL, ALL A-LONELY

Three little children sitting on the sand,
All, all a-lonely,
Three little children sitting on the sand,
All, all a-lonely,
Down in the green wood shady –
There came an old woman, said, Come on with me,
All, all a-lonely.
There came an old woman, said, Come on with me,
All, all a-lonely,
Down in the green wood shady –
She stuck her pen-knife through their heart,
All, all a-lonely,
She stuck her pen-knife through their heart,
All, all a-lonely,
Down in the green wood shady.

GIN BY PAILFULS

Gin by pailfuls, wine in rivers,
Dash the window-glass to shivers,
For three wild lads were we, brave boys,
And three wild lads were we;
Thou on the land, and I on the sand,
And Jack on the gallows-tree!

Sir Walter Scott

THE MILK-WHITE DOVE

Pew, pew,
My minny me slew,
My daddy me chew,
My sister gathered my banes,
And put them between twa milk-white stanes;
And I grew, and I grew,
To a milk-white doo,
And I took to my wings,
And away I flew.

A WITCH'S SPELL

Meare's milk and deer's milk
And every beast that bears milk,
Between St Johnston and Dundee,
Come a' to me, come a' to me.

MOTHER MAUDLIN THE WITCH

Within a gloomy dimble she doth dwell
Down in a pit o'ergrown with brakes and briars,
Close by the ruins of a shaken abbey
Torn, with an earthquake, down unto the ground,
'Mongst graves, and grots, near an old charnel house,
Where you shall find her sitting in her form,
As fearful, and melancholic, as that
She is about; with caterpillar's kells,
And knotty cobwebs, rounded in with spells;
Thence she steals forth to relief, in the fogs,
And rotten mists, upon the fens, and bogs,
Down to the drownèd lands of Lincolnshire;
To make ewes cast their lambs . . .

                                        Ben Jonson

dimble: *ravine or gully*; kells: *cocoons*; relief: *seek food*

THE WITCH'S BROOMSTICK SPELL

Horse and hattock
Horse and go
Horse and pelatis, ho, ho!

THE WITCHES

Heyhow for Hallow e'en
When all the witches are to be seen,
Some in black and some in green,
Heyhow for Hallow e'en.

THE HAUNTED PALACE

In the greenest of our valleys
    By good angels tenanted,
Once a fair and stately palace —
    Radiant palace — reared its head.
In the monarch Thought's dominion —
    It stood there!
Never seraph spread a pinion
    Over fabric half so fair!

Banners yellow, glorious, golden,
  On its roof did float and flow,
(This – all this – was in the olden
  Time long ago),
And every gentle air that dallied,
  In that sweet day,
Along the ramparts plumed and pallid,
  A wingéd odour went away.

Wanderers in that happy valley,
  Through two luminous windows, saw
Spirits moving musically,
  To a lute's well-tunéd law,
Round about a throne where, sitting
  (Porphyrogene!)
In state his glory well befitting,
  The ruler of the realm was seen.

And all with pearl and ruby glowing
    Was the fair palace door,
Through which came flowing, flowing, flowing
  And sparkling evermore,
A troop of Echoes, whose sweet duty
  Was but to sing,
In voices of surpassing beauty,
  The wit and wisdom of their king.

But evil things, in robes of sorrow,
  Assailed the monarch's high estate.
(Ah, let us mourn! – for never morrow
  Shall dawn upon him desolate!)
And round about his home the glory
  That blushed and bloomed,
Is but a dim-remembered story
  Of the old time entombed.

And travellers, now, within that valley,
  Through the red-litten windows see
Vast forms, that move fantastically
  To a discordant melody,
While, like a ghastly rapid river,
  Through the pale door
A hideous throng rush out forever
  And laugh – but smile no more.

Edgar Allan Poe

Be not frighted with our fashion,
　　Though we seem a tatter'd nation;
　　We account our rags our riches,
　　So our tricks exceed our stitches.

Give us bacon, rinds of walnuts,
　　Shells of cockles and of small nuts,
　　Ribands, bells, and saffron'd linen,
　　All the world is ours to win in.

Knacks we have that will delight you,
　　Sleights of hand that will invite you
　　To indure our tawny faces
　　And not cause you quit your places.

All your fortunes we can tell ye,
　　Be they for the back or belly,
　　In the moods too and the tenses
　　That may fit your fine five senses.

Draw but then your gloves, we pray you,
　　And sit still, we will not fray you.

Ben Jonson

JACKIE FAA

The gypsies they came to my lord Cassilis' yett,
　　And O but they sang bonnie!
They sang so sweet and so complete
　　Till down came our fair ladie.

She came tripping down the stairs,
　　And all her maids before her;
As soon as they saw her weel-far'd face,
　　They cast their glamourie owre her.

She gave them the good wheat bread,
　　And they give her the ginger;
But she give them a far better thing,
　　The gold rings of her finger.

'Will you go with me, my hinny and my heart?
　　Will you go with me, my dearie?
And I will swear, by the hilt of my spear,
　　That your lord shall no more come near thee.'

'Gar take from me my silk manteel,
    And bring to me a plaidie,
For I will travel the world owre
    Along with the gypsie laddie.

'I could sail the seas with my Jackie Faa,
    I could sail the seas with my dearie;
I could sail the seas with my Jackie Faa,
    And with pleasure could drown with my dearie.'

They wandred high, they wandred low,
    They wandred late and early,
Until they came to an old farmer's barn,
    And by this time she was weary.

'Last night I lay in a weel-made bed,
    And my noble lord beside me,
And now I must lie in an old farmer's barn,
    And the black crae glowring owre me.'

'Hold your tongue, my hinny and my heart,
    Hold your tongue, my dearie,
For I will swear, by the moon and the stars,
    That thy lord shall no more come near thee.'

They wandred high, they wandred low,
    They wandred late and early,
Until they came to that on-water,
    And by this time she was weary.

'Many a time have I rode that on-water,
  · And my lord Cassilis beside me,
And now I must set in my white feet and wade,
    And carry the gypsie laddie.'

By and by came home this noble lord,
    And asking for his ladie,
The one did cry, the other did reply,
    'She is gone with the gypsie laddie.'

'Go saddle to me the black,' he says,
    'The brown rides never so speedie,
And I will neither eat nor drink
    Till I bring home my ladie.'

He wandred high, he wandred low,
  He wandred late and early,
Until he came to that on-water,
  And there he spied his ladie.

'O wilt thou go home, my hinny and my heart,
  O wilt thou go home, my dearie?
And I'll close thee in a close room,
  Where no man shall come near thee.'

'I will not go home, my hinny and my heart,
  I will not go home, my dearie;
If I have brewn good beer, I will drink of the same,
  And my lord shall no more come near me.

'But I will swear, by the moon and the stars,
  And the sun that shines so clearly,
That I am as free of the gypsie gang
  As the hour my mother bore me.'

They were fifteen valiant men,
  Black, but very bonnie,
They lost all their lives for one,
  The Earl of Cassilis' ladie.

yett: *gate*; glamourie: *spell*; hinny: *honey*; crae: *crow*; on
water: *ford*

GIPSIES

The gipsies seek wide sheltering woods again,
With droves of horses flock to mark their lane,
And trample on dead leaves, and hear the sound,
And look and see the black clouds gather round,
And set their camps, and free from muck and mire,
And gather stolen sticks to make the fire.
The roasted hedgehog, bitter though as gall,
Is eaten up and relished by them all.
They know the woods and every fox's den
And get their living far away from men;
The shooters ask them where to find the game,
The rabbits know them and are almost tame.
The aged women, tawny with the smoke,
Go with the winds and crack the rotted oak.

John Clare

164

THE GIPSY CAMP

(In Epping Forest)

The snow falls deep; the Forest lies alone:
The boy goes hasty for his load of brakes,
Then thinks upon the fire and hurries back;
The Gipsy knocks his hands and tucks them up,
And seeks his squalid camp, half hid in snow,
Beneath the oak which breaks away the wind,
And pushes close, with snow-like hovel warm;
There stinking mutton roasts upon the coals,
And the half-roasted dog squats close and rubs,
Then feels the heat too strong and goes aloof;
He watches well, but none a bit can spare,
And vainly waits the morsel thrown away:
'Tis thus they live – a picture to the place;
A quiet, pilfering, unprotected race.

John Clare

THE TWO RIVERS

Says Tweed to Till
'What gars ye rin sae still?'
Says Till to Tweed
'Though ye rin with speed
And I rin slaw,
For a man that ye droon
I droon twa.'

THE THREE RAVENS

There were three ravens sat on a tree,
   Downe a downe, hay downe, hay downe.
There were three ravens sat on a tree,
   With a downe.
There were three ravens sat on a tree,
They were as black as they might be,
   With a downe derrie, derrie, derrie,
     downe, downe.

The one of them said to his mate,
'Where shall we our breakfast take?'

'Down in yonder green field,
There lies a knight slain under his shield.

'His hounds they lie down at his feet,
So well they can their master keep.

'His hawks they fly so eagerly,
There's no fowl dare him come nigh.'

Down there comes a fallow doe,
As great with young as she might go.

She lift up his bloody head,
And kissed his wounds that were so red.

She got him up upon her back,
And carried him to earthen lake.

She buried him before the prime,
She was dead herself ere evensong time.

God send every gentleman
Such hawks, such hounds, and such a leman.

COUNTING-OUT RHYME

Zeenty, peenty, heathery, mithery,
Bumfy, leery, over, Dover,
Saw the King of Heazle Peazle
Jumping o'er Jerusalem Dyke:
  Black fish, white trout
  Eerie, ourie, you're out.

EX AND SQUAREY

Ex and Squarey, Virgin Mary,
Vick, Vock, Little Stock,
O.U.T. spells out, so out goes . . .

THE ELDER TREE

Bourtree, bourtree, crookit rung,
Never straight, and never strong,
Ever bush, and never tree,
Since our Lord was nailed t' ye.

A CHARM

If ye fear to be affrighted
When ye are (by chance) benighted,
In your pocket for a trust
Carry nothing but a crust:
For that holy piece of bread
Charms the danger, and the dread.

Robert Herrick

A HOUSE BLESSING

Saint Francis and Saint Benedight
Bless this house from wicked wight,
From the nightmare, and the goblin,
That is hight Good-fellow Robin;
Keep it from all evil spirits,
Fairies, weasels, rats, and ferrets,
From curfew time
To the next prime.

William Cartright

THE NATIVITY CHANT

Canny moment, lucky fit;
Is the lady lighter yet?
Be it lad, or be it lass,
Sign wi' cross, and sain wi' mass.

Trefoil, vervain, John's-wort, dill,
Hinders witches of their will;
Weel is them, that weel may
Fast upon Saint Andrew's day.

Saint Bride and her brat,
Saint Colme and her cat,
Saint Michael and his spear,
Keep this house frae reif and wear.

Sir Walter Scott

sain: *sanctify*; reif: *robbery*

167

TEN COMMANDMENTS,
SEVEN DEADLY SINS,
AND FIVE WITS

Kepe well x, and flee fro vii,
Rule well v, and come to hevyn.

GRACE BEFORE MEAT

Here a little child I stand,
Heaving up my either hand;
Cold as paddocks though they be,
Here I lift them up to Thee,
For a benison to fall
On our meat, and on us all. *Amen.*

Robert Herrick

FIT ONLY FOR APOLLO

Shake off your heavy trance,
And leap into a dance
Such as no mortals use to tread:
Fit only for Apollo
To play to, for the moon to lead,
And all the stars to follow!

Francis Beaumont

THE SICK ROSE

O Rose, thou art sick!
The invisible worm
That flies in the night,
In the howling storm,
Has found out thy bed
Of crimson joy,
And his dark secret love
Does thy life destroy.

William Blake

11. ENCHANTMENTS

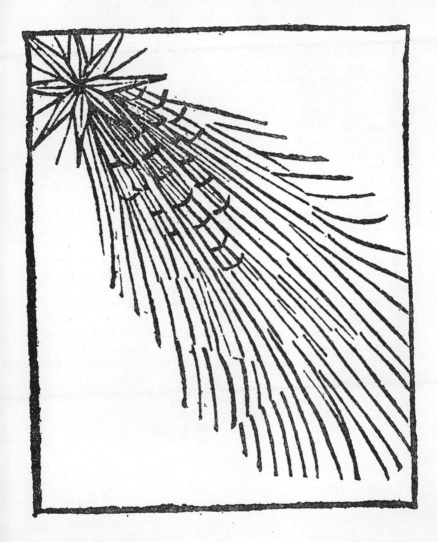

Enchantments

Here are more spellbinding or enchanting poems, introduced by a woodcut of a comet with a fiery tail – that rare kind of comet which glitters in a daylight sky.

If you are 'spellbound', you lose yourself for a while. It is not only creatures of more than natural power which can exert this binding. You can be spellbound by something especially beautiful, by the brilliance of the full moon on a summer night, for example – like Jessica and Lorenzo, in love, on the opposite page. In such a night as this, wonderful things happened (including the gathering of enchanted herbs by the witch Medea).

Look back again at the wonder-poems on pages 153 and 154. One moment in these poems we are spellbound, next moment we are back in the ordinary world. One moment I see a Venice glass fifteen fathoms deep, and a well full of men's tears, and red eyes all of a flaming fire. Push back the comma in the poem and I am returned to the ordinary world. I see a well fifteen fathoms deep, and red eyes full of tears, and a house all of a flaming fire.

Poets are not just eating Turkish delight when they indulge themselves with strangeness and wonder – in such a night as this. They may be seeing into things, and making rhythms of a 'vision of reality', in

> A hunger for the apple on the bough
> Most out of reach.
>
> (W. B. Yeats)

IN SUCH A NIGHT

Lorenzo   The moon shines bright. In such a night as this,
When the sweet wind did gently kiss the trees,
And they did make no noise, – in such a night
Troilus methinks mounted the Troyan walls,
And sigh'd his soul toward the Grecian tents,
Where Cressid lay that night.

Jessica   In such a night
Did Thisbe fearfully o'ertrip the dew,
And saw the lion's shadow ere himself,
And ran dismay'd away.

Lorenzo   In such a night
Stood Dido with a willow in her hand
Upon the wild sea-banks, and waft her love
To come again to Carthage.

Jessica   In such a night
Medea gather'd the enchanted herbs
That did renew old Æson.

Lorenzo   In such a night
Did Jessica steal from the wealthy Jew,
And with an unthrift love did run from Venice,
As far as Belmont.

Jessica   In such a night
Did young Lorenzo swear he loved her well,
Stealing her soul with many vows of faith,
And n'er a true one.

Lorenzo   In such a night
Did pretty Jessica (like a little shrew)
Slander her love, and he forgave it her.

Jessica   I would out-night you, did no body come:
But hark, I hear the footing of a man . . .

William Shakespeare

TOM O'BEDLAM'S SONG

From the hag and hungry goblin
That into rags would rend ye,
And the spirit that stands by the naked man
In the Book of Moons defend ye!
That of your five sound senses
You never be forsaken,
Nor wander from yourselves with Tom
Abroad to beg your bacon,
    While I do sing *Any food, any feeding,*
    Feeding, drink or clothing,
    Come dame or maid, be not afraid,
    Poor Tom will injure nothing.

Of thirty bare years have I
Twice twenty bin enragèd,
And of forty bin three times fifteen
In durance soundly cagèd
On the lordly lofts of Bedlam,
With stubble soft and dainty,
Brave bracelets strong, sweet whips ding-dong,
With wholesome hunger plenty.
    And now I sing, etc.

With a thought I took for Maudlin,
And a cruse of cockle pottage,
With a thing thus tall, sky bless you all,
I befell into this dotage,
I slept not since the Conquest,
Till then I never wakèd,
Till the roguish boy of love where I lay
Me found and stripped me naked.
    And now I sing, etc.

When I short have shorn my sour face
And swigged my horny barrel,
In an oaken inn I pound my skin
As a suit of gilt apparel.
The moon's my constant Mistress,
And the lowly owl my morrow,
The flaming drake and the nightcrow make
Me music to my sorrow.
    While I do sing, etc.

The palsy plagues my pulses
When I prig your pigs or pullen,
Your culvers take, or matchless make
Your chanticlere, or sullen.
When I want provant, with Humfrie
I sup, and when benighted,
I repose in Powl's with waking souls,
Yet never am affrighted.
    But I do sing, etc.

I know more than Apollo,
For oft, when he lies sleeping,
I see the stars at bloody wars
In the wounded welkin weeping;
The moon embrace her shepherd,
And the Queen of Love her warrior.
While the first doth horn the star of morn,
And the next the heavenly Farrier.
    While I do sing, etc.

The gipsy Snap and Pedro
Are none of Tom's comradoes.
The punk I scorn and the cutpurse sworn
And the roaring boys' bravado.
The meek, the white, the gentle,
Me handle, touch, and spare not,
But those that cross Tom Rynosseros
Do what the panther dare not.
    Although I sing, etc.

With an host of furious fancies,
Whereof I am commander,
With a burning spear, and a horse of air,
To the wilderness I wander.
By a knight of ghosts and shadows
I summoned am to tourney
Ten leagues beyond the wild world's end,
Methinks it is no journey.

    Yet will I sing *Any food, any feeding,*
    Feeding, drink or clothing,
    Come, dame or maid, be not afraid,
    Poor Tom will injure nothing.

    hag: witch; pullen: poultry; provant: *provender*

173

THE VOICE FROM THE WELL OF LIFE
SPEAKS TO THE MAIDEN

Gently dip: but not too deep;
For fear you make the golden beard to weep.

(*A head comes up with ears of corn,*
and she combs them in her lap.)

Fair maiden white and red,
Comb me smooth, and stroke my head:
And thou shalt have some cockell bread.
Gently dip, but not too deep,
For fear thou make the golden beard to weep.

Fair maid, white, and red,
Comb me smooth, and stroke my head;
And every hair, a sheave shall be,
And every sheave a golden tree.

(*A head comes up full of gold,*
she combs it into her lap) . . .

George Peele

GOOSE AND GANDER

Grey goose and gander,
Weft your wings together,
And carry the king's fair daughter
Over the one-strand river.

ENITHARMON'S SONG

I seize the sphery harp. I strike the strings.

At the first sound the golden sun arises from the deep
And shakes his awful hair,
The echo wakes the moon to unbind her silver locks,
The golden sun bears on my song
And nine bright spheres of harmony rise round the
fiery king . . .

William Blake

THOMAS RYMER AND THE QUEEN
OF ELFLAND

True Thomas lay o'er yond grassy bank,
   And he beheld a ladie gay,
A ladie that was brisk and bold,
   Come riding o'er the fernie brae.

Her skirt was of the grass-green silk,
   Her mantle of the velvet fine,
At ilka tett of her horse's mane
   Hung fifty silver bells and nine.

True Thomas he took off his hat,
   And bowed him low down till his knee:
'All hail, thou mighty Queen of Heaven!
   For your peer on earth I never did see.'

'O no, O no, True Thomas', she says,
   'That name does not belong to me;
I am but the queen of fair Elfland,
   And I'm come here for to visit thee.

'But ye maun go wi me now, Thomas,
   True Thomas, ye maun go wi me,
For ye maun serve me seven years,
   Thro weel or wae as may chance to be.'

She turned about her milk-white steed,
   And took true Thomas up behind,
And aye whene'er her bridle rang,
   The steed flew swifter than the wind.

For forty days and forty nights
   He wade thro red blude to the knee,
And he saw neither sun nor moon,
   But heard the roaring of the sea.

O they rade on, and farther on,
   Until they came to a garden green:
'Light down, light down, ye ladie free,
   Some of that fruit let me pull to thee.'

'O no, O no, True Thomas', she says.
　'That fruit maun not be touched by thee,
For a' the plagues that are in hell
　Light on the fruit of this countrie.

'But I have a loaf here in my lap,
　Likewise a bottle of claret wine,
And now ere we go farther on,
　We'll rest a while, and ye may dine.'

When he had eaten and drunk his fill,
　'Lay down your head upon my knee',
The lady sayd, 'ere we climb yon hill,
　And I will show you fairlies three.

'O see not ye yon narrow road,
　So thick beset wi thorns and briers?
That is the path of righteousness,
　Tho after it but few enquires.

'And see not ye that braid braid road,
　That lies across yon lillie leven?
That is the path of wickedness,
　Tho some call it the road to heaven.

'And see not ye that bonny road,
　Which winds about the fernie brae?
That is the road to fair Elfland,
　Where you and I this night maun gae.

'But, Thomas, ye maun hold your tongue,
　Whatever you may hear or see,
For gin ae word you should chance to speak,
　Ye will ne'er get back to your ain countrie.'

He has gotten a coat of the even cloth,
　And a pair of shoes of velvet green,
And till seven years were past and gone
　True Thomas on earth was never seen.

fairlies: *wonders*; lillie leven: *lovely lawn or glade*

In Xanadu did Kubla Khan
  A stately pleasure-dome decree:
Where Alph, the sacred river, ran
Through caverns measureless to man
  Down to a sunless sea.
So twice five miles of fertile ground
With walls and towers were girdled round:
And here were gardens bright with sinuous rills,
Where blossomed many an incense-bearing tree;
And here were forests ancient as the hills,
Enfolding sunny spots of greenery.

But oh! that deep romantic chasm which slanted
Down the green hill athwart a cedarn cover!
A savage place! as holy and enchanted
As e'er beneath a waning moon was haunted
By woman wailing for her demon-lover!
And from this chasm, with ceaseless turmoil seething,
As if this earth in fast thick pants were breathing,
Amid whose swift half-intermitted burst
Huge fragments vaulted like rebounding hail,
Or chaffy grain beneath the thresher's flail:
And 'mid these dancing rocks at once and ever
It flung up momently the sacred river.
Five miles meandering with a mazy motion
Through wood and dale the sacred river ran,
Then reached the caverns measureless to man,
And sank in tumult to a lifeless ocean:
And 'mid this tumult Kubla heard from far
Ancestral voices prophesying war!

    The shadow of the dome of pleasure
    Floated midway on the waves;
    Where was heard the mingled measure
    From the fountain and the caves.
It was a miracle of rare device,
A sunny pleasure-dome with caves of ice!

    A damsel with a dulcimer
    In a vision once I saw:
    It was an Abyssinian maid,
    And on her dulcimer she played,

Singing of Mount Abora.
Could I revive within me
Her symphony and song,
To such a deep delight 'twould win me,
That with music loud and long,
I would build that dome in air,
That sunny dome! those caves of ice!
And all who heard should see them there,
And all should cry, Beware! Beware!
His flashing eyes, his floating hair!
Weave a circle round him thrice,
And close your eyes with holy dread,
For he on honey-dew hath fed,
And drunk the milk of Paradise.

Samuel Taylor Coleridge

LA BELLE DAME SANS MERCI

O what can ail thee, knight-at-arms,
    Alone and palely loitering?
The sedge has wither'd from the lake,
    And no birds sing.

O what can ail thee, knight-at-arms,
    So haggard and so woe-begone?
The squirrel's granary is full,
    And the harvest's done.

I see a lily on thy brow
    With anguish moist and fever dew,
And on thy cheeks a fading rose
    Fast withereth too.

I met a lady in the meads,
    Full beautiful — a faery's child,
Her hair was long, her foot was light,
    And her eyes were wild.

I made a garland for her head,
  And bracelets too, and fragrant zone;
She look'd at me as she did love,
  And made sweet moan.

I set her on my pacing steed,
  And nothing else saw all day long,
For sidelong would she bend, and sing
  A faery's song.

She found me roots of relish sweet,
  And honey wild, and manna dew,
And sure in language strange she said —
  'I love thee true!'

She took me to her elfin grot,
  And there she wept and sigh'd full sore,
And there I shut her wild, wild eyes
  With kisses four.

And there she lulléd me asleep,
  And there I dream'd — ah! woe betide!
The latest dream I ever dream'd
  On the cold hill's side.

I saw pale kings and princes too.
  Pale warriors, death-pale were they all;
They cried — 'La Belle Dame sans Merci
  Hath thee in thrall!'

I saw their starved lips in the gloam,
With horrid warning gapéd wide,
And I awoke and found me here,
  On the cold hill's side.

And this is why I sojourn here,
  Alone and palely loitering,
Though the sedge is wither'd from the lake
  And no birds sing.

John Keats

TO ENTERTAIN DIVINE
ZENOCRATE

Black is the beauty of the brightest day,
The golden ball of heaven's eternal fire
That danc'd with glory on the silver waves,
Now wants the fuel that enflam'd his beams
And all with faintness and for foul disgrace
He binds his temples with a frowning cloud,
Ready to darken earth with endless night:
Zenocrate that gave him light and life,
Whose eyes shot fire from their ivory bowers,
And tempered every soul with lively heat,
Now by the malice of the angry skies,
Whose jealousy admits no second mate,
Draws in the comfort of her latest breath
All dazzled with the hellish mists of death.
Now walk the angels on the walls of heaven,
As sentinels to warn th'immortal souls
To entertain divine Zenocrate.
Apollo, Cynthia, and the ceaseless lamps
That gently look'd upon this loathsome earth,
Shine downwards now no more, but deck the heavens
To entertain divine Zenocrate.
The crystal springs whose taste illuminates
Refined eyes with an eternal sight,
Like triéd silver runs through Paradise
To entertain divine Zenocrate.
The Cherubins and holy Seraphins
That sing and play before the king of kings,
Use all their voices and their instruments
To entertain divine Zenocrate.
And in this sweet and curious harmony
The God that tunes this music to our souls,
Holds out his hand in highest majesty
To entertain divine Zenocrate.

Then let some holy trance convey my thoughts,
Up to the palace of th'imperial heaven,
That this my life may be as short to me
As are the days of sweet Zenocrate . . .

Christopher Marlowe

DIDO MY DEAR, ALAS, IS DEAD

Up then, Melpomene, thou mournfulst Muse of nine,
Such cause of mourning never hadst afore:
Up, grieslie ghosts! and up, my rueful rhyme!
Matter of mirth now shalt thou have no more;
For dead she is, that mirth thee made of yore.
   Dido my dear, alas, is dead,
   Dead, and lieth wrapt in lead:
      O heavy hearse!
Let streaming tears be pourèd out in store:
      O careful verse!

Shepherds, that by your flocks on Kentish downs abide,
Wail ye this woeful waste of nature's warke:
Wail we the wight whose presence was our pride:
Wail we the wight whose absence is our carke.
The sun of all the world is dim and dark:
   The earth now lacks her wonted light,
   And all we dwell in deadly night,
      O heavy hearse!
Break we our pipes, that shrilled as loud as lark,
      O careful verse!

Why do we longer live, (ah, why live we so long)
Whose better days death hath shut up in woe?
The fairest floure our gyrlond all emong,
Is faded quite and into dust ygoe.
Sing now, ye shepherds' daughters, sing no moe
   The songs that Colin made you in her praise,
   But into weeping turn your wanton lays,
      O heavy hearse!
Now is time to die. Nay, time was long ygoe,
      O careful verse!

Whence is it, that the flouret of the field doth fade,
And lyeth buried long in winter's bale:
Yet soon as spring his mantle doth display,
It floureth fresh, as it should never fail?
But thing on earth that is of most avail,
   As virtue's braunch and beauty's bud,
    Reliven not for any good,
       O heavy hearse!
The branch once dead, the bud eke needs must quail,
       O careful verse!

She, while she was, (that *was*, a woeful word to sayne)
For beauty's praise and plesaunce had no peer:
So well she couth the shepherds entertain,
With cakes and cracknels and such country cheer.
Ne would she scorn the simple shepherds' swain,
   For she would call hem often heme
    And give hem curds and clouted cream.
       O heavy hearse!
Als Colin Cloute she would not once disdain.
       O careful verse!

But now sike happy cheer is turn'd to heavy chaunce,
Such plesaunce now displaced by dolor's dint:
All music sleeps, where Death doth lead the daunce,
And shepherds' wonted solace is extinct.
The blue in black, the green in grey is tinct,
   The gaudie gyrlonds deck her grave,
    The faded flowres her corse embrave.
       O heavy hearse!
Mourn now, my Muse, now mourn with tears besprint.
       O careful verse!

O thou great shepherd, Lobbin, how great is thy grief!
Where bene the nosegays that she dight for thee?
The colourd chapelets wrought with a chief,
The knotted rush-rings, and gilt rosemaree?
For she deemed no thing too dear for thee.
   Ah, they bene all yclad in clay,
    One bitter blast blew all away.
       O heavy hearse!
Thereof nought remains but the memoree.
       O careful verse!

Ay me, that dreary Death should strike so mortal stroke,
That can undo Dame Nature's kindly course:
The faded locks fall from the lofty oak,
The floods do gasp, for dryèd is their source,
And floods of tears flow in their stead perforce.
  The mantled meadows mourn,
  Their sundry colours tourn.
    O heavy hearse!
The heavens do melt in tears without remorse.
    O careful verse!

The feeble flocks in field refuse their former food,
And hang their heads, as they would learn to weep:
The beasts in forest wail as they were woode,
Except the wolves, that chase the wandring sheep:
Now she is gone that safely did them keep,
  The turtle on the barèd braunch,
  Laments the wound, that Death did launch.
    O heavy hearse,
And Philomele her song with tears doth steep.
    O careful verse!

The water nymphs, that wont with her to sing and daunce,
And for her gyrlond olive braunches bear,
Now baleful boughs of cypress doen advaunce:
The Muses, that were wont green bays to wear,
Now bringen bitter elder braunches sear,
  The Fatal Sisters eke repent,
  Her vital thread so soon was spent.
    O heavy hearse,
Mourn now, my Muse, now mourn with heavy cheer.
    O careful verse!

O trustless state of earthly things, and slipper hope
Of mortal men, that swink and sweat for nought,
And shooting wide, do miss the markèd scope:
Now have I learned, (a lesson dearly bought)
That nys on earth assuraunce to be sought:
  For what might be in earthy mould,
  That did her buried body hold,
    O heavy hearse,
Yet saw I on the bier when it was brought.
    O careful verse!

But maugre Death, and dreaded sisters' deadly spite,
And gates of Hell, and fiery Furies' force:
She hath the bonds broke of eternal night,
Her soul unbodied of the burdenous corpse.
Why then weeps Lobbin so without remorse?
  O Lobb, thy loss no longer lament,
  Dido nis dead, but into Heaven hent.
    O happy hearse!
Cease now, my Muse, now cease thy sorrow's source.
    O joyful verse!

Why wail we then? Why weary we the gods with plaints,
As if some evil were to her betight?
She reigns a goddess now emong the saints,
That whilom was the saint of shepherds' light:
And is enstallèd now in Heaven's height.
  I see thee, blessèd soul, I see,
  Walk in Elysian fields so free.
    O happy hearse!
Might I once come to thee! (O that I might!)
    O joyful verse!

Unwise and wretched men, to weet what's good or ill,
We deem of death as doom of ill desert:
But knew we fools, what it us brings until,
Die would we daily, once it to expert.
No daunger there the shepherd can astert:
  Fair fields and pleasaunt lays there bene,
  The fields ay fresh, the grass ay green:
    O happy hearse!
Make haste, ye shepherds, thither to revert,
    O joyful verse!

Dido is gone afore (whose turn shall be the next?)
There lives she with the blessed gods in bliss,
There drinks she nectar with ambrosia mixt,
And joys enjoys, that mortal men do miss.
The honour now of highest gods she is,
  That whilom was poor shepherd's pride,
  While here on earth she did abide.
    O happy hearse!
Cease now my song, my woe now wasted is.
    O joyful verse! . . .

                              Edmund Spenser

All under the leaves, the leaves of life,
    I met with virgins seven,
And one of them was Mary mild,
    Our Lord's mother from heaven.

'O what are you seeking, you seven fair maids,
    All under the leaves of life?
Come tell, come tell me what seek you
    All under the leaves of life.'

'We're seeking for no leaves, Thomas,
    But for a friend of thine;
We're seeking for sweet Jesus Christ,
    To be our guide and thine.'

'Go you down, go you down to yonder town,
    And sit in the gallery;
And there you'll find sweet Jesus Christ,
    Nailed to a big yew-tree.'

So down they went to yonder town,
    As fast as foot could fall,
And many a grievous bitter tear,
    From the virgins' eyes did fall.

'O peace, mother, O peace, mother,
    Your weeping doth me grieve;
O I must suffer this', he said,
    'For Adam and for Eve.'

'O how can I my weeping leave,
    Or my sorrows undergo,
While I do see my own son die,
    When sons I have no mo'?'

'Dear mother, dear mother, you must take John,
    All for to be your son,
And he will comfort you sometimes,
    Mother, as I have done.'

'O come, thou John Evangelist,
    Thou'rt welcome unto me,
But more welcome my own dear son,
    That I nursed upon my knee.'

Then he laid his head on his right shoulder,
  Seeing death it struck him nigh;
'The Holy Ghost be with your soul, —
  I die, mother dear, I die.'

Oh the rose, the rose, the gentle rose,
  And the fennel that grows so green!
God give us grace in every place
  To pray for our king and queen.

Furthermore for our enemies all
  Our prayers they should be strong.
Amen, Good Lord, your charity
  Is the ending of my song.

THE KNIGHT IN THE BOWER

The heron flew east, the heron flew west,
The heron flew to the fair forest;
She flew o'er streams and meadows green,
And a' to see what could be seen:
And when she saw the faithful pair,
Her breast grew sick, her head grew sair;
For there she saw a lovely bower,
Was a' clad o'er wi' lilly-flower;
And in the bower there was a bed
With silken sheets, and weel down spread:
And in the bed there lay a knight,
Whose wounds did bleed both day and night;
And by the bed there stood a stane,
And there was set a leal maiden,
With silver needle and silken thread,
Stemming the wounds when they did bleed.

CORPUS CHRISTI CAROL

  Lully, lulley; lully, lulley;
  The fawcon hath born my mak away.

He bare hym up, he bare hym down;
He bare hym into an orchard brown.

In that orchard ther was an hall,
That was hangid with purpill and pall.

And in that hall ther was a bede;
Hit was hangid with gold so rede.

And yn that bed ther lythe a knyght,
His wowndes bledyng day and nyght.

By that bedes side ther kneleth a may,
And she wepeth both nyght and day.

And by that beddes side ther stondith a ston.
'Corpus Christi' wretyn theron.

mak: *mate*; may: *maid*

GOOD FRIDAY
(*A Gypsy Song*)

Christ made a trance on Friday view,
   He made it with his hand,
And made the sun clear all off the moon,
   Like water on dry land.

Like water on dry land, man Christ,
   That died upon the cross.
What can we do for our dear lord
   As he has done for us?

O hell is deep and hell is dark,
   And hell is full of mice,
So we'll do as much for our saviour
   As he has done for us.

God was in France all Friday too.
   All with his holy hand
He made the sun clear all off the moon,
   Like the water on dry land.

THE WHITE ISLAND

In this world (the Isle of Dreams)
While we sit by sorrow's streams,
Tears and terrors are our themes
   Reciting:

But when once from hence we fly,
More and more approaching nigh
Unto young Eternity
   Uniting:

187

In that whiter Island, where
Things are evermore sincere;
Candor here, and lustre there
    Delighting:

There no monstrous fancies shall
Out of hell an horror call,
To create (or cause at all)
    Affrighting.

There in calm and cooling sleep
We our eyes shall never steep;
But eternal watch shall keep,
    Attending

Pleasures, such as shall pursue
Me immortaliz'd, and you;
And fresh joys, as never too
    Have ending.

                      Robert Herrick

AND SHE WASHED HIS FEET WITH HER TEARS, AND WIPED THEM WITH THE HAIRS OF HER HEAD

The proud Ægyptian Queen, her Roman guest,
(T'express her love in height of state, and pleasure)
  With pearl dissolv'd in gold did feast,
    Both food, and treasure.

And now (dear Lord!) thy lover, on the fair
And silver tables of thy feet, behold!
  Pearl in her tears, and in her hair
    Offers thee gold.

              Sir Edward Sherburne (from the
                Italian of Giambattista Marino)

12. SHORE AND SEA

Shore and Sea

Here, first, are poems about the broad brims and beaches of the sea. American poets, living in a continent shut in by great inscrutable oceans, have been good at making poetry of those feelings which come to us as we walk along the beaches. So here are poems by Longfellow, Thoreau, Edgar Allan Poe, Robert Frost, Walt Whitman, and Herman Melville, who wrote the ocean epic of *Moby Dick*, the white whale.

After beach poems, poems about denizens of the sea, especially mermaids and whales, which visit sea depths we cannot enter. Have you opened a church door and seen on the wall opposite a huge St Christopher, striding through water and carrying the infant Christ against his neck? St Christopher, ogre changed to Christian ferryman, was painted opposite the doors of churches so that men could see him easily on their way to work each morning. He protected men on journeys. Often on a rock, near his feet, in such a medieval painting, you will see one of the dangers he protected them against – a mermaid, looking in a mirror and combing her hair. Mermaids are beautiful, they sing beautifully (pages 201 and 205) – and they drown the unwary.

> *A mermaid found a swimming lad,*
> *Picked him for her own,*
> *Pressed her body to his body,*
> *Laughed; and plunging down*
> *Forgot in cruel happiness*
> *That even lovers drown.*
>
> (*W. B. Yeats*)

The sea denizen in the woodcut is a Dolphin (from an Italian book of 1505). A dolphin saved a poet. In the Greek story Arion, poet and musician, was thrown overboard, and carried ashore by a dolphin. In gratitude the particular dolphin was immortalized into a constellation, and can be seen, a hump-backed group of faint stars, near Altair, in the summer sky.

THE TIDE RISES, THE TIDE FALLS

The tide rises, the tide falls,
The twilight darkens, the curlew calls;
Along the sea-sands damp and brown
The traveller hastens towards the town,
    And the tide rises, the tide falls.

Darkness settles on roofs and walls,
But the sea, the sea in the darkness calls;
The little waves, with their soft, white hands,
Efface the footprints in the sands,
    And the tide rises, the tide falls.

The morning breaks; the steeds in their stalls
Stamp and neigh, as the hostler calls;
The day returns, but never more
Returns the traveller to the shore,
    And the tide rises, the tide falls.

H. W. Longfellow

THE DANCING SEA

For lo! the sea that fleets about the land,
   And like a girdle clips her solid waist,
Music and measure both doth understand;
   For his great crystal eye is always cast
   Up to the moon, and on her fixèd fast;
    And as she danceth in her pallid sphere,
    So danceth he about the centre here.

Sometimes his proud green waves in order set,
   One after other, flow unto the shore;
Which when they have with many kisses wet,
   They ebb away in order, as before;
   And to make known his courtly love the more,
    He oft doth lay aside his three-forked mace,
    And with his arms the timorous earth embrace.

Only the earth doth stand for ever still:
  Her rocks remove not, nor her mountains meet,
Although some wits enriched with learning's skill
  Say heaven stands firm and that the earth doth fleet,
  And swiftly turneth underneath their feet . . .

Sir John Davies

NEITHER OUT FAR NOR IN DEEP

The people along the sand
All turn and look one way.
They turn their back on the land.
They look at the sea all day.

As long as it takes to pass
A ship keeps raising its hull;
The wetter ground like glass
Reflects a standing gull.

The land may vary more;
But wherever the truth may be —
The water comes ashore,
And the people look at the sea.

They cannot look out far.
They cannot look in deep.
But when was that ever a bar
To any watch they keep?

Robert Frost

THE FISHER'S BOY

My life is like a stroll upon the beach,
  As near the ocean's edge as I can go;
My tardy steps its waves sometimes o'erreach,
  Sometimes I stay to let them overflow.

My sole employment is, and scrupulous care,
  To place my gains beyond the reach of tides,
Each smoother pebble, and each shell more rare,
  Which Ocean kindly to my hand confides.

I have but few companions on the shore:
  They scorn the strand who sail upon the sea;
Yet oft I think the ocean they've sailed o'er
  Is deeper known upon the strand to me.

192

The middle sea contains no crimson dulse,
  Its deeper waves cast up no pearls to view;
Along the shore my hand is on its pulse,
  And I converse with many a shipwrecked crew.

H. D. Thoreau

SEA-SAND AND SORROW

What are heavy? Sea-sand and sorrow:
What are brief? To-day and to-morrow:
What are frail? Spring blossoms and youth:
What are deep? The ocean and truth.

Christina Rossetti

A DREAM WITHIN A DREAM

I stand amid the roar
Of a surf-tormented shore,
And I hold within my hand
Grains of the golden sand —
How few! yet how they creep
Through my fingers to the deep,
While I weep — while I weep!
O God! can I not grasp
Them with a tighter clasp?
O God! can I not save
One from the pitiless wave?
Is all that we see or seem
But a dream within a dream?

Edgar Allan Poe

DEEP AND DARK BLUE OCEAN

There is a pleasure in the pathless woods,
There is a rapture on the lonely shore,
There is society, where none intrudes,
By the deep Sea, and music in its roar:
I love not Man the less, but Nature more,
From these our interviews, in which I steal
From all I may be, or have been before,
To mingle with the Universe, and feel
What I can ne'er express, yet cannot all conceal.

Roll on, thou deep and dark blue Ocean — roll!
Ten thousand fleets sweep over thee in vain;
Man marks the earth with ruin — his control
Stops with the shore; upon the watery plain
The wrecks are all thy deed, nor doth remain
A shadow of man's ravage, save his own,
When, for a moment, like a drop of rain,
He sinks into thy depths with bubbling groan,
Without a grave, unknell'd, uncoffin'd, and unknown.

His steps are not upon thy paths, — thy fields
Are not a spoil for him, — thou dost arise
And shake him from thee; the vile strength he wields
For earth's destruction thou dost all despise,
Spurning him from thy bosom to the skies,
And send'st him, shivering in thy playful spray
And howling, to his Gods, where haply lies
His petty hope in some near port or bay,
And dashest him again to earth: — there let him lay.

The armaments which thunderstrike the walls
Of rock-built cities, bidding nations quake,
And monarchs tremble in their capitals,
The oak leviathans, whose huge ribs make
Their clay creator the vain title take
Of lord of thee, and arbiter of war —
These are thy toys, and, as the snowy flake,
They melt into thy yeast of waves, which mar
Alike the Armada's pride or spoils of Trafalgàr.

Thy shores are empires, changed in all save thee —
Assyria, Greece, Rome, Carthage, what are they?
Thy waters wash'd them power while they were free,
And many a tyrant since; their shores obey
The stranger, slave, or savage; their decay
Has dried up realms to deserts: — not so thou; —
Unchangeable, save to thy wild waves' play,
Time writes no wrinkle on thine azure brow:
Such as creation's dawn beheld, thou rollest now.

Thou glorious mirror, where the Almighty's form
Glasses itself in tempests; in all time —
Calm or convulsed, in breeze, or gale, or storm,
Icing the pole, or in the torrid clime

Dark-heaving — boundless, endless, and sublime,
The image of eternity, the throne
Of the Invisible; even from out thy slime
The monsters of the deep are made; each zone
Obeys thee; thou goest forth, dread, fathomless, alone.

And I have loved thee, Ocean! and my joy
Of youthful sports was on thy breast to be
Borne, like thy bubbles, onward: from a boy
I wanton'd with thy breakers — they to me
Were a delight; and if the freshening sea
Made them a terror — 't was a pleasing fear,
For I was as it were a child of thee,
And trusted to thy billows far and near,
And laid my hand upon thy mane — as I do here . . .

George Gordon, Lord Byron

A DIRGE

Rough wind, that moanest loud
   Grief too sad for song;
Wild wind, when sullen cloud
   Knells all the night long;
Sad storm, whose tears are vain,
Bare woods, whose branches strain,
Deep caves and dreary main, —
   Wail, for the world's wrong.

P. B. Shelley

IT IS A BEAUTEOUS EVENING

It is a beauteous evening, calm and free,
The holy time is quiet as a Nun
Breathless with adoration; the broad sun
Is sinking down in its tranquillity;
The gentleness of heaven broods o'er the Sea:
Listen! the mighty Being is awake,
And doth with his eternal motion make
A sound like thunder — everlastingly . . .

William Wordsworth

LIKE AS THE WAVES MAKE TOWARDS THE PEBBLED SHORE

Like as the waves make towards the pebbled shore,
   So do our minutes hasten to their end;
Each changing place with that which goes before,
   In sequent toil all forwards do contend.
Nativity, once in the main of light,
   Crawls to maturity, wherewith being crowned,
Crooked eclipses 'gainst his glory fight,
   And Time that gave doth now his gift confound.
Time doth transfix the flourish set on youth
   And delves the parallels in beauty's brow,
Feeds on the rarities of nature's truth,
   And nothing stands but for his scythe to mow.
     And yet to times in hope my verse shall stand,
     Praising thy worth, despite his cruel hand.

William Shakespeare

FRUTTA DI MARE

I am a sea-shell flung
Up from the ancient sea;
Now I lie here, among
Roots of a tamarisk tree;
No one listens to me.

I sing to myself all day
In a husky voice, quite low,
Things the great fishes say
And you most need to know;
All night I sing just so.

But lift me from the ground,
And hearken at my rim,
Only your sorrow's sound,
Amazed, perplexed and dim,
Comes coiling to the brim;

For what the wise whales ponder
Awaking from sleep,
The key to all your wonder,
The answers of the deep,
These to myself I keep.

Geoffrey Scott

THE TUFT OF KELP

All dripping in tangles green,
    Cast up by a lonely sea,
If purer for that, O Weed,
    Bitterer, too, are ye?

Herman Melville

ON THE BEACH AT NIGHT

On the beach at night,
Stands a child with her father,
Watching the east, the autumn sky.

Up through the darkness,
While ravening clouds, the burial clouds, in black masses
    spreading,
Lower sullen and fast athwart and down the sky,
Amid a transparent clear belt of ether yet left in the east,
Ascends large and calm the lord-star Jupiter,
And nigh at hand, only a very little above,
Swim the delicate sisters the Pleiades.

From the beach the child holding the hand of her father,
Those burial clouds that lower victorious soon to devour all
Watching, silently weeps.

Weep not, child,
Weep not, my darling,
With these kisses let me remove your tears,

The ravening clouds shall not long be victorious,
They shall not long possess the sky, they devour the stars only
    in apparition,
Jupiter shall emerge, be patient, watch again another night,
    the Pleiades shall emerge,
They are immortal, all those stars both silvery and golden
    shall shine out again,
The great stars and the little ones shall shine out again, they
    endure,
The vast immortal suns and the long-enduring pensive moons
    shall again shine.

Then, dearest child, mournest thou only for Jupiter?
Considerest thou alone the burial of the stars?

Something there is,
(With my lips soothing thee, adding I whisper,
I give thee the first suggestion, the problem and indirection,)
Something there is more immortal even than the stars,
(Many the burials, many the days and nights, passing away,)
Something that shall endure longer even than lustrous Jupiter,
Longer than sun or any revolving satellite,
Or the radiant sisters the Pleiades.

Walt Whitman

SUNRISE ON THE SEA

I with the morning's love have oft made sport,
And, like a forester, the groves may tread,
Even till the eastern gate, all fiery-red,
Opening on Neptune with fair blessed beams,
Turns into yellow gold his salt green streams . . .

William Shakespeare

HER HEARDS BE THOUSAND FISHES

So to the sea we came; the sea, that is
A world of waters heapèd up on high,
Rolling like mountains in wide wilderness,
Horrible, hideous, roaring with hoarse cry.
   'And is the sea (quoth Coridon) so fearful?'
   'Fearful much more (quoth he) than heart can fear:
Thousand wild beasts with deep mouths gaping direful
Therein still wait poor passengers to tear.
Who life doth loathe, and longs death to behold,
Before he die, already dead with fear,
And yet would live with heart half stony cold,
Let him to sea, and he shall see it there.
And yet as ghastly dreadful, as it seems,
Bold men, presuming life for gain to sell,
Dare tempt that gulf, and in those wandring streams
Seek ways unknown, ways leading down to hell.
For, as we stood there waiting on the strond,
Behold! an huge great vessel to us came,
Dauncing upon the waters back to lond,
As if it scorned the daunger of the same;
Yet was it but a wooden frame and frail,
Gluèd togither with some subtile matter.
Yet it had arms and wings, and head and tail,
And life to move it self upon the water.
Strange thing! how bold and swift the monster was,
That neither car'd for wind, nor hail, nor rain,
Nor swelling waves, but thorough them did pass
So proudly, that she made them roar again.
The same aboard us gently did receive,
And without harm us far away did bear,
So far that land, our mother, us did leave,
And nought but sea and heaven to us appear.
Then heartless quite, and full of inward fear,
That shepheard I besought to me to tell,
Under what sky, or in what world we were,
In which I saw no living people dwell.

Who, me recomforting all that he might,
Told me that that same was the regiment
Of a great shepheardess, that Cynthia hight,
His liege, his lady, and his life's regent. –
  'If then (quoth I) a shepheardess she be,
Where be the flocks and herds, which she doth keep?
And where may I the hills and pastures see,
On which she useth for to feed her sheep?'
  'These be the hills (quoth he), the surges high,
On which fair Cynthia her heards doth feed:
Her heards be thousand fishes with their fry,
Which in the bosom of the billows breed.
Of them the shepheard which hath charge in chief,
Is Triton, blowing loud his wreathèd horn:
At sound whereof, they all for their relief
Wend to and fro at evening and at morn.
And Proteus eke with him does drive his heard
Of stinking seals and porcpisces together,
With hoary head and dewy dropping beard,
Compelling them which way he list, and whether.
And I among the rest, of many least
Have in the Ocean charge to me assign'd;
Where I will live or die at her beheast,
And serve and honour her with faithful mind.
Besides an hundred nymphs all heavenly born,
And of immortal race, do still attend
To wash fair Cynthia's sheep, when they be shorn,
And fold them up, when they have made an end.
Those be the shepheards which my Cynthia serve
At sea, beside a thousand moe at land:
For land and sea my Cynthia doth deserve
To have in her commandëment at hand. . . .'

Edmund Spenser

relief: feeding

The world is too much with us; late and soon,
Getting and spending, we lay waste our powers:
Little we see in Nature that is ours;
We have given our hearts away, a sordid boon!
This Sea that bares her bosom to the moon;
The winds that will be howling at all hours,
And are up-gathered now like sleeping flowers;
For this, for every thing, we are out of tune;
It moves us not. — Great God! I'd rather be
A Pagan suckled in a creed outworn;
So might I, standing on this pleasant lea,
Have glimpses that would make me less forlorn;
Have sight of Proteus rising from the sea;
Or hear old Triton blow his wreathèd horn.

William Wordsworth

THE MERMAIDS

And now they nigh approachèd to the stead,
  Where as those mermaids dwelt: it was a still
And calmy bay, on th'one side shelterèd
  With the broad shadow of an hoary hill,
  On th'other side an high rock towred still,
That twixt them both a pleasaunt port they made,
  And did like an half theatre fulfill:
There those five sisters had continual trade,
And used to bath themselves in that deceitful shade.

They were fair ladies, till they fondly striv'd
  With th'Heliconian maids for maistery;
Of whom they over-comen, were depriv'd
  Of their proud beauty, and th'one moiety
  Transform'd to fish, for their bold surquedry;
But th'upper half their hue retainèd still,
  And their sweet skill in wonted melody;
Which ever after they abused to ill,
T'allure weak travellers, whom gotten they did kill . . .

Edmund Spenser

surquedry: *wantonness*

Nor safe their dwellings were; for, sapped by floods,
Their houses fell upon their household gods.
The solid piles, too strongly built to fall,
High o'er their heads, behold a wat'ry wall:
Now seas and earth were in confusion lost;
A world of waters, and without a coast.
  One climbs a cliff; one in his boat is born,
And ploughs above, where late he sow'd his corn.
Others o'er chimney tops and turrets row,
And drop their anchors on the meads below,
Or downwards driv'n, they bruise the tender vine,
Or tost aloft, are knock't against a pine.
And where of late the kids had cropt the grass,
The monsters of the deep now take their place.
Insulting Nereids on the cities ride,
And wond'ring dolphins o'er the palace glide.
On leaves and masts of mighty oaks they brouse,
And their broad fins entangle in the boughs.
The frighted wolf now swims amongst the sheep;
The yellow lion wanders in the deep . . .

John Dryden (after Ovid)

THE CHARACTER OF HOLLAND

Holland, that scarce deserves the name of land,
As but th'offscouring of the British sand,
And so much earth as was contributed
By English pilots when they heav'd the lead,
Or what by th'ocean's slow alluvion fell
Of shipwrackt cockle and the mussel-shell —
This indigested vomit of the sea
Fell to the Dutch by just propriety.
  Glad then, as miners that have found the ore,
They with mad labour fish'd the land to shore,
And div'd as desperately for each piece
Of earth, as if't had been of ambergreece;
Collecting anxiously small loads of clay,
Less than what building swallows bear away,
Or than those pills which sordid beetles roll,
Transfusing into them their dunghill soul.
  How did they rivet, with gigantic piles,
Thorough the centre their new-catchèd miles;

And to the stake a struggling country bound,
Where barking waves still bait the forcèd ground;
Building their wat'ry Babel far more high
To reach the sea, than those to reach the sky.
    Yet still his claim the injur'd ocean laid,
And oft at leap-frog o'er their steeples played,
As if on purpose it on land had come
To shew them what's their *Mare Liberum*.
A daily deluge over them does boil;
The earth and water play at level-coil;
The fish oft-times the burgher dispossest,
And sat not as a meat but as a guest;
And oft the Tritons and the Sea-nymphs saw
Whole shoals of Dutch serv'd up for cabillau;
Or as they over the new level rang'd
For pickled herring, pickled Heeren chang'd.
Nature, it seem'd, asham'd of her mistake,
Would throw their land away at duck and drake.
    Therefore Necessity, that first made kings,
Something like government among them brings.
For as with pigmies who best kills the crane,
Among the hungry he that treasures grain,
Among the blind the one-eye'd blinkard reigns,
So rules among the drownèd he that drains.
Not who first see the rising sun commands,
But who could first discern the rising lands.
Who best could know to pump an earth so leak
Him they their lord and country's father speak.
To make a bank was a great plot of state;
Invent a shov'l and be a magistrate. . . .

Andrew Marvell

level-coil: *a game of scrambling for position*; cabillau: *cod*

SONG OF THE SYRENS

Steer, hither steer, your wingèd pines,
    All beaten mariners,
Here lie Love's undiscovered mines,
    A prey to passengers;
    Perfumes far sweeter than the best
Which make the Phoenix' urn and nest.

Fear not your ships,
Nor any to oppose you save our lips,
But come on shore,
Where no joy dies till love hath gotten more.

For swelling waves, our panting breasts
Where never storms arise,
Exchange; and be a while our guests:
For stars, gaze on our eyes.
The compass love shall hourly sing,
And as he goes about the ring,
We will not miss
To tell each point he nameth with a kiss.

William Browne

THE GREAT SILKIE OF SULE SKERRY

An eartly nourris sits and sings,
And aye she sings, Ba, lily wean!
Little ken I my bairnis father,
Far less the land that he staps in.

Then ane arose at her bed-fit,
An a grumly guest I'm sure was he:
'Here am I, thy bairnis father,
Although that I be not comelie.

'I am a man, upo the lan,
An I am a silkie in the sea;
And when I'm far and far frae lan,
My dwelling is in Sule Skerrie.'

'It was na weel', quo the maiden fair,
'It was na weel, indeed', quo she,
'That the Great Silkie of Sule Skerrie
Suld hae come and aught a bairn to me.'

Now he has taen a purse of goud,
And he has pat it upo her knee,
Sayin, 'Gie to me my little young son,
An tak thee up thy nourris-fee.

'An it sall come to pass on a simmer's day,
When the sin shines het on evera stane,
That I will tak my little young son,
An teach him for to swim the faem.

206

'An thu sall marry a proud gunner,
   An a proud gunner I'm sure he'll be,
An the very first schot that ere he schoots,
   He'll schoot baith my young son and me.'

      silkie: *seal*; lily wean: *lovely child*;
      aught a bairn to me: *had a child by me*

SEA MONSTERS

Eftsoons they saw an hideous host array'd
Of huge sea monsters, such as living sense dismay'd.

Most ugly shapes and horrible aspects,
   Such as Dame Nature self mote fear to see,
Or shame that ever should so foul defects
   From her most cunning hand escapèd be;
   All dreadful pourtraits of deformity:
Spring-headed hydras, and sea-should'ring whales,
   Great whirlpools which all fishes make to flee,
Bright scolopendras, arm'd with silver scales,
Mighty monoceroes with immeasured tails.

The dreadful fish, that hath deserv'd the name
   Of Death, and like him looks in dreadful hue,
The grisly wasserman, that makes his game
   The flying ships with swiftness to pursue,
   The horrible sea-satyr, that doth shew
His fearful face in time of greatest storm,
   Huge ziffius, whom mariners eschew
No less than rocks (as travellers inform)
And greedy rosmarines with visages deform . . .

                              Edmund Spenser

THE HUGE LEVIATHAN

Toward the sea turning my troubled eye,
I saw the fish (if fish I may it cleep)
That makes the sea before his face to fly,
And with his flaggy fins doth seem to sweep
The foamy waves out of the dreadful deep,
The huge Leviathan, dame Nature's wonder,
Making his sport, that many makes to weep:
A sword-fish small him from the rest did sunder,

That, in his throat him pricking softly under,
His wide abyss him forcèd forth to spew,
That all the sea did roar like heaven's thunder,
And all the waves were stain'd with filthy hue.
　　Hereby I learnèd have not to despise
　　Whatever thing seems small in common eyes . . .

Edmund *Spenser*

THE WHALE

'Twas in the year of forty-nine,
　　On March, the twentieth day,
Our gallant ship her anchor weigh'd,
　　And to the sea she bore away,
　　　　Brave boys,
And to the sea she bore away.
　　　　With a fa la la la la la la
　　　　Fa la la la la la la
　　　　Fa la la fa la la
　　　　Fa la la la la.

Old Blowhard was our captain's name,
　　Our ship the Lion bold,
And we were bound to the North Country
　　To face the frost and the cold,
　　　　Brave boys, etc.

And when we came to that cold country
　　Where the ice and the snow do lie,
Where there's ice and snow, and the great whales blow,
　　And the daylight does not die,
　　　　Brave boys, etc.

Our mate went up to the topmast head
　　With a spyglass in his hand:
'A whale, a whale, a whale', he cries,
　　'And she spouts at every span,'
　　　　Brave boys, etc.

Up jumped old Blowhard on the deck –
And a clever little man was he –
'Overhaul, overhaul, let your main-tackle fall,
And launch your boat to sea,'
Brave boys, etc.

We struck that fish and away she flew
With a flourish of her tail;
But oh! and alas! we lost one man
And we did not catch that whale,
Brave boys, etc.

Now when the news to our captain came
He called up all his crew,
And for the losing of that man
He down his colours drew,
Brave boys, etc.

Says he: 'My men, be not dismayed
At the losing of one man,
For Providence will have his will,
Let man do what he can,'
Brave boys, etc.

Now the losing of that prentice boy
It grieved our captain sore,
But the losing of that great big whale
It grieved him a damned sight more,
Brave boys,
It grieved him a damned sight more.
With a fa la la la la la la la
Fa la la la la la la la
Fa la la fa la la
Fa la la la la la.

DOTH NOT A TENARIF, OR HIGHER HILL

Doth not a Tenarif, or higher hill
Rise so high like a rock, that one might think
The floating Moon would shipwreck there, and sink?
Seas are so deep, that Whales being strook to-day,
Perchance to-morrow, scarce at middle way

Of their wish'd journey's end, the bottom, die.
And men, to sound depths, so much line untie,
As one might justly think, that there would rise
At end thereof, one of th' Antipodies . . .

John Donne

THE WHALE

At every stroke his brazen fins do take,
More circles in the broken sea they make
Than cannons' voices, when the air they tear:
His ribs are pillars, and his high arch'd roof
Of bark that blunts best steel, is thunder-proof:
Swim in him swallow'd dolphins, without fear,
And feel no sides, as if his vast womb were
Some inland sea, and ever as he went
He spouted rivers up, as if he meant
   To join our seas with seas above the firmament.

He hunts not fish, but as an officer,
Stays in his court, at his own net, and there
All suitors of all sorts themselves enthrall;
So on his back lies this whale wantoning,
And in his gulf-like throat sucks every thing
That passeth near. Fish chaseth fish, and all,
Flyer and follower, in this whirlpool fall;
O might not states of more equality
Consist? and is it of necessity
   That thousand guiltless smalls, to make one great, must die?

Now drinks he up seas, and he eats up flocks,
He jostles islands, and he shakes firm rocks.
Now in a roomful house this Soul doth float,
And like a prince she sends her faculties
To all her limbs, distant as provinces.
The sun hath twenty times both Crab and Goat
Parched, since first launched forth this living boat;
'Tis greatest now, and to destruction
Nearest; there's no pause at perfection;
   Greatness a period hath, but hath no station.

Two little fishes whom he never harm'd,
Nor fed on their kind, two not throughly arm'd
With hope that they could kill him, nor could do
Good to themselves by his death (they did not eat
His flesh, nor suck those oils which thence outstreat)
Conspir'd against him, and it might undo
The plot of all, that the plotters were two,
But that they fishes were, and could not speak.
How shall a tyrant wise strong projects break,
    If wretches can on them the common anger wreak?

The flail-finn'd Thresher, and steel-beak'd Sword-fish
Only attempt to do, what all do wish.
The Thresher backs him, and to beat begins;
The sluggard Whale yields to oppression,
And t'hide himself from shame and danger, down
Begins to sink; the Sword-fish upward spins,
And gores him with his beak; his staff-like fins,
So well the one, his sword the other plies,
That now a scoffe, and prey, this tyrant dies,
    And (his own dole) feeds with himself all companies . . .

                                                John Donne

JONAH

A cream of phosphorescent light
Floats on the wash that to and fro
Slides round his feet – enough to show
Many a pendulous stalactite
Of naked mucus, whorls and wreaths
And huge festoons of mottled tripes
And smaller palpitating pipes
Through which a yeasty liquor seethes.

Seated upon the convex mound
Of one vast kidney, Jonah prays
And sings his canticles and hymns,
Making the hollow vault resound
God's goodness and mysterious ways,
Till the great fish spouts music as he swims.

                                                Aldous Huxley

THE FISH, THE MAN, AND THE SPIRIT

To Fish

You strange, astonish'd-looking, angle-faced,
  Dreary-mouth'd, gaping wretches of the sea,
  Gulping salt water everlastingly,
Cold-blooded, though with red your blood be graced,
And mute, though dwellers in the roaring waste;
  And you, all shapes beside, that fishy be, —
  Some round, some flat, some long, all devilry,
Legless, unloving, infamously chaste: —

O scaly, slippery, wet, swift, staring wights,
  What is't ye do? What life lead? eh, dull goggles?
How do ye vary your vile days and nights?
  How pass your Sundays? Are ye still but joggles
In ceaseless wash? Still nought but gapes, and bites,
  And drinks, and stares, diversified with boggles?

A Fish answers

Amazing monster! that, for aught I know,
  With the first sight of thee didst make our race
  For ever stare! O flat and shocking face,
Grimly divided from the breast below!
Thou that on dry land horribly dost go
  With a split body and most ridiculous pace,
  Prong after prong, disgracer of all grace,
Long-useless-finned, hair'd, upright, unwet, slow!

O breather of unbreathable, sword-sharp air,
  How canst exist? How bear thyself, thou dry
And dreary sloth? What particle canst share
  ⸱ Of the only blessed life, the watery?
I sometimes see of ye an actual pair
  Go by! link'd fin by fin! most odiously.

The Fish turns into a Man, and then into a Spirit, and again speaks

Indulge thy smiling scorn, if smiling still,
  O man! and loathe, but with a sort of love;
  For difference must its use by difference prove,
And, in sweet clang, the spheres with music fill.

One of the spirits am I, that at his will
  Lives in whate'er has life — fish, eagles, dove —
  No hate, no pride, beneath nought, nor above,
A visitor of the rounds of God's sweet skill.

Man's life is warm, glad, sad, 'twixt loves and graves,
  Boundless in hope, honour'd with pangs austere,
Heaven-gazing; and his angel-wings he craves: —
  The fish is swift, small-needing, vague yet clear,
A cold, sweet, silver life, wrapp'd in round waves,
  Quicken'd with touches of transporting fear.

Leigh Hunt

THE FLYING FISH

Of the birds that fly in the farthest sea
six are stranger than others be:
under its tumble, among the fish,
six are a marvel passing wish.

First is a hawk, exceeding great;
he dwelleth alone; he hath no mate;
his neck is a wound with a yellow ring;
on his breast is the crest of a former king.

The second bird is exceeding pale,
from little head to scanty tail;
she is striped with black on either wing,
which is rose-lined, like a princely thing.

Though small the bulk of the brilliant third,
of all blue birds 'tis the bluest bird:
they fly in bands; and, seen by day,
by the side of them the sky is grey.

I mind the fifth, I forget the fourth,
unless that it comes from the east by north.
The fifth is an orange white-billed duck;
he diveth for fish like the god of Luck;

he hath never a foot on which to stand;
for water yields and he loves not land.
This is the end of many words
Save one, concerning marvellous birds.

The great-faced dolphin is first of fish;
he is devil-eyed and devilish;
of all the fishes is he most brave,
he walks the sea like an angry wave.

The second the fishes call their lord;
himself a bow, his face is a sword;
his sword is armed with a hundred teeth,
fifty above and fifty beneath.

The third hath a scarlet suit of mail;
the fourth is naught but a feeble tail;
the fifth is a whip with a hundred strands,
and every arm hath a hundred hands.

The last strange fish is the last strange bird;
of him no sage hath ever heard;
he roams the sea in a gleaming horde
in fear of the dolphin and him of the sword.

He leaps from the sea with a silken swish;
he beats the air does the flying fish.
His eyes are round with excess of fright,
bright as the drops of his pinions' flight.

In sea and sky he hath no peace;
for the five strange fish are his enemies;
and the five strange fowls keep watch for him;
they know him well by his crystal gleam.

Oftwhiles, sir Sage, on my junk's white deck
have I seen this fish-bird come to wreck,
oftwhiles (fair deck) 'twixt bow and poop
have I seen this piteous sky-fish stoop.

Scaled bird, how his snout and gills dilate,
all quivering and roseate:
he pants in crystal and mother-of-pearl
while his body shrinks and his pinions furl.

His beauty passes like bubbles blown;
the white bright bird is a fish of stone;
the bird so fair, for its putrid sake,
is flung to the dogs in the junk's white wake.

John Gray

Ships on the Sea

The excellence of the ship in the woodcut (from a German book of chronicles of 1486) is that it floats so gaily and decidedly, is so much on the sea. A wind sends it scudding along. But if the wind freshened into a gale? Older poets (as in the psalm on the next page) were more concerned about their cockle ships coming safe into the haven, life's journey done. Later poets liked to think of launching out into the huge sea, good weather or bad, in life or in death. Next to the psalm I have put a poem by Arthur Hugh Clough. His ship sailed – who knows where to? Or where from? And its sailors liked both the quiet sea, and the pride of fighting with the chances of death.

Both attitudes are open to our imagination. Sometimes we feel one way, sometimes the other. D. H. Lawrence in his last poem put his soul into a small Ship of Death, with provisions, to row into oblivion. Emily Brontë, who wrote *Wuthering Heights*, imagined herself in a poem as a Stormy Petrel floating in solitude in the middle ocean and revelling in dreams. But listen to the wild sermon preached to the whalemen in *Moby Dick*, by Herman Melville (in which Captain Ahab drives his ship over the ocean after the white whale of fate, which has already bitten off his leg) –

But oh! shipmates! on the starboard hand of every woe, there is a sure delight; and higher the top of that delight, than the bottom of the woe is deep. Is not the main-truck higher than the kelson is low? Delight is to him – a far, far upward, and inward delight – who against the proud gods and commodores of this earth, ever stands forth his own inexorable self. Delight is to him whose strong arms yet support him, when the ship of this base treacherous world has gone down beneath him.

THEY THAT GO DOWN TO THE SEA

They that go down to the sea in ships: and
  occupy their business in great waters;

These men see the works of the Lord: and his
  wonders in the deep.

For at his word the stormy wind ariseth: which
  lifteth up the waves thereof.

They are carried up to the heaven, and down again to the deep;
  their soul melteth away because of the trouble.

They reel to and fro, and stagger like a drunken man:
  and are at their wit's end.

So when they cry unto the Lord in their trouble:
  he delivereth them out of their distress.

For he maketh the storm to cease: so that the waves thereof
  are still.

Then are they glad, because they are at rest:
  and so he bringeth them unto the haven where
  they would be.

O that men would therefore praise the Lord for his goodness:
  and declare the wonders that he doeth for the children
  of men! . . .

The Psalms

WHERE LIES THE LAND?

Where lies the land to which the ship would go?
Far, far ahead, is all her seamen know,
And where the land she travels from? Away,
Far, far behind, is all that they can say.

On sunny noons upon the deck's smooth face,
Linked arm in arm, how pleasant here to pace;
Or, o'er the stern reclining, watch below
The foaming wake far widening as we go.

On stormy nights when wild north-westers rave,
How proud a thing to fight with wind and wave!
The dripping sailor on the reeling mast
Exults to bear, and scorns to wish it past.

Where lies the land to which the ship would go?
Far, far ahead, is all her seamen know.
And where the land she travels from? Away,
Far, far behind, is all that they can say.

A. H. Clough

THE FROLIC MARINERS OF DEVON

Hail thou, my native soil! thou blessed plot
Whose equal all the world affordeth not!
Show me who can so many crystal rills,
Such sweet-cloth'd valleys, or aspiring hills,
Such wood-ground, pastures, quarries, wealthy mines,
Such rocks in whom the diamond fairly shines;
And if the earth can show the like again,
Yet will she fail in her sea-ruling men.
Time never can produce men to o'ertake
The fames of Greenvil, Davies, Gilbert, Drake,
Or worthy Hawkins, or of thousands more
That by their power made the Devonian shore
Mock the proud Tagus; for whose richest spoil
The boasting Spaniard left the Indian soil
Bankrupt of store, knowing it would quit cost
By winning this, though all the rest were lost.
As oft the sea-nymphs on her strand have set
Learning of fishermen to knit a net
Wherein to wind up their dishevell'd hairs,
They have beheld the frolic mariners
For exercise (got from their early beds)
Pitch bars of silver, and cast golden sleds . . .

William Browne

sleds: *sledge-hammers*

218

What joy attends the fisher's life,
    Blow, winds, blow,
The fisher and his faithful wife,
    Row, boys, row.
He drives no plough on stubborn land,
His fields are ready to his hand;
No nipping frosts his orchards fear,
He has his autumn all the year.

The husbandman has rent to pay,
    Blow, winds, blow,
And seed to purchase every day,
    Row, boys, row.
But he who farms the rolling deeps,
Though never sowing, always reaps.
The ocean's fields are fair and free,
There are no rent days on the sea.

MINE ARGOSY FROM ALEXANDRIA

Give me the merchants of the Indian mines,
That trade in metal of the purest mould;
The wealthy Moor, that in the eastern rocks
Without control can pick his riches up,
And in his house heap pearl like pibble-stones;
Receive them free, and sell them by the weight,
Bags of fiery Opals, Sapphires, Amatists,
Jacints, hard Topaz, grass-green Emeraulds,
Beauteous Rubies, sparkling Diamonds,
And seildseen costly stones of so great price,
As one of them indifferently rated,
And of a carrect of this quantity,
May serve in peril of calamity
To ransom great Kings from captivity.
This is the ware wherein consists my wealth:
And thus methinks should men of judgement frame
Their means of traffic from the vulgar trade,
And as their wealth increaseth, so inclose
Infinite riches in a little room.
But now how stands the wind?
Into what corner peers my halcyon's bill?
Ha, to the east? yes: See how stands the vanes?

219

East and by south: why then I hope my ships
I sent for Egypt and the bordering Isles
Are gotten up by Nilus' winding banks:
Mine argosie from Alexandria,
Loaden with spice and silks, now under sail,
Are smoothly gliding down by Candy shore
To Malta, through our Mediterranean sea . .

Christopher Marlowe

carrect: *carat*

WE'LL GO TO SEA NO MORE

Oh blithely shines the bonny sun
  Upon the Isle of May,
And blithely comes the morning tide
  Into St Andrew's Bay.
Then up, gude-man, the breeze is fair,
  And up, my braw bairns three;
There's gold in yonder bonny boat
  That sails so well the sea.
      When life's last sun goes feebly down,
      And death comes to our door,
      When all the world's a dream to us,
      We'll go to sea no more.

I've seen the waves as blue as air,
  I've seen them green as grass;
But I never feared their heaving yet,
  From Grangemouth to the Bass.
I've seen the sea as black as pitch,
  I've seen it white as snow:
But I never feared its foaming yet,
  Though the winds blew high or low.
      When life's last sun goes feebly down,
      And death comes to our door,
      When all the world's a dream to us,
      We'll go to sea no more.

I never liked the landsman's life,
  The earth is aye the same;
Give me the ocean for my dower,
  My vessel for my hame.
Give me the fields that no man ploughs,
  The farm that pays no fee:

Give me the bonny fish that glance
   So gladly through the sea.
      When life's last sun goes feebly down,
      And death comes to our door,
      When all the world's a dream to us,
      We'll go to sea no more.

The sun is up, and round Inchkeith
   The breezes softly blaw;
The gude-man has his lines aboard —
   Awa, my bairns, awa.
An ye'll be back by gloaming grey,
   An bright the fire will low,
An in your tales and songs we'll tell
   How weel the boat ye row.
      When life's last sun goes feebly down,
      And death comes to our door,
      When all the world's a dream to us,
      We'll go to sea no more.

CARRYING THEIR CORACLES

   But now the salmon-fishers moist
   Their leathern boats begin to hoist;
   And, like Antipodes in shoes,
   Have shod their heads in their canoes.
   How tortoise-like, but not so slow,
   These rational amphibii go!
   Let's in: for the dark hemisphere
   Does now like one of them appear . . .

                              Andrew Marvell

THE CORACLE

The moistened osier of the hoary willow
Is woven first into a little boat:
Then cloth'd in bullock's hide, upon the billow
Of a proud river, lightly doth it float
Under the waterman:
So on the lakes of over-swelling Po
Sails the Venetian: and the Briton so
On th'outspread ocean.

                  Sir Walter Ralegh (after Lucan)

221

THE VIKINGS

Bitter the storm to-night.
It hurls the white locks of the sea,
So I fear no wild men of Norway
Who sail on the Irish sea.

From the Irish

O'ER THE WILD GANNET'S BATH

O'er the wild gannet's bath
Come the Norse coursers!
O'er the whale's heritance
Gloriously steering!
With beaked heads peering,
Deep-plunging, high-rearing,
Tossing their foam abroad,
Shaking white manes aloft,
Creamy-neck'd, pitchy-ribb'd,
Steeds of the ocean!

O'er the Sun's mirror green
Come the Norse coursers!
Trampling its glassy breadth
Into bright fragments!
Hollow-back'd, huge-bosom'd,
Fraught with mail'd riders,
Clanging with hauberks,
Shield, spear, and battleaxe,
Canvas-wing'd, cable-rein'd,
Steeds of the Ocean!

O'er the Wind's ploughing-field
Come the Norse coursers!
By a hundred each ridden,
To the bloody feast bidden,
They rush in their fierceness
And ravine all round them!
Their shoulders enriching
With fleecy-light plunder,
Fire-spreading, foe-spurning,
Steeds of the Ocean!

George Darley

222

We pulled for you when the wind was against us and the sails
were low.
Will you never let us go?
We ate bread and onions when you took towns, or ran aboard
quickly when you were beaten back by the foe.
The Captains walked up and down the deck in fair weather
singing songs, but we were below.
We fainted with our chins on the oars and you did not see
that we were idle, for we still swung to and fro.
Will you never let us go?
The salt made the oar-handles like shark-skin; our knees were
cut to the bone with salt-cracks; our hair was stuck to our
foreheads; and our lips were cut to the gums, and you
whipped us because we could not row.
Will you never let us go?
But, in a little time, we shall run out of the port-holes as the
water runs along the oar-blade, and though you tell the
others to row after us you will never catch us till you
catch the oar-thresh and tie up the winds in the belly of
the sail. Aho!
Will you never let us go?

Rudyard Kipling

THE PRESS-GANG

Here's the tender coming,
   Pressing all the men;
     O, dear honey,
   What shall we do then?
Here's the tender coming,
   Off at Shields Bar.
Here's the tender coming,
   Full of men of war.

Here's the tender coming,
   Stealing of my dear;
     O dear honey,
They'll ship you out of here,
   They'll ship you foreign,
For that is what it means.
Here's the tender coming,
   Full of red marines.

THE SALCOMBE SEAMAN'S FLAUNT TO THE
PROUD PIRATE

A lofty ship from Salcombe came,
  Blow high, blow low, and so sailed we;
She had golden trucks that shone like flame,
  On the bonny coasts of Barbary.

'Masthead, masthead', the captains hail,
  Blow high, blow low, and so sailed we;
'Look out and round; d'ye see a sail?'
  On the bonny coasts of Barbary.

'There's a ship what looms like Beachy Head',
  Blow high, blow low, and so sailed we;
'Her banner aloft it blows out red',
  On the bonny coasts of Barbary.

'Oh, ship ahoy, and where do you steer?'
  Blow high, blow low, and so sailed we;
'Are you man-of-war, or privateer?'
  On the bonny coasts of Barbary.

'I am neither one of the two', said she,
  Blow high, blow low, and so sailed we;
'I'm a pirate looking for my fee',
  On the bonny coasts of Barbary.

'I'm a jolly pirate, out for gold':
  Blow high, blow low, and so sailed we;
'I will rummage through your after hold',
  On the bonny coasts of Barbary.

The grumbling guns they flashed and roared,
  Blow high, blow low, and so sailed we;
Till the pirate's mast went overboard,
  On the bonny coasts of Barbary.

They fired shot till the pirate's deck,
  Blow high, blow low, and so sailed we;
Was blood and spars and broken wreck,
  On the bonny coasts of Barbary.

'O do not haul the red flag down',
  Blow high, blow low, and so sailed we;
'O keep all fast until we drown',
  On the bonny coasts of Barbary.

They called for cans of wine, and drank,
  Blow high, blow low, and so sailed we;
They sang their songs until she sank,
  On the bonny coasts of Barbary.

Now let us brew good cans of flip,
  Blow high, blow low, and so sailed we;
And drink a bowl to the Salcombe ship,
  On the bonny coasts of Barbary.

And drink a bowl to the lad of fame,
  Blow high, blow low, and so sailed we;
Who put the pirate ship to shame,
  On the bonny coasts of Barbary.

BY THE DEEP NINE

For England, when with fav'ring gale
  Our gallant ship up channel steer'd,
And scudding under easy sail,
  The high blue western land appear'd,
To heave the lead the seaman sprung,
And to the pilot cheerly sung,
                              By the deep nine.

And bearing up to gain the port,
  Some well-known object kept in view,
An abbey tow'r, an harbour fort,
  Or beacon, to the vessel true:
While oft the lead the seaman flung,
And to the pilot cheerly sung,
                              By the mark seven.

And as the much-lov'd shore we near,
  With transports we behold the roof
Where dwelt a friend or partner dear,
  Of faith and love a matchless proof:
The lead once more the seaman flung,
And to the watchful pilot sung,
                              Quarter less five.

                              W. Pearce

NEVER WEATHER-BEATEN SAIL

Never weather-beaten sail more willing bent to shore,
  Never tired pilgrim's limbs affected slumber more,
Than my weary spright now longs to fly out of my troubled
    breast.
  O! come quickly, sweetest Lord, and take my soul to rest.

Ever blooming are the joys of Heaven's high Paradise.
  Cold age deafs not there our ears, nor vapour dims our
    eyes;
Glory there the sun outshines, whose beams the blessed only
    see.
  O! come quickly, glorious Lord, and raise my spright to
    thee.

Thomas Campion

14. A THOUSAND
FEARFUL WRECKS

A Thousand Fearful Wrecks

The figure I have chosen for A Thousand Fearful Wrecks was cut by Hans Holbein the Younger, who came to England from Switzerland to make the most living portraits of noble Englishmen, and of the cruel square face of their master, Henry VIII. Plague in the narrow cities made life sweeter and death more terrible; and men liked to dwell on the dance of death through life. So Holbein devised a book of *Imagines Mortis*, images or figures of Death. In woodcut after woodcut, Death as a skeleton invades the pursuits of life. Here in this cut, the ship floats deep, the waves jump and curl, the sail has gone, the mast has cracked; and Skeleton Death holds the mast with his fleshless fingers, and will let go at any moment. The same fingers came and plucked at Holbein's elbow in London, for he died there of the plague in 1543.

The poem by Francis Quarles (on page 231) saying that the world is like a sea, rather resembles a Holbein woodcut. It was one of the emblems or hieroglyphs in a book of 'hieroglyphics on the life of man'. Shakespeare (pages 229 and 231) goes under the waves, after the wreck; and down there he shines the light of his great imagination on the skulls of the drowned, and catches the reflection from the pearls and jewels which rest in their deep eye-sockets. The dreamer of the thousand fearful wrecks (in *Richard the Third*, in the first act), who was pushed overboard in his dream while passing from England to France, also dreamt that he tried to die among all these wonders and horrors under the English Channel, but the sea would not let his soul escape from his body. Before the scene has finished, his murderers — this is no dream — have come into his room in the Tower of London, have stabbed him, and tipped him into the butt of malmsey wine. Read another wreck poem or ballad — a very strange one — on page 359, about the drowning of a Duke of Grafton.

A DREAM OF WRECKS

O Lord! methought, what pain it was to drown!
What dreadful noise of water in mine ears!
What sights of ugly death within mine eyes!
Methought I saw a thousand fearful wrecks;
A thousand men that fishes gnaw'd upon;
Wedges of gold, great anchors, heaps of pearl,
Inestimable stones, unvalued jewels,
All scatt'red in the bottom of the sea.
Some lay in dead men's skulls; and, in the holes
Where eyes did once inhabit, there were crept,
As 't were in scorn of eyes, reflecting gems,
That woo'd the slimy bottom of the deep,
And mock'd the dead bones that lay scatter'd by . . .

William Shakespeare

IN WINTRY MIDNIGHT, O'ER A STORMY MAIN

In wintry midnight, o'er a stormy main
   A ship I, laden with oblivion, go
By whirlpool and by rock, while love my foe,
   And Sovereign ruler, at the helm must reign,
And ardent thoughts and vain intentions strain
   Each oar, and scorn the storm and waves below,
And winds of sighs and hopes, and wishes, blow
   With endless rage and rending sails in twain,
And storms of tears and clouds of scorn make slack
   And spoil my feeble cordage, which is found
Of nought but ignorance and error twined;
   And those two lovely eyes that lit my track
Are gone, and reason in the wars is drowned,
   And I cannot the destined haven find.

William Barnes,
from the Italian of Petrarch

LOWLANDS
(A Halliard Chanty)

I dreamt a dream the other night,
   Lowlands, Lowlands, hurrah, my John;
I dreamt a dream the other night,
   My Lowlands a-ray.

I dreamt I saw my own true love,
  Lowlands, Lowlands, hurrah, my John;
I dreamt I saw my own true love,
  My Lowlands a-ray.

He was green and wet with weeds so cold,
  Lowlands, Lowlands, hurrah, my John;
He was green and wet with weeds so cold,
  My Lowlands a-ray.

'I am drowned in the Lowland seas', he said,
  Lowlands, Lowlands, hurrah, my John;
'I am drowned in the Lowland seas', he said,
  My Lowlands a-ray.

'I shall never kiss you again', he said,
  Lowlands, Lowlands, hurrah, my John;
'I shall never kiss you again', he said,
  My Lowlands a-ray.

I will cut my breasts until they bleed,
  Lowlands, Lowlands, hurrah, my John;
I will cut my breasts until they bleed,
  My Lowlands a-ray.

I will cut away my bonny hair,
  Lowlands, Lowlands, hurrah, my John;
I will cut away my bonny hair,
  My Lowlands a-ray.

No other man shall think me fair,
  Lowlands, Lowlands, hurrah, my John;
No other man shall think me fair,
  My Lowlands a-ray.

O my love lies drowned in the windy Lowlands,
  Lowlands, Lowlands, hurrah, my John;
O my love lies drowned in the windy Lowlands,
  My Lowlands a-ray.

SLEEP AFTER TOIL

He there does now enjoy eternal rest
  And happy ease which thou dost want and crave,
And further from it daily wanderest:
  What if some little pain the passage have,
  That makes frail flesh to fear the bitter wave,

Is not short pain well born, that brings long ease,
    And lays the soul to sleep in quiet grave?
Sleep after toil, port after stormy seas,
Ease after war, death after life, does greatly please . . .

Edmund Spenser

AN INSCRIPTION BY THE SEA
(After a poem in the Greek Anthology)

No dust have I to cover me,
    My grave no man may show;
My tomb is this unending sea,
    And I lie far below.
My fate, O stranger, was to drown;
And where it was the ship went down
    Is what the sea-birds know.

Edwin Arlington Robinson

FULL FATHOM FIVE

Full fadom five thy father lies,
Of his bones are coral made;
Those are pearls that were his eyes,
Nothing of him that doth fade,
But doth suffer a sea-change
Into something rich, and strange;
Sea nymphs hourly ring his knell.
                Ding-dong!
Hark! now I hear them:
                Ding-dong, bell!

William Shakespeare

THE WORLD'S A SEA

The world's a sea; my flesh a ship that's mann'd
With lab'ring thoughts, and steer'd by Reason's hand:
My heart's the seaman's card, whereby she sails,
My loose affections are the greater sails:
The topsail is my fancy; and the gusts
That fill these wanton sheets are worldly lusts:
Pray'r is the cable, at whose end appears
The anchor Hope, ne'er slipp'd but in our fears:
My will's th'inconstant pilot, that commands

231

The stagg'ring keel; my sins are like the sands:
Repentance is the bucket; and my eye
The pump, unus'd (but in extremes) and dry:
My conscience is the plummet, that doth press
The deeps, but seldom cries, 'A fathom less!'
Smooth calm's security; the gulf, despair;
My freight's corruption, and this life's my fare:
My soul's the passenger, confus'dly driv'n
From fear to fright; her landing port is Heav'n.
My seas are stormy, and my ship doth leak;
My sailors rude; my steersman faint and weak:
My canvas torn, it flaps from side to side:
My cable's crack'd; my anchor's slightly tied:
My pilot's craz'd; my shipwreck sands are cloak'd;
My bucket's broken, and my pump is chok'd;
My calm's deceitful, and my gulf too near;
My wares are slubber'd, and my fare's too dear:
My plummet's light, it cannot sink nor sound;
Oh, shall my rock-bethreaten'd soul be drown'd?
Lord, still the seas, and shield my ship from harm!
Instruct my sailors, guide my steersman's arm:
Touch thou my compass, and renew my sails;
Send stiffer courage, or send milder gales:
Make strong my cable, bind my anchor faster;
Direct my pilot, and be thou his master:
Object the sands to my more serious view;
Make sound my bucket, bore my pump anew:
New-cast my plummet, make it apt to try
Where the rocks lurk, and where the quicksands lie;
Guard thou the gulf with love, my claims with care:
Cleanse thou my freight; accept my slender fare;
Refresh the sea-sick passenger; cut short
His voyage; land him in his wished port:
Thou, thou whom winds and stormy seas obey,
That through the deeps gav'st grumbling Isr'el way,
Say to my soul, Be safe; and then mine eye
Shall scorn grim Death, although grim Death stand by.
O thou whose strength-reviving arm did cherish
Thy sinking Peter, at the point to perish,
Reach forth thy hand, or bid me tread the wave;
I'll come, I'll come: the voice that calls will save.

Francis Quarles

15. THE SUMMER

The Summer

The Summer, and Flowers, and the Garden: all of the poems in these three sections ought to be gay, but sadness does break into summers; and as I read again through these poems, I see that of their writers, one became blind, one lived to become dull and pompous, one took to drink, one was murdered, one was killed in the First World War, and three went mad. English poets sometimes read to themselves Wordsworth's *Resolution and Independence*. Wordsworth remembered Burns who (like himself) lapsed into melancholy, and Chatterton, 'the marvellous Boy' who killed himself; and he wrote:

> We Poets in our youth begin in gladness;
> But thereof come in the end despondency and madness.

But the important thing is to begin in gladness; which is the parent of some (not all) of the best poems.

In sadness, even in madness, poets have remembered the summer gladness – for instance, the great German poet Hölderlin. *Life Half Lived* by Hölderlin, of which I have made an English version (page 244), he wrote when his mind had already broken, and when he was living in a tower at Tübingen, among willows, on the edge of a river he had always loved. I think the 'lake' which reflected his yellow pears and his wild roses, was that still river, which scarcely moves under his window, and below gardens and orchards. William Cowper (page 239) and John Clare (pages 255 and 264 – and see the index for more poems by him) are the two others who went mad. The Elizabethan poem next to Hölderlin's (page 243) sadly in its first line imitates the sucking noise which scythes make as they cut across a summer hayfield.

I shall describe the book from which the woodcut comes at the beginning of the Garden poems (on page 266).

RIDDLES

i

I am within as white as snow,
Without as green as herbs that grow;
I am higher than a house
And yet am lesser than a mouse.

ii

A long white barn,
Two roofs on it,
And no door at all, at all.

iii

I washed my face in water
That neither rained nor run;
I dried my face on a towel
That was neither wove nor spun.

(*A walnut; a hen's egg; dew, and the sun*)

PRELUDE

Still south I went and west and south again,
Through Wicklow from the morning till the night,
And far from cities, and the sights of men,
Lived with the sunshine, and the moon's delight.

I knew the stars, the flowers, and the birds,
The grey and wintry sides of many glens,
And did but half remember human words,
In converse with the mountains, moors, and fens.

J. M. Synge

HEAVEN AND EARTH

The azur'd vault, the crystal circles bright,
The gleaming fiery torches powdered there,
The changing round, the shining beamy light,
The sad and bearded fires, the monsters fair:

The prodigies appearing in the air,
The rearding thunders, and the blustering winds,
The fowls, in hue, in shape, in nature rare,
The pretty notes that wing'd musicians finds:
In earth the sav'ry flowers, the metall'd minds,
The wholesome herbs, the haughty pleasant trees,
The silver streams, the beasts of sundry kinds,
The bounded roars, and fishes of the seas:
   All these, for teaching man, the Lord did frame,
   To do his will, whose glory shines in thame.

King James I

THE HEAVENS

The heavens declare the glory of God:
   and the firmament sheweth his handy-work.

One day telleth another: and one night
   certifieth another.

There is neither speech nor language:
   but their voices are heard among them.

Their sound is gone out into all lands: and
   their words into the ends of the world.

In them hath he set a tabernacle for the sun:
   which cometh forth as a bridegroom out
   of his chamber, and rejoiceth as a giant
   to run his course.

It goeth forth from the uttermost part of
   the heaven, and runneth about unto the
   end of it again: and there is nothing hid
   from the heat thereof . . .

The Psalms

I AM HE THAT WALKS WITH THE TENDER AND GROWING NIGHT

I am he that walks with the tender and growing night,
I call to the earth and sea half held by the night.

Press close bare-bosom'd night — press close magnetic nourish-
   ing night!
Night of south winds — night of the large few stars!
Still nodding night — mad naked summer night.

Smile O voluptuous cool-breath'd earth!
Earth of the slumbering and liquid trees!
Earth of departed sunset — earth of the mountains misty-topt!
Earth of the vitreous pour of the full moon just tinged with
  blue!
Earth of shine and dark mottling the tide of the river!
Earth of the limpid gray of clouds brighter and clearer for my
  sake!
Far-swooping elbow'd earth — rich apple-blossom'd earth!
Smile, for your lover comes.

Prodigal, you have given me love — therefore I to you give
  love!
O unspeakable passionate love . . .

Walt Whitman

THE SHOWER

Waters above! Eternal springs!
The dew that silvers the Dove's wings!
O welcome, welcome to the sad:
Give dry dust drink, drink that makes glad!
Many fair ev'nings, many flow'rs
Sweetened with rich and gentle showers,
Have I enjoyed, and down have run
Many a fine and shining sun;
But never, till this happy hour,
Was blest with such an evening-shower!

Henry Vaughan

TALL NETTLES

Tall nettles cover up, as they have done
These many springs, the rusty harrow, the plough
Long worn out, and the roller made of stone:
Only the elm butt tops the nettles now.

This corner of the farmyard I like most:
As well as any bloom upon a flower
I like the dust on the nettles, never lost
Except to prove the sweetness of a shower.

Edward Thomas

237

ARRAN
(From the Old Irish)

Arran of the many stags,
the sea reaches to its shoulder;
island where companies are fed,
ridges whereon blue spears are reddened.

Wanton deer upon its peaks,
mellow blaeberries on its heaths,
cold water in its streams,
mast upon its brown oaks.

Hunting dogs are there, and hounds,
blackberries and sloes of the dark blackthorn,
dense thorn-bushes in its woods,
stags astray among its oak-groves.

Gathering of purple lichen on its rocks,
grass without blemish on its slopes;
over its fair shapely crags
gambolling of dappled fawns leaping.

Smooth is its lowland, fat are its swine,
pleasant its fields, a tale to be believed;
its nuts on the boughs of its hazel-wood,
sailing of long galleys past it.

It is delightful when fine weather comes,
trout under the banks of its streams,
seagulls answer each other round its white cliff;
delightful at all times is Arran.

Translated by Kenneth Jackson

RIVERS ARISE: A FRAGMENT

Rivers arise; whether thou be the son
Of utmost Tweed, or Oose, or gulphié Dun,
Or Trent, who like some earthborn giant spreads
His thirty arms along the indented meads,
Or sullen Mole that runneth underneath,
Or Severn swift, guilty of maiden's death,
Or rockie Avon, or of sedgie Lee,
Or coaly Tine, or antient hallowed Dee,
Or Humber loud that keeps the Scythians' name,
Or Medway smooth, or royal towred Thame.

John Milton

As Severn lately in her ebbs that sank,
Vast and forsaken leaves th'uncovered sands,
Fetching full tides, luxurious, high, and rank,
Seems in her pride t'invade the neighbouring lands,
Breaking her limits, covering all her banks,
Threat'neth the proud hills with her wat'ry hands,
　As though she meant her empyrie to have
　Where even but lately she beheld her grave . . .

Michael Drayton

THE POPLAR-FIELD

The poplars are fell'd, farewell to the shade
And the whispering sound of the cool colonnade,
The winds play no longer, and sing in the leaves,
Nor Ouse on his bosom their image receives.

Twelve years have elaps'd since I first took a view
Of my favourite field and the bank where they grew,
And now in the grass behold they are laid,
And the tree is my seat that once lent me a shade.

The blackbird has fled to another retreat
Where the hazels afford him a screen from the heat,
And the scene where his melody charm'd me before,
Resounds with his sweet-flowing ditty no more.

My fugitive years are all hasting away,
And I must ere long lie as lowly as they,
With a turf on my breast, and a stone at my head,
Ere another such grove shall arise in its stead.

'Tis a sight to engage me, if any thing can,
To muse on the perishing pleasures of man;
Though his life be a dream, his enjoyments, I see,
Have a being less durable even than he.

William Cowper

Silent Nymph, with curious eye!
Who, the purple ev'ning, lie
On the mountain's lonely van,
Beyond the noise of busy man,
Painting fair the form of things,
While the yellow linnet sings;
Or the tuneful nightingale
Charms the forest with her tale;
Come with all thy various hues,
Come, and aid thy sister Muse;
Now while Phoebus riding high
Gives lustre to the land and sky!
Grongar Hill invites my song,
Draw the landskip bright and strong;
Grongar, in whose mossy cells
Sweetly-musing Quiet dwells;
Grongar, in whose silent shade,
For the modest Muses made,
So oft I have, the evening still,
At the fountain of a rill,
Sate upon a flow'ry bed,
With my hand beneath my head;
While stray'd my eyes o'er Towy's flood,
Over mead, and over wood,
From house to house, from hill to hill,
Till Contemplation had her fill.

About his chequer'd sides I wind,
And leave his brooks and meads behind,
And groves, and grottoes, where I lay,
And vistoes shooting beams of day:
Wide and wider spreads the vale;
As circles on a smooth canal:
The mountains round, unhappy fate!
Sooner or later, of all height,
Withdraw their summits from the skies,
And lessen as the others rise:
Still the prospect wider spreads,
Adds a thousand woods and meads,
Still it widens, widens still,
And sinks the newly risen hill.

Now, I gain the mountain's brow,
What a landskip lies below!
No clouds, no vapours intervene,
But the gay, the open scene
Does the face of nature show,
In all the hues of heaven's bow!
And, swelling to embrace the light,
Spreads around beneath the sight.

Old castles on the cliffs arise,
Proudly tow'ring in the skies!
Rushing from the woods, the spires
Seem from hence ascending fires!
Half his beams Apollo sheds
On the yellow mountain-heads!
Gilds the fleeces of the flocks:
And glitters on the broken rocks!

Below me trees unnumber'd rise,
Beautiful in various dyes:
The gloomy pine, the poplar blue,
The yellow beech, the sable yew,
The slender fir, that taper grows,
The sturdy oak with broad-spread boughs.
And beyond the purple grove,
Haunt of Phillis, queen of love!
Gaudy as the op'ning dawn,
Lies a long and level lawn
On which a dark hill, steep and high,
Holds and charms the wand'ring eye!
Deep are his feet in Towy's flood,
His sides are cloath'd with waving wood,
And ancient towers crown his brow,
That cast an aweful look below;
Whose ragged walls the ivy creeps,
And with her arms from falling keeps;
So both a safety from the wind
Our mutual dependence find.

'Tis now the raven's bleak abode;
'Tis now th'apartment of the toad;
And there the fox securely feeds;
And there the pois'nous adder breeds
Conceal'd in ruins, moss and weeds;
While, ever and anon, there falls
Huge heaps of hoary moulder'd walls.

Yet time has seen, that lifts the low,
And level lays the lofty brow,
Has seen this broken pile compleat,
Big with the vanity of state;
But transient is the smile of fate!
A little rule, a little sway,
A sun beam in a winter's day,
Is all the proud and mighty have
Between the cradle and the grave.

And see the rivers how they run,
Thro' woods and meads, in shade and sun,
Sometimes swift, sometimes slow,
Wave succeeding wave, they go
A various journey to the deep,
Like human life to endless sleep!
Thus is nature's vesture wrought,
To instruct our wand'ring thought;
Thus she dresses green and gay,
To disperse our cares away.

Ever charming, ever new,
When will the landskip tire the view!
The fountain's fall, the river's flow,
The woody vallies, warm and low;
The windy summit, wild and high,
Roughly rushing on the sky!
The pleasant seat, the ruin'd tow'r,
The naked rock, the shady bow'r;
The town and village, dome and farm,
Each give each a double charm,
Like pearls upon an Aethiop's arm.

See on the mountain's southern side,
Where the prospect opens wide,
Where the evening gilds the tide;
How close and small the hedges lie!
What streaks of meadows cross the eye!
A step methinks may pass the stream,
So little distant dangers seem;
So we mistake the future's face,
Ey'd thro' hope's deluding glass;
As yon summit soft and fair
Clad in colours of the air,
Which to those who journey near,
Barren, brown, and rough appear;

Still we tread the same coarse way,
The present's still a cloudy day.
   O may I with myself agree,
And never covet what I see:
Content me with an humble shade,
My passions tam'd, my wishes laid;
For while our wishes wildly roll,
We banish quiet from the soul:
'Tis thus the busy beat the air;
And misers gather wealth and care.
   Now, ev'n now, my joys run high,
As on the mountain-turf I lie;
While the wanton Zephyr sings,
And in the vale perfumes his wings;
While the waters murmur deep;
While the shepherd charms his sheep;
While the birds unbounded fly,
And with musick fill the sky,
Now, ev'n now, my joys run high.
   Be full, ye courts, be great who will;
Search for Peace with all your skill:
Open wide the lofty door,
Seek her on the marble floor,
In vain you search, she is not there;
In vain ye search the domes of care!
Grass and flowers Quiet treads,
On the meads, and mountain-heads,
Along with Pleasure, close allied,
Ever by each other's side:
And often, by the murm'ring rill,
Hears the thrush, while all is still,
Within the groves of Grongar Hill.

                                          John Dyer

HOW TIME CONSUMETH ALL
EARTHLY THINGS

Ay me, ay me, I sigh to see the scythe afield.
   Down goeth the grass, soon wrought to withered hay;
Ay me alas, ay me alas, that beauty needs must yield
   And princes pass, as grass doth fade away.

Ay me, ay me, that life cannot have lasting leave,
 Nor gold take hold of everlasting joy:
Ay me alas, ay me alas, that Time hath talents to receive,
 And yet no time can make a sure stay.

Ay me, ay me, that wit cannot have wishèd choice,
 Nor wish can win that will desires to see:
Ay me alas, ay me alas, that mirth can promise no rejoice,
 Nor study tell what afterward shall be.

Ay me, ay me, that no sure staff is given to age
 Nor age can give sure wit that youth will take:
Ay me alas, ay me alas, that no counsel wise and sage
 Will shun the show that all doth mar and make.

Ay me, ay me, come Time, shear on, and shake thy hay,
 It is no boot to baulk thy bitter blows:
Ay me alas, ay me alas, come Time, take everything away,
 For all is thine, be it good or bad, that grows.

Thomas Proctor (?)

LIFE HALF LIVED

With yellow pears,
And with wild roses full
The land
Hangs in the lake:

You exquisite swans,
Tipsy with kisses,
Steep your heads
Deep in the holy
Water's soberness.

 O where, if the winter
Comes, shall I get the flowers,
O where
Earth's shine and shadiness?

The walls are cold and stand
And do not speak,
The windvanes
Clap and creak.

From the German of
J. C. F. Hölderlin

16. THE FLOWERS

The Flowers

Proserpina makes an appearance in these flower poems, in Shakespeare's (page 249), Swinburne's, and Spenser's (pages 262 and 263). The sun comes, the showers fall, and the flowers grow, bending this way and that (as in the rough Italian woodcut of 1495) — and poems recall Proserpina or Persephone in the field of Enna.

She is young and lovable, daughter of the goddess of the earth. She is picking flowers when black Pluto, Rector of the Damned, breaks out of Etna in his chariot, drawn by black-buttocked horses, and carries her off out of sunlight, to be his wife and Queen of the Dead. To black Pluto or Dis (another of his names) white Persephone acts as the girl acts to the nasty, husky, dusky, musty, fusky coal black smith in The Two Magicians, on page 68.

But what flowers did Persephone and her friends pick in the field of Enna? According to the poet Claudian, an April wind had infused into the flowers

> Whatever scents the dry Arabia
> Breathes from her spices on the morning grey,

and near a stream and a wood of oak and cypress and bay and box and (of course) cherry-trees, the flowers included violets, roses, lilies, marjoram, privet, hyacinth, and narcissi (which are Shakespeare's daffodils) —

> The Lily to the darker Violet
> One weaves; another to her breast doth set
> The soft-sweet Marjoram; a third must go
> Star-deckt with Roses; this in diff'ring show
> Pranks up her self with Privet white; and thee
> They gather, and thy weeping tragedy,
> Poor Hyacinth, renew; nor do they spare
> Narcissus —

Proserpina, as she fills her baskets, is rapt away with a garland of flowers round her head.

Pluto allowed her — since the flowers on earth all died when she was detained in hell — to spend eight months of each year on earth or in heaven. Her return to earth is spring, flowers, summer; her return to her black husband, and to hell, is autumn and the dying of the flowers and winter, and the burying of the seed.

THE IDLE FLOWERS

I have sown upon the fields
Eyebright and Pimpernel,
And Pansy and Poppy-seed
Ripen'd and scatter'd well,

And silver Lady-smock
The meads with light to fill,
Cowslip and Buttercup,
Daisy and Daffodil;

King-cup and Fleur-de-lys
Upon the marsh to meet
With Comfrey, Watermint,
Loose-strife and Meadowsweet;

And all along the stream
My care hath not forgot
Crowfoot's white galaxy
And love's Forget-me-not:

And where high grasses wave
Shall great Moon-daisies blink,
With Rattle and Sorrel sharp
And Robin's ragged pink.

Thick on the woodland floor,
Gay company shall be,
Primrose and Hyacinth
And frail Anemone,

Perennial Strawberry-bloom,
Woodsorrel's pencilled veil,
Dishevel'd Willow-weed
And Orchis purple and pale,

Bugle, that blushes blue,
And Woodruff's snowy gem,
Proud Foxglove's finger-bells
And Spurge with milky stem.

High on the downs so bare,
Where thou dost love to climb,
Pink Thrift and Milkwort are,
Lotus and scented Thyme;

And in the shady lanes
Bold Arum's hood of green,
Herb Robert, Violet,
Starwort and Celandine;

And by the dusty road
Bedstraw and Mullein tall,
With red Valerian
And Toadflax on the wall,

Yarrow and Chicory,
That hath for hue no like,
Silene and Mallow mild
And Agrimony's spike,

Blue-eyed Veronicas
And grey-faced Scabious
And downy Silverweed
And striped Convolvulus:

Harebell shall haunt the banks,
And thro' the hedgerow peer
Withwind and Snapdragon
And Nightshade's flower of fear.

And where men never sow,
Have I my Thistles set,
Ragwort and stiff Wormwood
And straggling Mignonette,

Bugloss and Burdock rank
And prickly Teasel high,
With Umbels yellow and white,
That come to kexes dry.

Pale Chlora shalt thou find,
Sun-loving Centaury,
Cranesbill and Sinjunwort,
Cinquefoil and Betony:

Shock-headed Dandelion,
That drank the fire of the sun:
Hawkweed and Marigold,
Cornflower and Campion.

Let Oak and Ash grow strong,
Let Beech her branches spread;
Let Grass and Barley throng
And waving Wheat for bread;

Be share and sickle bright
To labour at all hours;
For thee and thy delight
I have made the idle flowers.

But now 'tis Winter, child,
And bitter northwinds blow,
The ways are wet and wild,
The land is laid in snow.

Robert Bridges

THE BEE-ORCHIS

I saw a bee, I saw a flower;
I looked again and said, For sure
Never was flower, never was bee
Locked in such immobility.

The loud bees lurched about the hill,
But this flower-buried bee was still;
I said, O Love, has love the power
To change a bee into a flower.

Andrew Young

SOME FLOWERS O' THE SPRING

Now, my fair'st friend,
I would I had some flowers o' the spring that might
Become your time of day; — and yours, and yours,
That wear upon your virgin branches yet

Your maidenheads growing: – O Proserpina,
For the flowers now, that frighted, thou lett'st fall
From Dis's wagon! daffodils
That come before the swallow dares, and take
The winds of March with beauty; violets dim,
But sweeter than the lids of Juno's eyes
Or Cytherea's breath; pale primroses,
That die unmarried, ere they can behold
Bright Phoebus in his strength, – a malady
Most incident to maids; bold oxlips and
The crown-imperial; lilies of all kinds,
The flower-de-luce being one! . . .

William Shakespeare

LYCIDAS

(In this Monody the Author bewails a learned Friend, unfortunately drown'd in his passage from Chester on the Irish Seas, 1637.)

Yet once more, O ye laurels, and once more
Ye myrtles brown, with ivy never-sear,
I come to pluck your berries harsh and crude,
And with forc'd fingers rude,
Shatter your leaves before the mellowing year.
Bitter constraint, and sad occasion dear,
Compels me to disturb your season due:
For Lycidas is dead, dead ere his prime
Young Lycidas, and hath not left his peer:
Who would not sing for Lycidas? he knew
Himself to sing, and build the lofty rhyme.
He must not float upon his wat'ry bier
Unwept, and welter to the parching wind,
Without the meed of some melodious tear.
    Begin then, Sisters of the sacred well,
That from beneath the seat of Jove doth spring,
Begin, and somewhat loudly sweep the string.
Hence with denial vain, and coy excuse,
So may some gentle Muse
With lucky words favour my destin'd Urn,
And as he passes turn,
And bid fair peace be to my sable shroud.
For we were nurst upon the selfsame hill,
Fed the same flock, by fountain, shade, and rill.

Together both, ere the high lawns appear'd
Under the opening eye-lids of the morn,
We drove afield, and both together heard
What time the gray-fly winds her sultry horn,
Batt'ning our flocks with the fresh dews of night,
Oft till the star that rose, at ev'ning, bright
Towards heav'ns descent had slop'd his westering wheel.
Meanwhile the rural ditties were not mute,
Temper'd to th'oaten flute;
Rough satyrs danc'd, and fauns with clov'n heel,
From the glad sound would not be absent long,
And old Damaetas lov'd to hear our song.

But O the heavy change, now thou art gone,
Now thou art gone, and never must return!
Thee shepherd, thee the woods, and desert caves,
With wild thyme and the gadding vine o'ergrown,
And all their echoes mourn.
The willows, and the hazel copses green,
Shall now no more be seen,
Fanning their joyous leaves to thy soft lays.
As killing as the canker to the rose,
Or taint-worm to the weanling herds that graze,
Or frost to flowers, that their gay wardrobe wear,
When first the whitethorn blows;
Such, Lycidas, thy loss to shepherd's ear.

Where were ye, nymphs, when the remorseless deep
Clos'd o'er the head of your lov'd Lycidas?
For neither were ye playing on the steep,
Where your old bards, the famous druids lie,
Nor on the shaggy top of Mona high,
Nor yet where Deva spreads her wizard stream:
Ay me, I fondly dream!
Had ye bin there — for what could that have done?
What could the muse herself that Orpheus bore,
The muse herself, for her inchanting son
Whom universal nature did lament,
When by the rout that made the hideous roar,
His goary visage down the stream was sent,
Down the swift Hebrus to the Lesbian shore.

Alas! What boots it with uncessant care
To tend the homely slighted shepherd's trade,
And strictly meditate the thankless muse,
Were it not better done as others use,

To sport with Amaryllis in the shade,
Or with the tangles of Neaera's hair?
Fame is the spur that the clear spirit doth raise
(That last infirmity of noble mind)
To scorn delights, and live laborious days;
But the fair guerdon when we hope to find,
And think to burst out into sudden blaze,
Comes the blind fury with th'abhorrèd shears,
And slits the thin spun life. But not the praise,
Phoebus repli'd, and touch'd my trembling ears;
Fame is no plant that grows on mortal soil,
Nor in the glistering foil
Set off to th'world, nor in broad rumour lies,
But lives and spreads aloft by those pure eyes,
And perfet witness of all judging Jove;
As he pronounces lastly on each deed,
Of so much fame in heav'n expect thy meed.

    O fountain Arethuse, and thou honour'd flood,
Smooth-sliding Mincius, crown'd with vocal reeds,
That strain I heard was of a higher mood:
But now my oat proceeds,
And listens to the herald of the sea
That came in Neptune's plea,
He ask'd the waves, and ask'd the felon winds,
What hard mishap hath doom'd this gentle swain?
And question'd every gust of rugged wings
That blows from off each beakèd promontory,
They knew not of his story,
And sage Hippotades their answer brings,
That not a blast was from his dungeon stray'd,
The air was calm, and on the level brine,
Sleek Panope with all her sisters play'd,
It was that fatal and perfidious bark
Built in th'eclipse, and rigg'd with curses dark,
That sunk so low that sacred head of thine.

    Next Camus, reverend sire, went footing slow,
His mantle hairy, and his bonnet sedge,
Inwrought with figures dim, and on the edge
Like to that sanguine flower inscribed with woe.
Ah; Who hath reft (quoth he) my dearest pledge?
Last came and last did go,
The pilot of the Galilaean lake,
Two massy keys he bore of metals twain,

(The golden opes, the iron shuts amain)
He shook his miter'd locks, and stern bespake,
How well could I have spar'd for thee, young swain,
Anow of such as for their bellies sake,
Creep and intrude, and climb into the fold?
Of other care they little reck'ning make,
Than how to scramble at the shearers' feast,
And shove away the worthy bidden guest.
Blind mouths! that scarce themselves know how to hold
A sheep-hook, or have learn'd aught else the least
That to the faithful herdman's art belongs!
What recks it them? What need they? They are sped;
And when they list, their lean and flashy songs
Grate on their scrannel pipes of wretched straw,
The hungry sheep look up, and are not fed,
But swoll'n with wind, and the rank mist they draw,
Rot inwardly, and foul contagion spread:
Besides what the grim Wolf with privy paw
Daily devours apace, and nothing said,
But that two-handed engine at the door,
Stands ready to smite once, and smite no more.
    Return, Alpheus, the dread voice is past,
That shrunk thy streams; Return, Sicilian muse,
And call the vales, and bid them hither cast
Their bells, and flow'rets of a thousand hues.
Ye valleys low where the mild whispers use,
Of shades and wanton winds, and gushing brooks,
On whose fresh lap the swart star sparely looks,
Throw hither all your quaint enamel'd eyes,
That on the green turf suck the honied showers,
And purple all the ground with vernal flowers.
Bring the rathe primrose that forsaken dies.
The tufted crow-toe, and pale jessamine,
The white pink, and the pansy freak'd with jet,
The glowing violet.
The musk-rose, and the well attir'd woodbine.
With cowslips wan that hang the pensive head,
And every flower that sad embroidery wears:
Bid amaranthus all his beauty shed,
And daffadillies fill their cups with tears,
To strew the laureate hearse where Lycid lies.
For so to interpose a little ease,
Let our frail thoughts dally with false surmise.

Ay me! Whilst thee the shores, and sounding seas
Wash far away, where ere thy bones are hurl'd,
Whether beyond the stormy Hebrides,
Where thou perhaps under the whelming tide
Visit'st the bottom of the monstrous world;
Or whether thou to our moist vows denied,
Sleep'st by the fable of Bellerus old,
Where the great vision of the guarded mount
Looks towards Namancos and Bayona's hold;
Look homeward Angel now, and melt with ruth.
And, O ye dolphins, waft the hapless youth.
   Weep no more, woeful shepherds weep no more,
For Lycidas your sorrow is not dead,
Sunk though he be beneath the wat'ry floor,
So sinks the day-star in the Ocean bed,
And yet anon repairs his drooping head,
And tricks his beams, and with new spangled ore,
Flames in the forehead of the morning sky:
So Lycidas sunk low, but mounted high,
Through the dear might of him that walk'd the waves
Where other groves, and other streams along,
With nectar pure his oozy locks he laves,
And hears the unexpressive nuptial song,
In the blest kingdoms meek of joy and love.
There entertain him all the saints above,
In solemn troops, and sweet societies
That sing, and singing in their glory move,
And wipe the tears for ever from his eyes.
Now Lycidas the shepherds weep no more;
Henceforth thou art the genius of the shore,
In thy large recompense, and shalt be good
To all that wander in that perilous flood.
   Thus sang the uncouth swain to th'oaks and rills,
While the still morn went out with sandles gray,
He touch'd the tender stops of various quills,
With eager thought warbling his doric lay:
And now the sun had stretch'd out all the hills,
And now was dropp'd into the western bay;
At last he rose, and twitch'd his mantle blue:
To-morrow to fresh woods, and pastures new.

John Milton

THE RAGWORT

Ragwort, thou humble flower with tattered leaves,
I love to see thee come and litter gold
What time the summer binds her russet sheaves,
Decking rude spots in beauties manifold,
That without thee were dreary to behold,
Sunburnt and bare — the meadow bank, the baulk
That leads a wagon-way through mellow fields
Rich with the tints that harvest's plenty yields,
Browns of all hues; and everywhere I walk
Thy waste of shining blossoms richly shields
The sun-tanned sward in splendid hues that burn
So bright and glaring that the very light
Of the rich sunshine doth to paleness turn,
And seems but very shadows in thy sight.

John Clare

THE SUN-FLOWER

Ah, Sun-flower! weary of time,
Who countest the steps of the sun,
Seeking after that sweet golden clime
Where the traveller's journey is done:

Where the youth pined away with desire,
And the pale virgin shrouded in snow
Arise from their graves, and aspire
Where my Sun-flower wishes to go.

William Blake

THE SCHOLAR GIPSY

Go, for they call you, Shepherd, from the hill;
Go, Shepherd, and untie the wattled cotes:
No longer leave thy wistful flock unfed,
Nor let thy bawling fellows rack their throats,
Nor the cropp'd grasses shoot another head.
But when the fields are still,
And the tired men and dogs all gone to rest,
And only the white sheep are sometimes seen
Cross and recross the strips of moon-blanch'd green;
Come, Shepherd, and again renew the quest.

Here, where the reaper was at work of late,
　In this high field's dark corner, where he leaves
　　His coat, his basket, and his earthen cruse,
　And in the sun all morning binds the sheaves,
　　Then here, at noon, comes back his stores to use;
　　Here will I sit and wait,
　While to my ear from uplands far away
　　The bleating of the folded flocks is borne,
　　With distant cries of reapers in the corn —
　All the live murmur of a summer's day.

Screen'd is this nook o'er the high, half-reap'd field,
　And here till sun-down, Shepherd, will I be.
　　Through the thick corn the scarlet poppies peep,
　And round green roots and yellowing stalks I see
　　Pale blue convolvulus in tendrils creep:
　　And air-swept lindens yield
　Their scent, and rustle down their perfum'd showers
　　Of bloom on the bent grass where I am laid,
　　And bower me from the August sun with shade;
　And the eye travels down to Oxford's towers:

And near me on the grass lies Glanvil's book —
　Come, let me read the oft-read tale again,
　　The story of that Oxford scholar poor
　Of pregnant parts and quick inventive brain,
　　Who, tir'd of knocking at Preferment's door,
　　One summer morn forsook
　His friends, and went to learn the Gipsy lore,
　　And roam'd the world with that wild brotherhood,
　　And came, as most men deem'd, to little good,
　But came to Oxford and his friends no more.

But once, years after, in the country lanes,
　Two scholars whom at college erst he knew
　　Met him, and of his way of life inquir'd.
　Whereat he answer'd, that the Gipsy crew,
　　His mates, had arts to rule as they desir'd
　　The workings of men's brains;
　And they can bind them to what thoughts they will:
　　'And I', he said, 'the secret of their art,
　　When fully learn'd, will to the world impart:
　But it needs heaven-sent moments for this skill.'

This said, he left them, and return'd no more,
But rumours hung about the country side
That the lost Scholar long was seen to stray,
Seen by rare glimpses, pensive and tongue-tied,
In hat of antique shape, and cloak of grey,
The same the Gipsies wore.
Shepherds had met him on the Hurst in spring;
At some lone alehouse in the Berkshire moors,
On the warm ingle bench, the smock-frock'd boors
Had found him seated at their entering,

But, mid their drink and clatter, he would fly:
And I myself seem half to know thy looks,
And put the shepherds, Wanderer, on thy trace;
And boys who in lone wheatfields scare the rooks
I ask if thou hast pass'd their quiet place;
Or in my boat I lie
Moor'd to the cool bank in the summer heats,
Mid wide grass meadows which the sunshine fills,
And watch the warm green-muffled Cumner hills,
And wonder if thou haunt'st their shy retreats.

For most, I know, thou lov'st retired ground,
Thee, at the ferry, Oxford riders blithe,
Returning home on summer nights, have met
Crossing the stripling Thames at Bab-lock-hithe,
Trailing in the cool stream thy fingers wet,
As the slow punt swings round:
And leaning backwards in a pensive dream,
And fostering in thy lap a heap of flowers
Pluck'd in shy fields and distant Wychwood bowers,
And thine eyes resting on the moonlit stream:

And then they land, and thou art seen no more.
Maidens who from the distant hamlets come
To dance around the Fyfield elm in May,
Oft through the darkening fields have seen thee roam,
Or cross a stile into the public way.
Oft thou hast given them store
Of flowers — the frail-leaf'd, white anemone —
Dark bluebells drench'd with dews of summer eves —
And purple orchises with spotted leaves —
But none has words she can report of thee.

And, above Godstow Bridge, when hay-time's here
   In June, and many a scythe in sunshine flames,
      Men who through those wide fields of breezy grass
   Where black-wing'd swallows haunt the glittering Thames,
      To bathe in the abandon'd lasher pass,
         Have often pass'd thee near
   Sitting upon the river bank o'ergrown:
      Mark'd thy outlandish garb, thy figure spare,
      Thy dark vague eyes, and soft abstracted air;
         But, when they came from bathing, thou wert gone.

At some lone homestead in the Cumner hills,
   Where at her open door the housewife darns,
      Thou hast been seen, or hanging on a gate
   To watch the threshers in the mossy barns.
      Children, who early range these slopes and late
         For cresses from the rills,
   Have known thee watching, all an April day,
      The springing pastures and the feeding kine;
      And mark'd thee, when the stars come out and shine,
         Through the long dewy grass move slow away.

In Autumn, on the skirts of Bagley wood,
   Where most the Gipsies by the turf-edg'd way
      Pitch their smok'd tents, and every bush you see
   With scarlet patches tagg'd and shreds of grey,
      Above the forest ground call'd Thessaly —
         The blackbird picking food
   Sees thee, nor stops his meal, nor fears at all;
      So often has he known thee past him stray
      Rapt, twirling in thy hand a wither'd spray,
         And waiting for the spark from Heaven to fall.

And once, in winter, on the causeway chill
   Where home through flooded fields foot-travellers go,
      Have I not pass'd thee on the wooden bridge
   Wrapt in thy cloak and battling with the snow,
      Thy face towards Hinksey and its wintry ridge?
         And thou hast climb'd the hill
   And gain'd the white brow of the Cumner range,
      Turn'd once to watch, while thick the snowflakes fall,
      The line of festal light in Christ-Church hall —
         Then sought thy straw in some sequester'd grange.

But what — I dream! Two hundred years are flown
    Since first thy story ran through Oxford halls,
      And the grave Glanvil did the tale inscribe
    That thou wert wander'd from the studious walls
      To learn strange arts, and join a Gipsy tribe:
        And thou from earth art gone
    Long since, and in some quiet churchyard laid;
      Some country nook, where o'er thy unknown grave
      Tall grasses and white flowering nettles wave —
        Under a dark red-fruited yew-tree's shade.

— No, no, thou hast not felt the lapse of hours.
    For what wears out the life of mortal men?
      'Tis that from change to change their being rolls:
    'Tis that repeated shocks, again, again,
      Exhaust the energy of strongest souls,
        And numb the elastic powers.
   Till having us'd our nerves with bliss and teen,
      And tir'd upon a thousand schemes our wit,
      To the just-pausing Genius we remit
        Our worn-out life, and are — what we have been.

Thou hast not liv'd, why should'st thou perish, so?
    Thou hast one aim, one business, one desire:
      Else wert thou long since number'd with the dead —
    Else hadst thou spent, like other men, thy fire.
      The generations of thy peers are fled,
        And we ourselves shall go;
    But thou possessest an immortal lot,
      And we imagine thee exempt from age
      And living as thou liv'st on Glanvil's page,
        Because thou hadst — what we, alas, have not!

For early didst thou leave the world, with powers
    Fresh, undiverted to the world without,
      Firm to their mark, not spent on other things;
    Free from the sick fatigue, the languid doubt,
      Which much to have tried, in much been baffled, brings.
        O Life unlike to ours!
    Who fluctuate idly without term or scope,
      Of whom each strives, nor knows for what he strives,
      And each half lives a hundred different lives;
        Who wait like thee, but not, like thee, in hope.

Thou waitest for the spark from Heaven: and we,
    Vague half-believers of our casual creeds,
        Who never deeply felt, nor clearly will'd,
    Whose insight never has borne fruit in deeds,
        Whose weak resolves never have been fulfill'd;
            For whom each year we see
    Breeds new beginnings, disappointments new;
        Who hesitate and falter life away,
        And lose to-morrow the ground won to-day —
            Ah, do not we, Wanderer, await it too?

Yes, we await it, but it still delays,
    And then we suffer; and amongst us One,
        Who most has suffer'd, takes dejectedly
    His seat upon the intellectual throne;
        And all his store of sad experience he
            Lays bare of wretched days;
    Tells us his misery's birth and growth and signs,
        And how the dying spark of hope was fed,
        And how the breast was sooth'd, and how the head,
            And all his hourly varied anodynes.

This for our wisest: and we others pine,
    And wish the long unhappy dream would end,
        And waive all claim to bliss and try to bear,
    With close-lipp'd Patience for our only friend,
        Sad Patience, too near neighbour to Despair:
            But none has hope like thine.
    Thou through the fields and through the woods dost stray
        Roaming the country side, a truant boy,
        Nursing thy project in unclouded joy,
            And every doubt long blown by time away.

O born in days when wits were fresh and clear,
    And life ran gaily as the sparkling Thames;
        Before this strange disease of modern life,
    With its sick hurry, its divided aims,
        Its heads o'ertax'd, its palsied hearts, was rife —
            Fly hence, our contact fear!
    Still fly, plunge deeper in the bowering wood!
        Averse, as Dido did with gesture stern
        From her false friend's approach in Hades turn,
            Wave us away, and keep thy solitude.

Still nursing the unconquerable hope,
  Still clutching the inviolable shade,
    With a free onward impulse brushing through,
  By night, the silver'd branches of the glade –
    Far on the forest skirts, where none pursue,
      On some mild pastoral slope
  Emerge, and resting on the moonlit pales,
    Freshen thy flowers, as in former years,
    With dew, or listen with enchanted ears,
      From the dark dingles, to the nightingales

But fly our paths, our feverish contact fly!
  For strong the infection of our mental strife,
    Which, though it gives no bliss, yet spoils for rest;
  And we should win thee from thy own fair life,
    Like us distracted, and like us unblest.
      Soon, soon thy cheer would die,
  Thy hopes grow timorous, and unfix'd thy powers,
    And thy clear aims be cross and shifting made:
    And then thy glad perennial youth would fade,
      Fade, and grow old at last, and die like ours.

Then fly our greetings, fly our speech and smiles!
  – As some grave Tyrian trader, from the sea,
    Descried at sunrise an emerging prow
  Lifting the cool-hair'd creepers stealthily,
    The fringes of a southward-facing brow
      Among the Aegean isles;
  And saw the merry Grecian coaster come,
    Freighted with amber grapes, and Chian wine,
    Green bursting figs, and tunnies steep'd in brine;
      And knew the intruders on his ancient home,

The young light-hearted Masters of the waves;
  And snatch'd his rudder, and shook out more sail,
    And day and night held on indignantly
  O'er the blue Midland waters with the gale,
    Betwixt the Syrtes and soft Sicily,
      To where the Atlantic raves
  Outside the Western Straits, and unbent sails
    There, where down cloudy cliffs, through sheets of foam,
    Shy traffickers, the dark Iberians come;
      And on the beach undid his corded bales.

Matthew Arnold

A TALE

There once the walls
Of the ruined cottage stood.
The periwinkle crawls
With flowers in its hair into the wood.

In flowerless hours
Never will the bank fail,
With everlasting flowers
On fragments of blue plates, to tell the tale.

Edward Thomas

PROSERPINE

Pale, beyond porch and portal,
   Crowned with calm leaves, she stands
Who gathers all things mortal
   With cold immortal hands;
Her languid lips are sweeter
Than love's who fears to greet her
To men that mix and meet her
   From many times and lands.

She waits for each and other,
   She waits for all men born;
Forgets the earth her mother,
   The life of fruits and corn;
And spring and seed and swallow
Take wing for her and follow
Where summer songs ring hollow
   And flowers are put to scorn.

There go the loves that wither,
   The old loves with wearier wings;
And all dead years draw thither,
   And all disastrous things;
Dead dreams of days forsaken,
Blind buds that snows have shaken,
Wild leaves that winds have taken,
   Red strays of ruined springs.

We are not sure of sorrow,
   And joy was never sure;
To-day will die to-morrow;
   Time stoops to no man's lure;

And love, grown faint and fretful,
With lips but half regretful
Sighs, and with eyes forgetful
   Weeps that no loves endure.

From too much love of living,
   From hope and fear set free,
We thank with brief thanksgiving
   Whatever gods may be
That no life lives for ever;
That dead men rise up never;
That even the weariest river
   Winds somewhere safe to sea.

Then star nor sun shall waken,
   Nor any change of light:
Nor sound of waters shaken,
   Nor any sound or sight:
Nor wintry leaves nor vernal,
Nor days nor things diurnal;
Only the sleep eternal
   In an eternal night...

Algernon Charles Swinburne

THE GARDEN OF PROSERPINA

There mournful cypress grew in greatest store,
   And trees of bitter gall, and heben sad,
Dread sleeping poppy, and black hellebore,
   Cold coloquintida, and tetra mad,
   Mortal samnitis, and cicuta bad,
With which th'unjust Athenians made to die
   Wise Socrates, who thereof quaffing glad,
Pour'd out his life and last philosophy
To the fair Critias, his dearest belamy.

The Garden of Proserpina this hight;
   And in the midst thereof a silver seat,
With a thick arbour goodly overdight,
   In which she often us'd from open heat
   Her self to shroud, and pleasures to entreat ...

Edmund Spenser

HARK! HARK! THE LARK

Hark! hark! the lark at heaven's gate sings,
   And Phoebus 'gins arise,
His steeds to water at those springs
   On chaliced flowers that lies;
And winking Mary-buds begin
   To ope their golden eyes;
With everything that pretty is,
   My lady sweet, arise!
   Arise, arise!

William Shakespeare

TO MARY: IT IS THE EVENING HOUR

It is the evening hour,
   How silent all doth lie,
The hornèd moon he shews his face
   In the river with the sky.
Just by the path on which we pass
The flaggy lake lies still as glass.

Spirit of her I love,
   Whispering to me,
Stories of sweet visions, as I rove,
   Here stop, and crop with me
Sweet flowers that in the still hour grew,
We'll take them home, nor shake off the bright dew.

Mary, or sweet spirit of thee,
   As the bright sun shines to-morrow,
Thy dark eyes these flowers shall see,
   Gathered by me in sorrow,
In the still hour when my mind was free
To walk alone — yet wish I walk'd with thee.

John Clare

17. THE GARDEN

The Garden

The garden of the woodcut is such as they had in Italy, indeed in Venice, in the Quattrocento, the fifteenth century of the great painters, when eyes opened to flowers and men and clothes and all objects and shapes and outlines in colours. In 1499 Aldus Manutius, at his Aldine Press in Venice, the most exquisite of the world's cities, printed what is held to be one of the most exquisitely designed of the world's books, the Hypnerotomachia Poliphili, a dream about love by Francesco de Colonna. The woodcut is one of his illustrations.

This garden is enclosed; water trickles from a sealed fountain. There are fruit trees as well as an arbour with vines. I trecalls the Song of Solomon: *A garden inclosed is my sister, my spouse; a spring shut up, a fountain sealed. Thy plants are an orchard of pomegranates, with pleasant fruits.* Girls lie in the grass with their instruments of music. One offers flowers to Poliphilus, another offers him a garland. You can observe such gardens, coloured, with their flowers and fruit, in paintings of the Quattrocento in the great art galleries —

> *Quattrocento put in paint*
> *On backgrounds for a God or Saint*
> *Gardens where a soul's at ease;*
> *Where everything that meets the eye*
> *Flowers and grass and cloudless sky*
> *Resemble forms that are or seem*
> *When sleepers wake and yet still dream . . .*
>
> (*W. B. Yeats*)

MIDWAYS OF A WALLED GARDEN

Midways of a walled garden,
  In the happy poplar land,
  Did an ancient castle stand,
With an old knight for a warden.

Many scarlet bricks there were
  In its walls, and old grey stone;
  Over which red apples shone
At the right time of the year.

On the bricks the green moss grew,
  Yellow lichen on the stone,
  Over which red apples shone;
Little war that castle knew.

Deep green water fill'd the moat,
  Each side had a red-brick lip,
  Green and mossy was the drip
Of dew and rain; there was a boat

Of carven wood, with hangings green
  About the stern; it was great bliss
  For lovers to sit there and kiss
In the hot summer noons, not seen.

Across the moat the fresh west wind
  In very little ripples went;
  The way the heavy aspens bent
Towards it, was a thing to mind.

The painted drawbridge over it
  Went up and down with gilded chains,
  'Twas pleasant in the summer rains
Within the bridge-house there to sit.

There were five swans that ne'er did eat
  The water-weeds, for ladies came
  Each day, and young knights did the same,
And gave them cakes and bread for meat.

They had a house of painted wood,
  A red roof gold-spiked over it,
  Wherein upon their eggs to sit
Week after week; no drop of blood,

Drawn from men's bodies by sword-blows,
  Came there ever, or any tear;
  Most certainly from year to year
'Twas pleasant as a Provence rose . . .

William Morris

HOW ROSES CAME RED

'Tis said, as Cupid danced among
The Gods, he down the nectar flung;
Which, on the white rose being shed,
Made it ever after red.

Robert Herrick

HOW MARIGOLDS CAME YELLOW

Jealous girls these sometimes were,
While they lived, or lasted here:
Turned to flowers, still they be
Yellow, marked for jealousy.

Robert Herrick

THE GARDEN

What wond'rous life is this I lead!
Ripe apples drop about my head;
The luscious clusters of the vine
Upon my mouth do crush their wine;
The nectarine, and curious peach,
Into my hands themselves do reach;
Stumbling on melons, as I pass,
Ensnar'd with flow'rs, I fall on grass.

Meanwhile the mind, from pleasure less,
Withdraws into its happiness:
The mind, that ocean where each kind
Does straight its own resemblance find;

Yet it creates, transcending these,
Far other worlds, and other seas;
Annihilating all that's made
To a green thought in a green shade.

Here at the fountain's sliding foot,
Or at some fruit-tree's mossy root,
Casting the body's vest aside,
My soul into the boughs does glide:
There like a bird it sits, and sings,
Then whets and combs its silver wings;
And, till prepar'd for longer flight,
Waves in its plumes the various light . . .

Andrew Marvell

GREAT DIOCLETIAN

Methinks I see great Diocletian walk
In the Salonian garden's shade,
Which by his own imperial hands was made:
I see him smile methinks, as he does talk
With the ambassadors who come in vain,
    T'entice him to a throne again.
'If I, my friends', said he, 'should to you show
All the delights which in these gardens grow,
'Tis likelier much that you should with me stay
Than 'tis that you should carry me away:
And trust me not, my friends, if every day
    I walk not here with more delight
Than ever after the most happy fight,
In triumph to the Capitol I rode,
To thank the gods, and to be thought myself almost a god . . .'

Abraham Cowley

THANKSGIVING TO GOD, FOR HIS HOUSE

Lord, thou hast given me a cell
    Wherein to dwell;
A little house, whose humble roof
    Is weather-proof;
Under the spars of which I lie
    Both soft, and dry;

Where thou my chamber for to ward
Hast set a guard
Of harmless thoughts, to watch and keep
Me, while I sleep.
Low is my porch, as is my fate,
Both void of state;
And yet the threshold of my door
Is worn by th'poor,
Who thither come, and freely get
Good words, or meat:
Likeas my parlour, so my hall
And kitchen's small:
A little buttery, and therein
A little bin,
Which keeps my little loaf of bread
Unchipt, unflead:
Some brittle sticks of thorn or briar
Make me a fire,
Close by whose living coal I sit,
And glow like it.
Lord, I confess too, when I dine,
The pulse is thine,
And all those other bits, that be
There plac'd by thee;
The worts, the purslane, and the mess
Of water-cress,
Which of thy kindness thou hast sent;
And my content
Makes those, and my belovèd beet,
To be more sweet.
'Tis thou that crown'st my glittering hearth
With guiltless mirth;
And giv'st me wassail bowls to drink,
Spic'd to the brink.
Lord, 'tis thy plenty-dropping hand
That soils my land;
And giv'st me, for my bushel sown,
Twice ten for one:
Thou mak'st my teeming hen to lay
Her egg each day:
Besides my healthful ewes to bear
Me twins each year:
The while the conduits of my kine

Run cream, (for wine.)
All these, and better thou dost send
    Me, to this end,
That I should render, for my part,
    A thankful heart;
Which, fir'd with incense, I resign,
    As wholly thine;
But the acceptance, that must be,
    My Christ, by thee.

Robert Herrick

THE BROKEN-HEARTED GARDENER
(A Street Ballad)

I'm a broken-hearted Gardener, and don't know what to do,
My love she is inconstant, and a fickle jade, too,
One smile from her lips will never be forgot,
It refreshes, like a shower from a watering pot.
            Oh, Oh! she's a fickle wild rose,
            A damask, a cabbage, a young China rose.

She's my myrtle, my geranium,
My sun-flower, my sweet marjoram,
My honeysuckle, my tulip, my violet,
My hollyhock, my dahlia, my mignonette.

We grew up together like two apple trees,
And clung to each other like double sweet peas,
Now they're going to trim her, and plant her in a pot,
And I'm left to wither, neglected and forgot.

She's my snowdrop, my ranunculus,
My hyacinth, my gillyflower, my polyanthus,
My heartsease, my pink water-lily,
My buttercup, my daisy, my daffydowndilly.

I'm like a scarlet runner that has lost its stick,
Or a cherry that's left for the dickey to pick,
Like a waterpot I weep, like a paviour I sigh,
Like a mushroom I'll wither, like a cucumber, die.

I'm like a humble bee that doesn't know where to settle,
And she's a dandelion, and a stinging nettle,
My heart's like a beetroot choked with chickweed,
And my head's like a pumpkin running to seed.

271

I'm a great mind to make myself a felo-de-se,
And finish all my woes on the branch of a tree:
But I won't, for I know at my kicking you'd roar,
And honour my death with a double encore.
Oh, Oh! she's a fickle wild rose,
A damask, a cabbage, a young China rose.

I HAVE AN ORCHARD

I have an orchard that hath store of plums,
Brown almonds, services, ripe figs and dates,
Dewberries, apples, yellow oranges,
A garden where are bee hives full of honey,
Musk-roses, and a thousand sort of flowers,
And in the midst doth run a silver stream,
Where thou shalt see the red-gilled fishes leap,
White swans, and many lovely water fowls . . .

Christopher Marlowe

ON HIMSELF

Born I was to meet with age,
And to walk life's pilgrimage,
Much, I know, of time is spent.
Tell I can't what's resident.
Howsoever, cares, adieu;
I'll have nought to say to you:
But I'll spend my coming hours
Drinking wine, and crown'd with flowers.

Robert Herrick

Journeys

Some are journeys to love, some are journeys to strange places, some are journeys without an end, some are journeys remembered and regretted, some are pilgrimages away from hard life or to a better life, including (on page 281) the first lines of the most famous of all the journey poems in our language, Geoffrey Chaucer's *Canterbury Tales*, tales, the poet imagines, which were told on a pilgrimage to Canterbury and to St Thomas à Becket in a warm April about 1390.

Poems themselves are journeys from first word to last, life is a journey between birth and death, so there is no more favourite subject. Indeed journey poems occur all through this book.

A poet who felt this pilgrimage through life with particular strength was the proud, honest Sir Walter Ralegh. Tradition says – I believe it – that he wrote his *Passionate Man's Pilgrimage* (on page 283) in the Tower of London in 1603, where he waited every day in expectation of the axe. Though he was reprieved, it was only to be condemned again, and to be beheaded, years after. His widow begged Sir Walter's head of the executioner, wrapped it in salt and spices, and kept it all her days in a pouch of red leather. Ralegh's passionate pilgrim carries the scallop-shell of St James the Apostle, which means he was thinking of the great pilgrimage to the shrine of St James at Santiago de Compostella in Spain, where, say the Spaniards, the Milky Way comes to an end, the stars, too, travelling there as pilgrims. The old pilgrimages to Our Lady's Shrine at Walsingham in Norfolk, with palmers or pilgrims from all Europe, are remembered by Ralegh in his great poem about love (on page 55). The *Lament for Walsingham* (on page 327) recalls them too.

BABYLON

King and Queen of Cantelon,
How many miles to Babylon?
　Eight and eight, and other eight.
Will I be there by candlelight?
　If your horse be good
　And your spurs be bright.

INTO MY HEART AN AIR THAT KILLS

　　　　　　　air that kills
　From yon far　　　blows:
What are those blue　　　　hills,
　What spires, what farms are

That is the land of lost content,
　I see it shining plain,
The happy highways where I went
　And cannot come again.

A. E. Housman

THE WANDERING KNIGHT'S SONG

My ornaments are arms,
　My pastime is in war,
My bed is cold upon the wold,
　My lamp yon star:

My journeyings are long,
　My slumbers short and broken;
From hill to hill I wander still,
　Kissing thy token.

I ride from land to land,
　I sail from sea to sea;
Some day more kind I fate may find,
　Some night kiss thee.

J. G. Lockhart

Art thou gone in haste?
   I'll not forsake thee!
Runn'st thou ne'er so fast,
   I'll o'ertake thee!
O'er the dales or the downs,
   Through the green meadows,
From the fields, through the towns,
   To the dim shadows!

All along the plain,
   To the low fountains;
Up, and down again,
   From the high mountains:
Echo, then, shall again
   Tell her I follow,
And the floods to the woods
   Carry my holla.
       Holla!
Ce! la! ho! ho! hu!

SATAN JOURNEYS TO THE GARDEN OF EDEN

Now to th'ascent of that steep savage hill
Satan had journied on, pensive and slow;
But further way found none, so thick entwin'd,
As one continu'd brake, the undergrowth
Of shrubs and tangling bushes had perplext
All path of man or beast that passed that way:
One gate there only was, and that look'd east
On th'other side: which when th'arch-felon saw
Due entrance he disdain'd, and in contempt,
At one slight bound high overleap'd all bound
Of hill or highest wall, and sheer within
Lights on his feet. As when a prowling wolf,
Whom hunger drives to seek new haunt for prey,
Watching where shepherds pen their flocks at eve
In hurdl'd cotes amid the field secure,
Leaps o'er the fence with ease into the fold:
Or as a thief bent to unhoard the cash
Of some rich burgher, whose substantial doors,
Cross-barr'd and bolted fast, fear no assault,

In at the window climbs, or o'er the tiles:
So clomb this first grand thief into God's fold:
So since into his church lewd hirelings climb.
Thence up he flew, and on the Tree of Life,
The middle tree and highest there that grew,
Sat like a cormorant; yet not true life
Thereby regain'd, but sat devising death
To them who liv'd; nor on the virtue thought
Of that life-giving plant, but only us'd
For prospect, what well us'd had bin the pledge
Of immortality . . .

John Milton

EXPULSION FROM PARADISE

The brandish't sword of God before them blaz'd
Fierce as a comet; which with torrid heat,
And vapour as the Libyan air adust,
Began to parch that temperate clime; whereat
In either hand the hast'ning Angel caught
Our ling'ring parents, and to th' Eastern Gate
Led them direct, and down the cliff as fast
To the subjected plain; then disappear'd.
They looking back, all th'eastern side beheld
Of Paradise. so late their happy seat,
Wav'd over by that flaming brand, the Gate
With dreadful faces throng'd and fiery arms:
Some natural tears they dropped, but wiped them soon;
The world was all before them, where to choose
Their place of rest, and Providence their guide:
They hand in hand with wand'ring steps and slow,
Through Eden took their solitary way.

John Milton

BERMUDAS

Where the remote Bermudas ride
In th'ocean's bosom unespy'd,
From a small boat, that row'd along,
The listning winds receiv'd this song.

What should we do but sing his praise
That led us through the wat'ry maze,
Unto an isle so long unknown,
And yet far kinder than our own?
Where he the huge sea-monsters wracks,

That lift the deep upon their backs.
He lands us on a grassy stage;
Safe from the storms, and prelate's rage.
He gave us this eternal spring,
Which here enamels every thing;
And sends the fowls to us in care,
On daily visits through the air.
He hangs in shades the orange bright,
Like golden lamps in a green night,
And does in the pomegranates close
Jewels more rich than Ormus shows.
He makes the figs our mouths to meet;
And throws the melons at our feet.
But apples plants of such a price,
No tree could ever bear them twice.
With cedars, chosen by his hand,
From Lebanon, he stores the land.
And makes the hollow seas, that roar,
Proclaim the ambergris on shore.
He cast (of which we rather boast)
The gospel's pearl upon our coast.
And in these rocks for us did frame
A temple where to sound his name.
Oh let our voice his praise exalt,
Till it arrive at Heaven's vault:
Which thence (perhaps) rebounding, may
Echo beyond the Mexique Bay.

    Thus sung they, in the English boat,
An holy and a cheerful note,
And all the way, to guide their chime,
With falling oars they kept the time.

Andrew Marvell

THE LOTOS-EATERS

'Courage!' he said, and pointed toward the land,
'This mounting wave will roll us shoreward soon.'
In the afternoon they came unto a land
In which it seemed always afternoon.
All round the coast the languid air did swoon,
Breathing like one that hath a weary dream.
Full-faced above that valley stood the moon;

And like a downward smoke, the slender stream
Along the cliff to fall and pause and fall did seem.

A land of streams! some, like a downward smoke,
Slow-dropping veils of thinnest lawn, did go;
And some thro' wavering lights and shadows broke,
Rolling a slumbrous sheet of foam below.
They saw the gleaming river seaward flow
From the inner land: far off, three mountain-tops,
Three silent pinnacles of aged snow,
Stood sunset-flush'd: and, dew'd with showery drops,
Up-clomb the shadowy pine above the woven copse.

The charmed sunset linger'd low adown
In the red West: thro' mountain clefts the dale
Was seen far inland, and the yellow down
Border'd with palm, and many a winding vale
And meadow, set with slender galingale;
A land where all things always seem'd the same!
And round about the keel with faces pale,
Dark faces pale against that rosy flame,
The mild-eyed melancholy Lotos-eaters came.

Branches they bore of that enchanted stem,
Laden with flower and fruit, whereof they gave
To each, but whoso did receive of them,
And taste, to him the gushing of the wave
Far far away did seem to mourn and rave
On alien shores; and if his fellow spake,
His voice was thin, as voices from the grave;
And deep-asleep he seem'd, yet all awake,
And music in his ears his beating heart did make.

They sat them down upon the yellow sand,
Between the sun and moon upon the shore;
And sweet it was to dream of Fatherland,
Of child, and wife, and slave; but evermore
Most weary seem'd the sea, weary the oar,
Weary the wandering fields of barren foam.
Then some one said, 'We will return no more';
And all at once they sang, 'Our island home
Is far beyond the wave; we will no longer roam . . .'

Alfred, Lord Tennyson

THE BIG ROCK CANDY MOUNTAINS

One evening when the sun was low
And the jungle fires were burning
Down the track came a hobo hamming
And he said, Boys, I'm not turning;
I'm headed for a land that's far away
Beside the crystal fountains.
So come with me, we'll go and see
The Big Rock Candy Mountains.

In the Big Rock Candy Mountains
There's a land that's fair and bright,
Where the handouts grow on bushes
And you sleep out every night,
Where the box-cars all are empty
And the sun shines everyday
On the birds and the bees
And the cigarette trees,
The rock-and-rye springs
Where the whangdoodle sings,
In the Big Rock Candy Mountains.

In the Big Rock Candy Mountains
All the cops have wooden legs
And the bulldogs all have rubber teeth
And the hens lay hard-boiled eggs;
The farmers' trees are full of fruit
And the barns are full of hay:
O I'm bound to go
Where there ain't no snow,
And the rain don't fall,
The wind don't blow,
In the Big Rock Candy Mountains.

In the Big Rock Candy Mountains
You never change your socks
And the little streams of alkyhol
Come a-trickling down the rocks;
The shacks all have to tip their hats
And the railroad bulls are blind;
There's a lake of stew,
And of whisky too,

You can paddle all around
In a big canoe,
In the Big Rock Candy Mountains.

In the Big Rock Candy Mountains
The jails are made of tin
And you can bust right out again
As soon as they put you in;
There ain't no short-handled shovels,
No axes, saws or picks:
O I'm going to stay
Where you sleep all day,
Where they hung the Turk
That invented work,
In the Big Rock Candy Mountains.
I'll see you all
This coming fall
In the Big Rock Candy Mountains.

WHAN THAT APRILLE WITH HIS SHOURES SOTE

Whan that Aprille with his shoures sote
The droghte of Marche hath perced to the rote,
And bathed every veyne in swich licour,
Of which vertu engendred is the flour;
Whan Zephirus eek with his swete breeth
Inspired hath in every holt and heeth
The tendre croppes, and the yonge sonne
Hath in the Ram his halfe cours y-ronne,
And smale fowles maken melodye,
That slepen al the night with open ye,
(So priketh hem nature in hir corages):
Than longen folk to goon on pilgrimages
(And palmers for to seken straunge strondes)
To ferne halwes, couthe in sondry londes;
And specially, from every shires ende
Of Engelond, to Caunterbury they wende,
The holy blisful martir for to seke,
That hem hath holpen, whan that they were seke . . .

Geoffrey Chaucer

sote: *sweet*; ye: *eye*; corages: *minds*; ferne halwes: *far-off
hallowed places or shrines*; couthe: *well known*; seke: *ill*

THE PILGRIMAGE

I travell'd on, seeing the hill, where lay
　　　　My expectation.
　　A long it was and weary way.
　　The gloomy cave of Desperation
I left on th'one, and on the other side
　　　　The rock of Pride.

And so I came to Phansy's meadow strow'd
　　　　With many a flower:
　　Fain would I here have made abode,
　　But I was quicken'd by my hour.
So to Care's copse I came, and there got through
　　　　With much ado.

That led me to the wild of Passion; which
　　　　Some call the wold;
　　A wasted place, but sometimes rich.
　　Here I was robb'd of all my gold,
Save one good Angel, which a friend had tied
　　　　Close to my side.

At length I got unto the gladsome hill,
　　　　Where lay my hope,
　　Where lay my heart; and climbing still,
　　When I had gain'd the brow and top,
A lake of brackish waters on the ground
　　　　Was all I found.

With that abash'd and struck with many a sting
　　　　Of swarming fears,
　　I fell, and cry'd, Alas, my King,
　　Can both the way and end be tears?
Yet taking heart I rose, and then perceiv'd
　　　　I was deceiv'd.

My hill was further: so I flung away,
　　　　Yet heard a cry
　　Just as I went, *None goes that way*
　　And lives: If that be all, said I,
After so foul a journey death is fair,
　　　　And but a chair.

George Herbert

(Supposed to be written by one at the point of death)

Give me my scallop-shell of quiet,
My staff of faith to walk upon,
My scrip of joy, immortal diet,
My bottle of salvation:
My gown of glory, hope's true gage,
And thus I'll take my pilgrimage.

Blood must be my body's balmer,
No other balm will there be given
Whilst my soul like a white palmer
Travels to the land of heaven,
Over the silver mountains,
Where spring the nectar fountains:
And there I'll kiss
The bowl of bliss,
And drink my eternal fill
On every milken hill.
My soul will be a-dry before,
But after it, will ne'er thirst more.

And by the happy blissful way
More peaceful pilgrims I shall see,
That have shook off their gowns of clay,
And go apparelled fresh like me.
I'll bring them first
To slake their thirst,
And then to taste those nectar suckets
At the clear wells
Where sweetness dwells
Drawn up by saints in crystal buckets.
And when our bottles and all
Are filled with immortality,
Then the holy paths we'll travel
Strewed with rubies thick as gravel,
Ceilings of diamonds, sapphire floors,
High walls of coral and pearl bow'rs.

From thence to heaven's bribeless hall
Where no corrupted voices brawl,
No conscience molten into gold,
Nor forged accusers bought and sold,

No cause deferred, nor vain spent irony,
For there Christ is the King's attorney:
Who pleads for all without degrees,
And he hath angels, but no fees.

When the grand twelve million jury,
Of our sins and sinful fury,
'Gainst our souls black verdicts give,
Christ pleads his death, and then we live.
Be thou my speaker, taintless pleader,
Unblotted lawyer, true proceeder,
Thou movest salvation even for alms:
Not with a bribed lawyer's palms.

And this is my eternal plea,
To him that made Heaven, Earth and Sea,
Seeing my flesh must die so soon,
And want a head to dine next noon,
Just at the stroke when my veins start and spread
Set on my soul an everlasting head.
Then am I ready like a palmer fit,
To tread those blest paths which before I writ.

Sir Walter Ralegh

19. LONDON POEMS

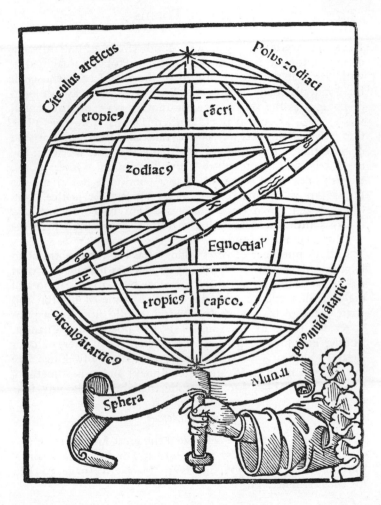

London Poems

The shape overleaf is the Sphera Mundi (from an Italian poem of 1505), the old figure of our system as Ptolemy imagined it, with Earth at the centre instead of the Sun. I have chosen it for London Poems, because the English have always thought of London as the very centre, in another way, of that central world. Even a Scottish poet, William Dunbar (on page 288), told London she was the flower of cities all. Other cities would dispute that; other cities would deny that the world in the twentieth century revolves around London. Other poets, English ones, have come to say that London is not all beauty (as we know) or marvel, kindness, honesty, or justice. John Clare looked down on London from Epping Forest and saw it like a little shrub among the hills, and preferred his trees and bracken and solitude.

Still, for hundreds of years London has been the centre of an English universe of poetry. No other city has managed to rival it – so far; and I do not think there has been any great poet of the English language who did not live some of his life and write some of his poems in London, or did not find a publisher for them in London. It is the poets' city. Chaucer, Donne, Ben Jonson, Milton, Blake, were born there. Shakespeare and Yeats worked there. Poets, not only kings, are buried in London in Westminster Abbey; and it is something to search the abbey for that stone inscribed with only four words:

O rare Ben Jonson

Two of her poets have celebrated the great fires of 1666 and the Second World War, from which London rose again – John Dryden (page 290), and Louis MacNeice (page 309) in his Streets of Laredo.

LONDON BRIDGE

London Bridge is broken down,
  Dance o'er my lady lee,
London Bridge is broken down,
  With a gay lady.

How shall we build it up again?
  Dance o'er my lady lee,
How shall we build it up again?
  With a gay lady.

Build it up with silver and gold,
  Dance o'er my lady lee,
Build it up with silver and gold,
  With a gay lady.

Silver and gold will be stole away,
  Dance o'er my lady lee,
Silver and gold will be stole away,
  With a gay lady.

Build it up again with iron and steel,
  Dance o'er my lady lee,
Build it up again with iron and steel,
  With a gay lady.

Iron and steel will bend and bow,
  Dance o'er my lady lee,
Iron and steel will bend and bow,
  With a gay lady.

Build it up with wood and clay,
  Dance o'er my lady lee,
Build it up with wood and clay,
  With a gay lady.

Wood and clay will wash away,
  Dance o'er my lady lee,
Wood and clay will wash away,
  With a gay lady.

Build it up with stone so strong,
Dance o'er my lady lee,
Huzza! 'twill last for ages long,
With a gay lady.

OF LONDON BRIDGE, AND THE STUPENDOUS SIGHT, AND STRUCTURE THEREOF

When Neptune from his billows London spied,
  Brought proudly thither by a high spring-tide,
  As through a floating wood he steer'd along,
  And dancing castles cluster'd in a throng;
  When he beheld a mighty bridge give law
  Unto his surges, and their fury awe,
  When such a shelf of cataracts did roar,
  As if the Thames with Nile had chang'd her shore,
  When he such massy walls, such tow'rs did eye,
  Such posts, such irons upon his back to lie,
  When such vast arches he observ'd, that might
  Nineteen Rialtos make for depth and height,
  When the Cerulean God these things survey'd,
  He shook his trident, and astonish'd said,
  Let the whole Earth now all her wonders count.
  This Bridge of Wonders is the paramount.

James Howell

Rialto: *the chief bridge in Venice*

TO THE CITY OF LONDON

London, thou art of townes A *per se.*
  Soveraign of cities, semeliest in sight,
Of high renoun, riches, and royaltie;
  Of lordis, barons, and many goodly knyght;
  Of most delectable lusty ladies bright;
Of famous prelatis in habitis clericall;
  Of merchauntis full of substaunce and myght:
London, thou art the flour of Cities all.

Gladdith anon, thou lusty Troy Novaunt,
  Citie that some tyme cleped was New Troy,
In all the erth, imperiall as thou stant,
  Pryncesse of townes, of pleasure, and of joy,

A richer restith under no Christen roy;
For manly power, with craftis naturall,
  Fourmeth none fairer sith the flode of Noy:
London, thou art the flour of Cities all.

Gemme of all joy, jasper of jocunditie,
  Most myghty carbuncle of vertue and valour;
Strong Troy in vigour and in strenuytie;
  Of royall cities rose and geraflour;
  Empresse of townes, exalt in honour;
In beawtie heryng the crone imperiall;
  Swete paradise precelling in pleasure:
London, thou art the flour of Cities all.

Above all ryvers thy Ryver hath renowne,
  Whose beryall stremys, pleasaunt and preclare,
Under thy lusty wallys renneth down,
  Where many a swanne doth swymme with wyngis fare;
  Where many a barge doth saile, and row with are,
Where many a ship doth rest with toppe-royall.
  O! towne of townes, patrone and not-compare:
London, thou art the flour of Cities all.

Upon thy lusty Brigge of pylers white
  Been merchauntis full royall to behold;
Upon thy stretis goth many a semely knyght
  In velvet gownes and cheynes of fyne gold.
  By Julyus Cesar thy Tour founded of old
May be the hous of Mars victoryall,
  Whos artillary with tonge may not be told:
London, thou art the flour of Cities all.

Strong be thy wallis that about the standis;
  Wise be the people that within the dwellis;
Fresh is thy ryver with his lusty strandis;
  Blith be thy chirches, wele sownyng be thy bellis;
  Riche be thy merchauntis in substance that excellis
Fair be thy wives, right lovesom, white and small;
  Clere be thy virgyns, lusty under kellis:
London, thou art the flour of Cities all.

Thy famous Maire, by pryncely governaunce,
  With swerd of justice the rulith prudently
No Lord of Parys, Venyce, or Floraunce
  In dignytie or honoure goeth to hym nye.

289

He is extempler, loode-ster, and guye;
Principall patrone and roose orygynalle,
　　Above all Maires as maister moost worthy:
London, thou art the flour of Cities all.

William Dunbar

roy: king; Noy: Noah; strenuytie: strength; geraflour: gilli-
flower; crone: crown; are: oar; sownyng: sounding; kellis:
coifs; guye: guide

COMPOSED UPON WESTMINSTER BRIDGE,
Sept. 3, 1802

Earth has not any thing to show more fair:
Dull would he be of soul who could pass by
A sight so touching in its majesty:
This City now doth, like a garment, wear
The beauty of the morning; silent, bare,
Ships, towers, domes, theatres, and temples lie
Open unto the fields, and to the sky;
All bright and glittering in the smokeless air.
Never did sun more beautifully steep
In his first splendour, valley, rock or hill;
Ne'er saw I, never felt, a calm so deep!
The river glideth at his own sweet will:
Dear God! the very houses seem asleep;
And all that mighty heart is lying still!

William Wordsworth

THE FIRE OF LONDON
(From 'Annus Mirabilis: The Year of Wonders MDCLXVI')

As when some dire usurper Heav'n provides
To scourge his country with a lawless sway,
His birth perhaps some petty village hides,
And sets his cradle out of fortune's way,

Till fully ripe his swelling fate breaks out,
And hurries him to mighty mischiefs on:
His Prince, surpris'd at first, no ill could doubt,
And wants the pow'r to meet it when 'tis known:

Such was the rise of this prodigious Fire,
Which in mean buildings first obscurely bred,
From thence did soon to open streets aspire,
And straight to palaces and temples spread.

The diligence of trades and noiseful gain,
And luxury, more late, asleep were laid:
All was the night's, and in her silent reign
No sound the rest of nature did invade.

In this deep quiet, from what source unknown,
Those seeds of fire their fatal birth disclose;
And first, few scatt'ring sparks about were blown,
Big with the flames that to our ruin rose.

Then, in some close-pent room it crept along,
And smould'ring as it went, in silence fed;
Till th'infant monster, with devouring strong,
Walk'd boldly upright with exalted head.

Now like some rich or mighty murderer,
Too great for prison, which he breaks with gold,
Who fresher for new mischiefs does appear
And dares the world to tax him with the old:

So scapes th'insulting Fire his narrow jail
And makes small out-lets into open air:
There the fierce winds his tender force assail,
And beat him downward to his first repair.

The winds, like crafty courtesans, withheld
His flames from burning but to blow them more:
And every fresh attempt he is repell'd
With faint denials weaker than before.

And now, no longer letted of his prey,
He leaps up at it with enrag'd desire:
O'erlooks the neighbours with a wide survey,
And nods at every house his threat'ning fire.

The ghosts of traitors from the Bridge descend,
With bold fanatic spectres to rejoice:
About the fire into a dance they bend,
And sing their Sabbath notes with feeble voice.

Our Guardian Angel saw them where he sate
Above the palace of our slumb'ring king;
He sigh'd, abandoning his charge to fate,
And, drooping, oft lookt back upon the wing.

At length the crackling noise and dreadful blaze
Call'd up some waking lover to the sight;
And long it was ere he the rest could raise,
Whose heavy eyelids yet were full of night.

The next to danger, hot pursued by fate,
Half cloth'd, half naked, hastily retire:
And frighted mothers strike their breasts, too late,
For helpless infants left amidst the fire.

Their cries soon waken all the dwellers near;
Now murmuring noises rise in every street;
The more remote run stumbling with their fear,
And, in the dark, men justle as they meet.

So weary bees in little cells repose;
But if night-robbers lift the well-stor'd hive,
An humming through their waxen city grows,
And out upon each other's wings they drive.

Now streets grow throng'd and busy as by day:
Some run for buckets to the hallow'd Quire:
Some cut the pipes, and some the engines play;
And some more bold mount ladders to the fire.

In vain: For from the east a Belgian wind
His hostile breath through the dry rafters sent;
The flames impell'd soon left their foes behind
And forward with a wanton fury went.

A quay of fire ran all along the shore,
And lighten'd all the river with a blaze:
The waken'd tides began again to roar,
And wond'ring fish in shining waters gaze.

Old Father Thames rais'd up his reverend head,
But fear'd the fate of Simois would return:
Deep in his ooze he sought his sedgy bed,
And shrunk his waters back into his urn.

The Fire, meantime, walks in a broader gross;
To either hand his wings he opens wide:
He wades the streets, and straight he reaches 'cross,
And plays his longing flames on th'other side.

At first they warm, then scorch, and then they take;
Now with long necks from side to side they feed:
At length, grown strong, their mother-fire forsake,
And a new colony of flames succeed.

To every nobler portion of the town
The curling billows roll their restless tide:
In parties now they straggle up and down,
As armies, unoppos'd, for prey divide.

One mighty squadron, with a side-wind sped,
Through narrow lanes his cumber'd fire does haste:
By pow'rful charms of gold and silver led,
The Lombard bankers and the Change to waste.

Another backward to the Tow'r would go,
And slowly eats his way against the wind:
But the main body of the marching foe
Against th'imperial palace is design'd.

Now day appears, and with the day the King,
Whose early care had robb'd him of his rest:
Far off the cracks of falling houses ring,
And shrieks of subjects pierce his tender breast.

Near as he draws, thick harbingers of smoke
With gloomy pillars cover all the place:
Whose little intervals of night are broke
By sparks, that drive against his sacred face . . .

Himself directs what first is to be done,
And orders all the succours which they bring:
The helpful and the good about him run,
And form an army worthy such a king.

He sees the dire contagion spread so fast
That where it seizes, all relief is vain:
And therefore must unwillingly lay waste
That country, which would, else, the foe maintain.

The powder blows up all before the fire:
Th'amazed flames stand gather'd on a heap;
And from the precipice's brink retire,
Afraid to venture on so large a leap.

Thus fighting fires awhile themselves consume,
But straight like Turks, forc'd on to win or die,
They first lay tender bridges of their fume,
And o'er the breach in unctuous vapours fly.

Part stays for passage, till a gust of wind
Ships o'er their forces in a shining sheet:
Part, creeping underground their journey blind,
And climbing from below, their fellows meet.

Thus to some desert plain, or old wood-side,
Dire night-hags come from far to dance their round:
And o'er broad rivers, on their fiends, they ride,
Or sweep in clouds above the blasted ground.

No help avails: for, Hydra-like, the Fire
Lifts up his hundred heads to aim his way:
And scarce the wealthy can one half retire
Before he rushes in to share the prey.

The rich grow suppliant, and the poor grow proud:
Those offer mighty gain, and these ask more;
So void of pity is th'ignoble crowd,
When others' ruin may increase their store.

As those who live by shores with joy behold
Some wealthy vessel split or stranded nigh,
And from the rocks leap down for shipwrack'd gold
And seek the tempest which the others fly,

So these but wait the owner's last despair,
And what's permitted to the flames invade:
Ev'n from their jaws they hungry morsels tear,
And on their backs the spoils of Vulcan lade.

The days were all in this lost labour spent;
And when the weary king gave place to night,
His beams he to his royal brother lent,
And so shone still in his reflective light.

Night came, but without darkness or repose,
A dismal picture of the gen'ral doom;
Where souls distracted when the trumpet blows
And half unready with their bodies come.

Those who have homes, when home they do repair,
To a last lodging call their wand'ring friends:
Their short uneasy sleeps are broke with care,
To look how near their own destruction tends.

Those who have none, sit round where once it was,
And with full eyes each wonted room require:
Haunting the yet warm ashes of the place,
As murder'd men walk where they did expire.

Some stir up coals, and watch the vestal fire,
Others in vain from sight of ruin run;
And while through burning lab'rinths they retire,
With loathing eyes repeat what they would shun.

The most in fields like herded beasts lie down,
To dews obnoxious on the grassy floor;
And while their babes in sleep their sorrows drown,
Sad parents watch the remnants of their store.

While by the motion of the flames they guess
What streets are burning now, and what are near,
An infant waking to the paps would press,
And meets, instead of milk, a falling tear . . .

John Dryden

THE FIELDS FROM ISLINGTON TO MARYBONE

The fields from Islington to Marybone,
To Primrose Hill and Saint John's Wood,
    Were builded over with pillars of gold,
And there Jerusalem's pillars stood.

    Her little ones ran on the fields,
The Lamb of God among them seen,
    And fair Jerusalem his bride,
Among the little meadows green.

    Pancras and Kentish Town repose
Among her golden pillars high,
    Among her golden arches which
Shine upon the starry sky.

The Jew's Harp house and the Green Man,
The ponds where boys to bathe delight,
   The fields of cows by Willan's Farm,
Shine in Jerusalem's pleasant sight.

   She walks upon our meadows green,
The Lamb of God walks by her side,
   And every English child is seen
Children of Jesus and his Bride . . .

William Blake

LONDON BELLS

Gay go up, and gay go down
To ring the bells of London town.

   Bull's eyes and targets,
   Say the bells of St Marg'ret's.

   Brickbats and tiles,
   Say the bells of St Giles'.

   Oranges and lemons,
   Say the bells of St Clement's.

   Pancakes and fritters,
   Say the bells of St Peter's.

   Two sticks and an apple,
   Say the bells at Whitechapel.

   Old Father Baldpate,
   Say the slow bells at Aldgate.

   Maids in white aprons,
   Say the bells of St Cath'rine's.

   Pokers and tongs,
   Say the bells at St John's.

   Kettles and pans,
   Say the bells at St Anne's.

   You owe me ten shillings,
   Say the bells at St Helen's.

When will you pay me?
Say the bells at Old Bailey.

When I grow rich,
Say the bells at Fleetditch

When will that be?
Say the bells at Stepney.

I'm sure I don't know,
Says the great bell at Bow.

When I am old,
Say the bells at St Paul's.

> Here comes a candle to light you to bed,
> And here comes a chopper to chop off your head.

TROYNOVANT

The New Troy or London transformed for King James I, 'upon the
day of his Majestyies Tryumphant Passage through his Honourable
Citie (and Chamber) of London, being the 15 of March 1603'

Troynovant is now no more a city:
   O great pity! is't not pity?
And yet her towers on tiptoe stand,
Like pageants built in fairy land,
   And her marble arms,
   Like to magic charms
Bind thousands fast unto her,
That for her wealth and beauty daily woo her.
   Yet for all this, is't not pity?
Troynovant is now no more a city.

Troynovant is now a summer arbour,
   Or the nest wherein doth harbour
The Eagle, of all birds that fly
The sovereign, for his piercing eye.
   If you wisely mark,
   'Tis beside a park
Where runs (being newly born)
With the fierce Lion, the fair Unicorn,
   Or else it is a wedding hall,
Where four great kingdoms hold a festival

297

Troynovant is now a bridal chamber,
   Whose roof is gold, floor is of amber,
By virtue of that holy light,
That burns in Hymen's hand, more bright
   Than the silver moon,
   Or the torch at noon.
Hark what the Echoes say!
Britain till now ne'er kept a holiday:
   For Jove dwells here. And 'tis no pity,
If Troynovant be now no more a city.

Thomas Dekker

THE LOVER TO THE THAMES OF LONDON, TO FAVOUR HIS LADY PASSING THEREON

Thou stately stream that with the swelling tide
   'Gainst London walls incessantly dost beat,
Thou Thames, I say, where barge and boat doth ride,
   And snow-white swans do fish for needful meat,

When so my Love, of force or pleasure, shall
   Flit on thy flood as custom is to do,
Seek not with dread her courage to appal,
   But calm thy tide, and smoothly let it go,
   As she may joy, arrived to siker shore,
   To pass the pleasant stream she did before.

To welter up and surge in wrathful wise,
   As did the flood where Helle drenchèd was
Would but procure defame of thee to rise.
   Wherefore let all such ruthless rigour pass,
   So wish I that thou mayst with bending side
   Have power for aye in wonted gulf to glide.

George Turberville

PROTHALAMION

i

Calm was the day, and through the trembling air,
Sweet breathing Zephyrus did softly play
A gentle spirit, that lightly did delay
Hot Titan's beams, which then did glister fair:

When I whom sullcin care,
Through discontent of my long fruitless stay
In Prince's court, and expectation vain
Of idle hopes, which still do fly away,
Like empty shadows, did afflict my brain,
Walkt forth to ease my pain
Along the shore of silver streaming Thames,
Whose rutty bank, the which his river hems,
Was painted all with variable flowers,
And all the meads adorned with dainty gems,
Fit to deck maidens' bowers,
And crown their paramours,
Against the bridal day, which is not long:
  Sweet Thames run softly, till I end my song.

ii

There, in a meadow, by the river's side,
A flock of nymphs I chauncèd to espy,
All lovely Daughters of the Flood thereby,
With goodly greenish locks all loose untied,
As each had been a bride,
And each one had a little wicker basket,
Made of fine twigs entrailèd curiously,
In which they gathered flowers to fill their flasket:
And with fine fingers, cropt full feateously
The tender stalks on high.
Of every sort, which in that meadow grew,
They gathered some; the Violet pallid blue,
The little Dazie, that at evening closes,
The virgin Lillie, and the Primrose true,
With store of vermeil Roses,
To deck their bridegroom's posies,
Against the bridal day, which was not long:
  Sweet Thames run softly, till I end my song.

iii

With that, I saw two swans of goodly hue,
Come softly swimming down along the lee;
Two fairer birds I yet did never see:
The snow which doth the top of Pindus strew,
Did never whiter shew,
Nor Jove himself when he a swan would be
For love of Leda, whiter did appear:
Yet Leda was, they say, as white as he,

Yet not so white as these, nor nothing near;
So purely white they were,
That even the gentle stream, the which them bare,
Seem'd foul to them, and bad his billows spare
To wet their silken feathers, least they might
Soil their fair plumes with water not so fair,
And marr their beauties bright,
That shone as heaven's light,
Against their bridal day, which was not long:
  Sweet Thames run softly, till I end my song.

iv

Eftsoons the nymphs, which now had flowers their fill,
Ran all in haste, to see that silver brood,
As they came floating on the crystal flood.
Whom when they saw, they stood amazèd still,
Their wondring eyes to fill,
Then seemed they never saw a sight so fair,
Of fowls so lovely, that they sure did deem
Them heavenly born, or to be that same pair
Which through the sky draw Venus' silver team,
For sure they did not seem
To be begot of any earthly seed,
But rather angels or of angel's breed:
Yet they were bred of summer's heat, they say,
In sweetest season, when each flower and weed
The earth did fresh array,
So fresh they seemed as day,
Even as their bridal day, which was not long;
  Sweet Thames run softly, till I end my song.

v

Then forth they all out of their baskets drew,
Great store of flowers, the honour of the field,
That to the sense did fragrant odours yield,
All which upon those goodly birds they threw,
And all the waves did strew,
That like old Peneus' waters they did seem,
When down along by pleasant Tempe's shore
Scattered with flowers, through Thessaly they stream,
That they appear through Lillies' plenteous store,
Like a bride's chamber floor:
Two of those nymphs, meanwhile, two garlands bound,

Of freshest flowers which in that mead they found,
The which presenting all in trim array,
Their snowy foreheads therewithal they crowned,
Whilst one did sing this lay,
Prepared against that day,
Against their bridal day, which was not long:
  Sweet Thames run softly, till I end my song.

vi

Ye gentle birds, the world's fair ornament,
And heaven's glory, whom this happy hower
Doth lead unto your lover's blissful bower,
Joy may you have and gentle heart's content
Of your love's couplement:
And let fair Venus, that is Queen of Love,
With her heart-quelling son upon you smile,
Whose smile they say, hath vertue to remove
All love's dislike, and friendship's faulty guile
For ever to assoil.
Let endless peace your steadfast hearts accord,
And blessed plenty wait upon your board,
And let your bed with pleasures chaste abound,
That fruitful issue may to you afford,
Which may your foes confound,
And make your joys redound,
Upon your bridal day, which is not long:
  Sweet Thames run softly, till I end my song.

vii

So ended she; and all the rest around
To her redoubled that her undersong,
Which said, their bridal day should not be long.
And gentle Echo from the neighbour ground,
Their accents did resound.
So forth those joyous birds did pass along,
Adown the lea, that to them murmured low,
As he would speak, but that he lacked a tong
Yet did by signs his glad affection show,
Making his stream run slow.
And all the fowl which in his flood did dwell
Gan flock about these twain, that did excell
The rest, so far, as Cynthia doth shend
The lesser stars. So they enrangèd well,

Did on those two attend,
And their best service lend,
Against their wedding day, which was not long:
  Sweet Thames run softly, till I end my song.

viii

At length they all to merry London came,
To merry London, my most kindly nurse,
That to me gave this life's first native source:
Though from another place I take my name,
An house of auncient fame.
There when they came, whereas those bricky towers,
The which on Thames' broad agèd back do ride,
Where now the studious lawyers have their bowers
There whilom wont the Templar Knights to bide,
Till they decayed through pride:
Next whereunto there stands a stately place,
Where oft I gainèd gifts and goodly grace
Of that great Lord, which therein wont to dwell,
Whose want too well now feels my friendless case:
But, ah, here fits not well
Old woes but joys to tell
Against the bridal day, which is not long:
  Sweet Thames run softly, till I end my song.

ix

Yet therein now doth lodge a noble peer,
Great England's glory and the world's wide wonder,
Whose dreadful name late through all Spain did thunder,
And Hercules' two pillars standing near,
Did make to quake and fear:
Fair branch of Honour, flower of Chevalry,
That fillest England with thy triumph's fame,
Joy have thou of thy noble victory,
And endless happiness of thine own name
That promiseth the same:
That through thy prowess and victorious arms,
Thy country may be freed from forraine harms:
And great Elisa's glorious name may ring
Through all the world, filled with thy wide alarms,
Which some brave muse may sing
To ages following,
Upon the bridal day, which is not long:
  Sweet Thames run softly, till I end my song.

From those high towers, this noble lord issuing,
Like radiant Hesper when his golden hair
In th'ocean billows he hath bathèd fair,
Descended to the river's open viewing,
With a great train ensuing.
Above the rest were goodly to be seen
Two gentle knights of lovely face and feature
Beseeming well the bower of any Queen,
With gifts of wit and ornaments of nature,
Fit for so goodly stature:
That like the twins of Jove they seemed in sight,
Which deck the baldrick of the heavens bright,
They two forth pacing to the river's side,
Received those two fair brides, their love's delight,
Which at th'appointed tide,
Each one did make his bride,
Against their bridal day, which is not long:
  Sweet Thames run softly, till I end my song.

Edmund Spenser

POVERTY IN LONDON

By numbers here from shame or censure free,
All crimes are safe, but hated poverty.
This, only this, the rigid law pursues,
This, only this, provokes the snarling muse.
The sober trader at a tatter'd cloak
Wakes from his dream, and labours for a joke;
With brisker air the silken courtiers gaze,
And turn the varied taunt a thousand ways.
Of all the griefs that harass the distress'd,
Sure the most bitter is a scornful jest;
Fate never wounds more deep the gen'rous heart
Than when a blockhead's insult points the dart.
  Has heaven reserv'd, in pity to the poor,
No pathless waste, or undiscover'd shore;
No secret island in the boundless main?
No peaceful desart yet unclaim'd by Spain?
Quick let us rise, the happy seats explore,
And bear oppression's insolence no more.
This mournful truth is ev'ry where confess'd,
Slow rises worth, by poverty depress'd:

But here more slow, where all are slaves to gold,
Where looks are merchandise, and smiles are sold;
Where won by bribes, by flatteries implor'd,
The groom retails the favours of his lord . . .

Samuel Johnson

LONDON

There souls of men are bought and sold,
And milk-fed infancy for gold;
And youth to slaughter houses led,
And beauty for a bit of bread . . .

William Blake

LONDON

I wander thro' each dirty street,
Near where the dirty Thames does flow.
And mark in every face I meet
Marks of weakness, marks of woe.

In every cry of every man,
In every infant's cry of fear,
In every voice, in every ban,
The mind forg'd manacles I hear . . .

William Blake

WHY SHOULD I CARE FOR THE MEN OF THAMES?

Why should I care for the men of Thames,
Or the cheating waves of charter'd streams,
Or shrink at the little blasts of fear
That the hireling blows into my ear?

Tho' born on the cheating banks of Thames,
Tho' his waters bathed my infant limbs,
The Ohio shall wash his stains from me:
I was born a slave, but I go to be free.

William Blake

In London there I was bent,
I saw myself where truth should be attaint,
Fast to Westminster ward I went
To a man of law, to make my complaint.
I said 'For Mary's love, that holy saint,
Have pity on the poor, that would proceed;
I would give silver, but my purse is faint;
For lack of money I may not speed.'

As I thrast throughout the throng
Among them all, my hood was gone.
Nathless I let not long
To Kings Bench till I come;
Before a judge I kneeled anon;
I prayed him for God's sake he would take heed.
Full ruefully to him I gan make my moan,
For lack of money I may not speed.

Beneath him sat clerks, a great rout;
Fast they writen by one assent.
There stood up one and cried round about
'Richard, Robert, and John of Kent.'
I wist not wele what he meant,
For he cried so thick there indeed.
There were strong thieves shamed and shent,
But they that lacked money might not speed.

Unto the Common Pleas I yode thoo
Where sat one with a silken hood.
I did him reverence as me ought to do.
I told him my case as well as I could
And said 'All my goods by norward and by sorward
I am defrauded with great falsehed.'
He would not give me a mum of his mouth.
For lack of money I may not speed.

Then I went me unto the Rollis
Before the clerks of the Chauncerie.
There were many qui tollis,
But I heard no man speak of me.
Before them I kneeled upon my knee,
Showed them mine evidence and they began to read;
They said truer things might there never be;
But for lack of money I may not speed.

In Westminster Hall I found one
Went in a long gown of ray.
I crouched, I kneeled before him anon.
For Mary's love, of help I gan him pray.
As he had be wroth, he voided away
Backward, his hand he gan me bid.
'I wot not what thou meanest', gan he say.
'Lay down silver, or here thou may not speed.'

In all Westminster Hall I could find never a one
That for me would do, though I should die.
Without the doors, where Flemings grete woon,
Upon me fast they gan to cry,
And said 'Master, what will ye copen or buy,
Fine felt hats, spectacles for to read
Of this gay gear'; a great cause why
For lack of money I might not speed.

Then to Westminster Gate I went
When the sun was at high prime.
Cooks to me, they took good intent,
Called me near, for to dine,
And proffered me good bread, ale, and wine;
A fair cloth they began to spread,
Ribs of beef both fat and fine.
But for lack of money I might not speed.

Into London I gan me to hie.
Of all the land it beareth the prize.
'Hot peascods', one gan cry.
'Strawberry ripe, and cherry in the ryse.'
One bad me come near and buy some spice;
Pepper and saffron they gan me bede,
Clove, grains, and flour of rice.
For lack of money I might not speed.

Then into Cheap I gan me drawn
Where I saw stand much people.
One bad me come near, and buy fine cloth of lawn,
Paris thread, cotton, and umple.
I said thereupon I could not skyle,
I am not wont thereto indeed.
One bad me buy an heure, my head to hele.
For lack of money I might not speed.

306

Then went I forth by London Stone
Throughout all Canywike Street.
Drapers to me they called anon;
Great cheap of clothe, they gan me hete.
Then come there one, and cried 'Hot sheep's feet!'
'Rishes fair and green!' another gan to greet.
Both melwell and mackerel I gan meet,
But for lack of money I might not speed.

Then I hied me into East Cheap,
One cried ribs of beef and many a pie,
Pewter pots they clattered in a heap;
There was harp, pipe, and sawtry:
'Yea, by cock!' 'Nay, by cock!' some began to cry;
Some sangen of Jenken and Julian, to get themselves mede;
Full fain I would had of that minstrelsie,
But for lack of money I could not speed.

Into Cornhill anon I yode,
Where is much stolne gear among;
I saw where hange mine own hood
That I had lost in Westminster among the throng.
Then I beheld it with looks full long,
I kenned it as well as I did my creed;
To buy mine own hood again me thought it wrong,
But for lack of money I might not speed.

Then came the taverner and took me by the sleeve
And said 'Sir, a pint of wine would you assay?'
'Sir', quod I, 'it may not grieve,
For a penny may do no more than it may.'
I drank a pint, and therefore gan pay.
Sore a-hungered away I yede,
For well London Lackpenny for once and aye.
For lack of money I may not speed.

Then I hied me to Billingsgate.
One cried 'Wag, wag you hence!'
I prayed a barge man for God's sake
That they would spare me mine expense.
He said 'Rise up, man, and get thee hence!
What winist thou I will do on thee my almes deed,
Here scapeth no man beneath two pence.'
For lack of money I might not speed.

Then I conveyed me into Kent,
For of the Law would I meddle no more
Because no man to me would take intent;
I dight me to the plough, even as I did before.
Jesus save London, that in Bethlehem was bore,
And every true man of law God graunt him soul's mede;
And they that be other, God their state restore;
For he that lacketh money, with them he shall not speed.

attaint: *attained*; proceed: *go to law*; let: *delayed*; shent:
disgraced; yode: *went*; thoo: *then*; mum: *mumble*; Rollis:
The Rolls, the Court of Chancery; ray: *striped cloth*; bid: *offer,
hold out*; grete woon: *chiefly dwell*; copen: *purchase*; in the
ryse: *on the bough*; bede: *bid*; umple: *linen cloth*; thereupon
I could not skyle: *I knew nothing about them*; heure: *skull-cap*;
hele: *cover, put a roof on*; great cheap of clothe: *cloth very
cheap*; hete: *promise*; rishes: *rushes*; melwell: *cod*; mede:
mead (*drink*); wag you hence: *move off, scram*; winist:
weenest (*thinkest*); dight me: *betook myself*; bore: *born*;
mede: *reward*.

Anon.
(15)

LONDON SNOW

When men were all asleep the snow came flying,
In large white flakes falling on the city brown,
Stealthily and perpetually settling and loosely lying,
    Hushing the latest traffic of the drowsy town;
Deadening, muffling, stifling its murmurs failing;
Lazily and incessantly floating down and down:
    Silently sifting and veiling road, roof and railing;
Hiding difference, making unevenness even,
Into angles and crevices softly drifting and sailing.
    All night it fell, and when full inches seven
It lay in the depth of its uncompacted lightness,
The clouds blew off from a high and frosty heaven;
    And all woke earlier for the unaccustomed brightness
Of the winter dawning, the strange unheavenly glare:
The eye marvelled — marvelled at the dazzling whiteness;
    The ear hearkened to the stillness of the solemn air;
No sound of wheel rumbling nor of foot falling,
And the busy morning cries came thin and spare.
    Then boys I heard, as they went to school, calling,
They gathered up the crystal manna to freeze
Their tongues with tasting, their hands with snowballing;
    Or rioted in a drift, plunging up to the knees;

Or peering up from under the white-mossed wonder,
'O look at the trees!' they cried, 'O look at the trees!'
   With lessened load a few carts creak and blunder,
Following along the white deserted way,
A country company long dispersed asunder:
   When now already the sun, in pale display
Standing by Paul's high dome, spread forth below
His sparkling beams, and awoke the stir of day.
   For now doors open, and war is waged with the snow;
And trains of sombre men, past tale of number,
Tread long brown paths, as toward their toil they go:
   But even for them awhile no cares encumber
Their minds diverted; the daily word is unspoken,
The daily thoughts of labour and sorrow slumber
At the sight of the beauty that greets them, for the charm they
      have broken.

Robert Bridges

THE STREETS OF LAREDO

O early one morning I walked out like Agag,
Early one morning to walk through the fire
Dodging the pythons that leaked on the pavements
With tinkle of glasses and tangle of wire;

When grimed to the eyebrows I met an old fireman
Who looked at me wryly and thus did he say:
'The streets of Laredo are closed to all traffic,
We won't never master this joker to-day.

'O hold the branch tightly and wield the axe brightly,
The bank is in powder, the banker's in hell,
But loot is still free on the streets of Laredo
And when we drive home we drive home on the bell.'

Then out from a doorway there sidled a cockney,
A rocking-chair rocking on top of his head:
'O fifty-five years I been feathering my love-nest
And look at it now – why, you'd sooner be dead.'

At which there arose from a wound in the asphalt,
His big wig a-smoulder, Sir Christopher Wren
Saying: 'Let them make hay of the streets of Laredo;
When your ground-rents expire I will build them again.'

Then twangling their bibles with wrath in their nostrils
From Bunhill Fields came Bunyan and Blake:
'Laredo the golden is fallen, is fallen;
Your flame shall not quench nor your thirst shall not slake.'

'I come to Laredo to find me asylum,'
Says Tom Dick and Harry the Wandering Jew;
'They tell me report at the first police station
But the station is pancaked — so what can I do?'

Thus eavesdropping sadly I strolled through Laredo
Perplexed by the dicta misfortunes inspire
Till one low last whisper inveigled my earhole —
The voice of the Angel, the voice of the fire:

O late, very late, have I come to Laredo
A whimsical bride in my new scarlet dress
But at last I took pity on those who were waiting
To see my regalia and feel my caress.

Now ring the bells gaily and play the hose daily,
Put splints on your legs, put a gag on your breath;
O you streets of Laredo, you streets of Laredo,
Lay down the red carpet — My dowry is death.

Louis MacNeice

FOOLS GAZE AT PAINTED COURTS

Fools gaze at painted courts, to th' country let me go,
To climb the easy hill, then walk the valley low;
No gold-embossèd roofs to me are like the woods;
No bed like to the grass, nor liquor like the floods:
A city's but a sink, gay houses gaudy graves,
The Muses have free leave to starve or live in caves . .

Michael Drayton

20. AUTUMN POEMS

Autumn Poems

Now it is autumn and the falling fruit
and the long journey towards oblivion.

The apples falling like great drops of dew
To bruise themselves an exit from themselves.

That is how D. H. Lawrence's last poem begins. But in autumn poems there is often not only calmness, rest, a sense of holiness, and a sense of passing, but exultation. Persephone — if you remember page 246 — now goes back to the underworld to rejoin her Rector of the Damned; but she takes the seed into the earth for the next spring. If we have no Italian or French grape harvest, and bother less than we used to about our harvest of wheat, I am sure it is still right to introduce these autumn poems with the wheaten sheaves which the man in the woodcut of 1495 threshes with a flail, and right as well to begin them with a harvest sonnet and a harvest song.

The wheat, which gives us food, and yet will grow into next year's harvest, symbolizes immortality, in spite of the dying year. The wheat is the colour of gold, which does not rust or tarnish; and the men who harvest it — *You sunburnt sicklemen, of August weary* — are themselves turned as golden and as tawny. In Kent Samuel Palmer, the friend of William Blake, dipped his brush into orange and ochre, and spread immortal golden wheat across his sheets of paper, below an autumn moon. In Herefordshire Thomas Traherne saw eternal wheatfields: *The corn was orient and immortal wheat, which never should be reaped, nor was ever sown. I thought it had stood from everlasting to everlasting.*

HURRAHING IN HARVEST

Summer ends now; now, barbarous in beauty, the stooks arise
   Around; up above, what wind-walks! what lovely behaviour
   Of silk-sack clouds! has wilder, wilful-wavier
Meal-drift moulded ever and melted across skies?

I walk, I lift up, I lift up heart, eyes,
   Down all that glory in the heavens to glean our Saviour;
   And, eyes, heart, what looks, what lips yet gave you a
Rapturous love's greeting of realer, of rounder replies?

And the azurous hung hills are his world-wielding shoulder
   Majestic – as a stallion stalwart, very-violet-sweet! –
These things, these things were here and but the beholder
   Wanting; which two when they once meet,
The heart rears wings bold and bolder
   And hurls for him, O half hurls earth for him off under his
     feet.

Gerard Manley Hopkins

THE RIPE AND BEARDED BARLEY

Come out, 'tis now September,
   The hunter's moon's begun,
And through the wheaten stubble
   We hear the frequent gun;
The leaves are turning yellow,
   And fading into red,
While the ripe and bearded barley
   Is hanging down its head.

All among the barley,
   Who would not be blithe,
While the ripe and bearded barley
   Is smiling on the scythe!

The wheat is like a rich man,
　　It's sleek and well-to-do;
The oats are like a pack of girls,
　　They're thin and dancing too,
The rye is like a miser,
　　Both sulky, lean, and small,
Whilst the ripe and bearded barley
　　Is the monarch of them all.

　　All among the barley,
　　　　Who would not be blithe,
　　While the ripe and bearded barley
　　　　Is smiling on the scythe!

The spring is like a young maid
　　That does not know her mind,
The summer is a tyrant
　　Of most ungracious kind;
The autumn is an old friend
　　That pleases all he can,
And brings the bearded barley
　　To glad the heart of man.

　　All among the barley,
　　　　Who would not be blithe,
　　While the ripe and bearded barley
　　　　Is smiling on the scythe!

RUSHES IN A WATERY PLACE

　　Rushes in a watery place,
　　　　And reeds in a hollow;
　　A soaring skylark in the sky,
　　　　A darting swallow;
　　And where pale blossom used to hang
　　　　Ripe fruit to follow.

                                   Christina Rossetti

THE ROAD NOT TAKEN

Two roads diverged in a yellow wood,
And sorry I could not travel both
And be one traveller, long I stood
And looked down one as far as I could
To where it bent in the undergrowth;

Then took the other, as just as fair,
And having perhaps the better claim,
Because it was grassy and wanted wear;
Though as for that the passing there
Had worn them really about the same,

And both that morning equally lay
In leaves no step had trodden black.
Oh, I kept the first for another day!
Yet knowing how way leads on to way,
I doubted if I should ever come back.

I shall be telling this with a sigh
Somewhere ages and ages hence:
Two roads diverged in a wood, and I —
I took the one less travelled by,
And that has made all the difference.

Robert Frost

CALM IS THE MORN

Calm is the morn without a sound,
   Calm as to suit a calmer grief,
   And only thro' the faded leaf
The chestnut pattering to the ground:

Calm and deep peace on this high wold,
   And on these dews that drench the furze,
   And all the silvery gossamers
That twinkle into green and gold:

Calm and still light on yon great plain
   That sweeps with all its autumn bowers,
   And crowded farms and lessening towers,
To mingle with the bounding main:

Calm and deep peace in this wide air,
   These leaves that redden to the fall;
   And in my heart, if calm at all,
If any calm, a calm despair:

Calm on the seas, and silver sleep,
   And waves that sway themselves in rest,
   And dead calm in that noble breast
Which heaves but with the heaving deep.

Alfred, Lord Tennyson

SPRING TO WINTER

How stately stand yon pines upon the hill;
How soft the murmurs of that living rill;
And o'er the park's tall paling, scarcely higher,
Peeps the low church and shows the modest spire.
Unnumber'd violets on those banks appear,
And all the first-born beauties of the year;
The grey-green blossoms of the willows bring
The large wild bees upon the labouring wing.
Then comes the summer with augmented pride,
Whose pure small streams along the valley glide;
Her richer flora their brief charms display,
And, as the fruit advances, fall away.
Then shall th'autumnal yellow clothe the leaf,
What time the reaper binds the burden'd sheaf;
Then silent groves denote the dying year,
The morning frost, and noon-tide gossamer;
And all be silent in the scene around —
All, save the distant sea's uncertain sound,
Or here and there the gun, whose loud report
Proclaims to man that death is but his sport.
And then the wintry winds begin to blow;
Then fall the flaky stars of gathering snow;
When on the thorn the ripening sloe, yet blue,
Takes the bright varnish of the morning dew;
The agèd moss grows brittle on the pale;
The dry boughs splinter in the windy gale;
And every changing season of the year
Stamps on the scene its English character . . .

George Crabbe

SONG

Why fadest thou in death,
    Oh yellow waning tree?
Gentle is autumn's breath,
    And green the oak by thee.

But with each wind that sighs
    The leaves from thee take wings;
And bare thy branches rise
    Above their drifted ring.

R. W. Dixon

THE LEAVES

Leaves of the summer, lovely summer's pride,
　Sweet is the shade below your silent tree,
Whether in waving copses, where ye hide
　My roamings, or in fields that let me see
　The open sky; and whether ye may be
Around the low-stemm'd oak, robust and wide;
Or taper ash upon the mountain side;
　Or lowland elm; your shade is sweet to me.

Whether ye wave above the early flow'rs
　In lively green; or whether, rustling sere,
Ye fly on playful winds, around my feet,

In dying autumn; lovely are your bow'rs,
　Ye early-dying children of the year;
　　Holy the silence of your calm retreat.

William Barnes

SPRING AND FALL:
to a young child

Márgarét, are you grieving
Over Goldengrove unleaving?
Leáves, líke the things of man, you
With your fresh thoughts care for, can you?
Áh! ás the heart grows older
It will come to such sights colder
By and by, nor spare a sigh
Though worlds of wanwood leafmeal lie;
And yet you will weep and know why.
Now no matter, child, the name:
Sórrow's springs áre the same.
Nor mouth had, no nor mind, expressed
What heart heard of, ghost guessed:
It ís the blight man was born for,
It is Margaret you mourn for.

Gerard Manley Hopkins

A LAMENT

O world! O life! O time!
On whose last steps I climb,
   Trembling at that where I had stood before;
When will return the glory of your prime?
   No more — Oh, never more!

Out of the day and night
A joy has taken flight;
   Fresh spring, and summer, and winter hoar,
Move my faint heart with grief, but with delight
   No more — Oh, never more!

Percy Bysshe Shelley

SLIEVE GUA

Slieve Gua, craggy and black wolf-den:
   In its clefts the wind howls,
   In its denes the wolves wail.

Autumn on Slieve Gua: and the angry
   Brown deer bells, and herons
   Croak across Slieve Gua's crags.

From the Old Irish

THAT TIME OF YEAR THOU MAYST IN ME BEHOLD

That time of year thou mayst in me behold
   When yellow leaves, or none, or few, do hang
Upon those boughs which shake against the cold,
   Bare ruined choirs, where late the sweet birds sang.
In me thou see'st the twilight of such day
   As after sunset fadeth in the west;
Which by and by black night doth take away,
   Death's second self, that seals up all the rest.
In me thou see'st the glowing of such fire,
   That on the ashes of his youth doth lie,
As the death-bed whereon it must expire,
   Consumed with that which it was nourished by.
      This thou perceivest, which makes thy love more strong,
      To love that well which thou must leave ere long.

William Shakespeare

21. THE CHERRY FAIR

The Cherry Fair

In the Middle Ages they thought of cherry fairs, or cherry feasts — fairs held in the cherry orchards in July, when the ripe cherries which had glittered on every branch were picked and sold — as a similitude of the short stay of man. Lovers went to the cherry fairs, which were on Sunday evenings, and strolled through the orchards, and there were summer games and games of chop-cherry, and dancing and singing and much laughter — 'boisterous gaiety and license'. In the Middle Ages they also wrote in Latin or in English on the theme of *ubi sunt*. Where are they now? Friar Thomas of Hales, a Franciscan, when he was asked for a love song, answered with an *ubi sunt*, in English instead of Latin, beginning *Where is Paris and Heleyne?* (page 321).

Of course the idea of passing away belongs to all times, all poetries; and here are poems ancient, less ancient, and modern, by poets English, Irish, American, Chinese, Persian. But changing from cherry feasts to roses I shall quote Jeremy Taylor — *But so have I seen a Rose newly springing from the clefts of its hood, and at first it was fair as the Morning, and full with the dew of Heaven, as a lamb's fleece; but when a ruder breath had forced open its virgin modesty, and dismantled its too youthful and unripe attachments, it began to put on darkness, and to decline to softness, and the symptoms of a sickly age; it bowed the head, and broke its stalk, and at night having lost some of its leaves,*[1] *and all its beauty, it fell into the portion of weeds and outworn faces.*

The ruins overleaf — another symbol of All is Vanity — are from that *Hypnerotomachia Poliphili* I described on page 266.

[1] i.e. petals

SLOW, SLOW, FRESH FOUNT

Slow, slow, fresh fount, keep time with my salt tears;
  Yet slower, yet, O faintly gentle springs:
List to the heavy part the music bears,
  Woe weeps out her division when she sings.
     Droop, herbs and flowers;
     Fall, grief, in showers;
     Our beauties are not ours:
       O, I could still
(Like melting snow upon some craggy hill)
     Drop, drop, drop, drop,
Since nature's pride is, now, a wither'd daffodil.

Ben Jonson

A CHERRY FAIR

This lyfe, I see, is but a cheyre feyre;
All thingis passen and so most I algate.
To-day I sat full ryall in a cheyere,
Tyll sotell deth knokyd at my gate,
And on-avysed he seyd to me, chek-mate!
Lo! how sotell he maketh a devors —
And worms to fede, he hath here leyd my cors .

    algate: *in any case*; on-avysed: *without warning*

WHERE IS PARIS AND HELEYNE?

  Where is Paris and Heleyne,
    That weren so bright and fair on bleo?
  Amadas and Ideyne,
    Tristram, Yseude and alle theo?
  Ector, with his scharpe meyne,
    And Cesar, rich of worlde's feo?
  He beoth iglyden out of the reyne
    So the sheaf is of the cleo . . .

Thomas of Hales

  bleo: *face*; theo: *those*; scharpe meyne: *bold company*;
feo: *wealth*; He beoth iglyden out of the reyne: *they have
glided out of the world*; so: *as*; of the cleo: *off the hillside*

REMEMBER NOW THY CREATOR

Remember now thy Creator in the days of thy youth, while the evil days come not, nor the years draw nigh, when thou shalt say, I have no pleasure in them;

While the sun, or the light, or the moon, or the stars, be not darkened, nor the clouds return after the rain:

In the day when the keepers of the house shall tremble, and the strong men shall bow themselves, and the grinders cease because they are few, and those that look out of the windows be darkened,

And the doors shall be shut in the streets, when the sound of the grinding is low, and he shall rise up at the voice of the bird, and all the daughters of musick shall be brought low;

Also when they shall be afraid of that which is high, and fears shall be in the way, and the almond tree shall flourish, and the grasshopper shall be a burden, and desire shall fail: because man goeth to his long home, and the mourners go about the streets;

Or ever the silver cord be loosed, or the golden bowl be broken, or the pitcher be broken at the cistern.

Then shall the dust return to the earth as it was: and the spirit shall return unto God who gave it.

Vanity of vanities, saith the preacher; all is vanity . . .

From Ecclesiastes or, The Preacher

TIME'S GLORY

Time's glory is to calm contending kings,
  To unmask falsehood and bring truth to light,
To stamp the seal of time in aged things,
  To wake the morn and sentinel the night,
  To wrong the wronger till he render right,
    To ruinate proud buildings with thy hours,
    And smear with dust their glittering golden towers;

To fill with worm-holes stately monuments,
  To feed oblivion with decay of things,
To blot old books and alter their contents,

To pluck the quills from ancient ravens' wings,
To dry the old oak's sap and cherish springs,
    To spoil antiquities of hammered steel,
    And turn the giddy round of Fortune's wheel;

To show the beldam daughters of her daughter,
    To make the child a man, the man a child,
To slay the tiger that doth live by slaughter,
    To tame the unicorn and lion wild,
    To mock the subtle, in themselves beguiled,
        To cheer the ploughman with increaseful crops,
        And waste huge stones with little water-drops . . .

William Shakespeare

THE FORT OF RATHANGAN
(From the Old Irish)

The fort by the oak trees there
    Was Bruidgi's, was Cathal's,
    Was Aed's and Ailill's,
    Cuilini's, and Conaing's,
        And Mael Duin's.
The fort in turn outlives
Each of these kings renowned
Whose hosts sleep in the ground.

Berchan

THE HEARTH OF URIEN
(From the Welsh of Llywarch the Aged)

Is not this hearth, where goats now feed?
Here chatt'ring tongues, with noisy speed,
Once talk'd around the yellow mead.

Is not this hearth this day among
Tall nettles? Once here stood a throng
Of Owen's suitors all day long.

Is not this hearth with grass o'erspread?
Ere noble Owen yet was dead,
The cauldron-heating flames were red.

323

Is not this hearth where toad-stools grow?
There Owen's warriors once did show
The swordblade dreaded by the foe.

Is not this hearth within a band
Of rushes? Once here blazed the brand,
And food was dealt with lib'ral hand.

Is not this hearth below the thorn?
Here, ere it thus was left forlorn,
Did once pass round the mead's deep horn.

Is not this hearth where emmets crawl?
Here blazed the torch upon the wall,
Around the crowded banquet hall.

Is not this hearth now cold among
Red sorrel-stems? Here once a throng
Of warriors drank with laugh and song.

Is not this hearth, where swine have plough'd?
Here once bold warriors' tongues were loud,
As mead-cups pass'd among the crowd.

Is not this hearth, where scrapes the hen?
No want was here among the men
Of brave Owen and Urien.

William Barnes

ELEGY

(Before his execution)

My prime of youth is but a frost of cares,
  My feast of joy is but a dish of pain,
My crop of corn is but a field of tares,
  And all my good is but vain hope of gain;
    The day is past, and yet I saw no sun,
    And now I live, and now my life is done.

My tale was heard and yet it was not told,
  My fruit is fallen and yet my leaves are green,
My youth is spent and yet I am not old,
  I saw the world and yet I was not seen;
    My thread is cut and yet it is not spun,
    And now I live, and now my life is done.

I sought my death and found it in my womb,
    I looked for life and saw it was a shade,
I trod the earth and knew it was my tomb,
    And now I die, and now I was but made;
        My glass is full, and now my glass is run.
        And now I live, and now my life is done.

Chidiock Tichborne

VITAE SUMMA BREVIS SPEM NOS VETAT INCOHARE LONGAM

They are not long, the weeping and the laughter,
    Love and desire and hate:
I think they have no portion in us after
    We pass the gate.

They are not long, the days of wine and roses:
    Out of a misty dream
Our path emerges for a while, then closes
    Within a dream.

Ernest Dowson

EARTH UPON EARTH

Earth out of earth is worldly wrought,
Earth hath gotten upon earth a dignity of nought,
Earth upon earth hath set all his thought
How that earth upon earth might be high brought.

Earth upon earth would be a king,
But how that earth shall to earth, he thinketh no thing;
When earth biddeth earth his rentis home bring,
Then shall earth for earth have a hard parting.

Earth upon earth winneth castles and towres,
Then saith earth unto earth 'This is all ours';
But when earth upon earth hath builded his bowres,
Then shall earth for earth suffer hard showres.

Earth upon earth hath wealth upon mould,
Earth goth upon earth glidring all in gold.
Like as he unto earth never turn should;
And yet shall earth unto earth sooner than he would.

325

Why that earth loveth earth, wonder I think;
Or why that earth will for earth sweat or swink;
For when earth upon earth is brought within the brink,
Then shall earth for earth suffer a foul stink.

As earth upon earth were the Worthies Nine,
And as earth upon earth in honour did shine;
But earth list not to know how they should encline,
And their crownis laid in earth, when death hath made his
    fine.

As earth upon earth, full worthy was Josue,
David the worthy king, Judas Machabe;
They were but earth upon earth, none of them three,
And so from earth unto earth they lost their dignity.

Alisander was but earth, that all the world wan,
And Ector upon earth was hold a worthy man,
And Julius Cesar that the empire first be-gan;
And now as earth within earth they lie pale and wan.

Arthur was but earth, for all his renown;
No more was king Charlys, ne Godfrey of Bolown;
But now earth hath turned their nobleness upsodown;
And thus earth goth to earth by short conclusion.

Who so reckon also of William Conquerowr,
King Harry the first, that was of knighthood flowr;
Earth hath closed them full straitly in his bowr;
Loo, the end of worthiness! here is no more socowr.

Now they that live upon earth, both young and old,
Think how ye shall to earth, be ye never so bold;
Ye be unsiker, whether it be in heat or cold,
Like as your brother did before, as I have told . . .

Now, sith by death we shall all pass, it is to us certain,
For of the earth we come all, and to the earth shall turn again,
Therefor to strive or grucche it were but in vain,
For all is earth, and shall be earth, no thing more certain.

Now earth upon earth consider thou may,
How earth cometh to earth naked all-way.
Why should earth upon earth go stout or gay,
Sith earth out of earth shall pass in poor array?

I counsel you, upon earth that wickedly hath wrought,
While that earth is on earth, turn up your thought,
And pray to God upon earth that all the earth hath wrought,
That earth out of earth to bliss may be brought.

Amen

BY WORLD LAID LOW

By world laid low
Great Caesar, Alexander and their men
By wind are blown like ash away:
Troy's gone, Tara's below the grass to-day.
Surely the English too
Will pass away,
Some day.

From the Irish of the seventeenth century

A LAMENT FOR THE PRIORY
OF WALSINGHAM

(3 stanzas are omitted)

Bitter was it, Oh to view
  The sacred vine,
While the gardeners played all close,
  Rooted up by the swine.

Bitter, bitter, Oh to behold
  The grass to grow
Where the walls of Walsingham
  So stately did shew.

Such were the works of Walsingham,
  While she did stand;
Such are the wracks as now do shew
  Of that holy land.

Level, level with the ground
  The towers do lie,
Which with their golden glittring tops
  Pierced out to the sky.

Where were gates no gates are now,
  The ways unknowen
Where the press of friars did pass,
  While her fame far was blowen.

Owls do scrike where the sweetest hymns
　　Lately were song;
Toads and serpents hold their dens
　　Where the palmers did throng.

Weep, weep, O Walsingham,
　　Whose days are nights,
Blessings turned to blasphemies,
　　Holy deeds to despites.

Sin is where our Lady sat,
　　Heaven turned to Hell;
Sathan sits where our Lord did sway:
　　Walsingham, Oh farewell! . . .

Anon. c. 1560

Supposed to be by Philip Howard, E. of Arundel

TO THE DRIVING CLOUD

Gloomy and dark art thou, O chief of the mighty Omahas;
Gloomy and dark, as the driving cloud, whose name thou hast
　　taken!
Wrapt in thy scarlet blanket, I see thee stalk through the city's
Narrow and populous streets, as once by the margin of rivers
Stalked those birds unknown, that have left us only their foot-
　　prints.
What, in a few short years, will remain of thy race but the
　　footprints?

How canst thou walk these streets, who hast trod the green
　　turf of the prairies?
How canst thou breathe this air, who hast breathed the sweet
　　air of the mountains?
Ah! 'tis in vain that with lordly looks of disdain thou dost
　　challenge
Looks of disdain in return, and question these walls and these
　　pavements,
Claiming the soil for thy hunting-grounds, while down-
　　trodden millions
Starve in the garrets of Europe, and cry from its caverns that
　　they, too,
Have been created heirs of the earth, and claim its division!

Back, then, back to thy woods in the regions west of the
　　Wabash!
There as a monarch thou reignest. In autumn the leaves of the
　　maple

328

Pave the floors of thy palace-halls with gold, and in summer
Pine trees waft through its chambers the odorous breath of
    their branches.
There thou art strong and great, a hero, a tamer of horses!
There thou chasest the stately stag on the banks of the Elk-horn,
Or by the roar of the Running-Water, or where the Omawhaw
Calls thee, and leaps through the wild ravine like a brave of the
    Blackfeet!

Hark! what murmurs arise from the heart of those mountainous
    deserts?
Is it the cry of the Foxes and Crows, or the mighty Behemoth,
Who, unharmed, on his tusks once caught the bolts of the
    thunder,
And now lurks in his lair to destroy the race of the red man?
Far more fatal to thee and thy race than the Crows and the
    Foxes,
Far more fatal to thee and thy race than the tread of Behemoth,
Lo! the big thunder-canoe, that steadily breasts the Missouri's
Merciless current! and yonder, afar on the prairies, the camp-
    fires
Gleam through the night; and the cloud of dust in the grey of
    the daybreak
Marks not the buffalo's track, nor the Mandan's dexterous
    horse-race;
It is a caravan, whitening the desert where dwell the Ca-
    manches!
Ha! how the breath of these Saxons and Celts, like the blast of
    the east-wind,
Drifts evermore to the west the scanty smokes of thy wigwams!

H. W. Longfellow

FROM THE RUBÁIYÁT OF OMAR KHAYYÁM

    Think, in this batter'd Caravanserai
    Whose Doorways are alternate Night and Day,
       How Sultán after Sultán with his Pomp
    Abode his Hour or two, and went his way.

    They say the Lion and the Lizard keep
    The Courts where Jamshýd gloried and drank deep:
       And Bahrám, that great Hunter — the Wild Ass
    Stamps o'er his Head, and he lies fast asleep.

I sometimes think that never blows so red
The Rose as where some buried Caesar bled;
   That every Hyacinth the Garden wears
Dropt in its Lap from some once lovely Head.

And this delightful Herb whose tender Green
Fledges the River's Lip on which we lean —
   Ah, lean upon it lightly! for who knows
From what once lovely Lip it springs unseen!

Ah, my Belovèd, fill the Cup that clears
To-day of past Regrets and future Fears —
   To-morrow? — Why, To-morrow I may be
Myself with Yesterday's Sev'n Thousand Years.

Lo! some we loved, the loveliest and best
That Time and Fate of all their Vintage prest,
   Have drunk their Cup a Round or two before,
And one by one crept silently to Rest.

And we, that now make merry in the Room
They left, and Summer dresses in new Bloom,
   Ourselves must we beneath the Couch of Earth
Descend, ourselves to make a Couch — for whom?

Ah, make the most of what we yet may spend,
Before we too into the Dust descend;
   Dust into Dust, and under Dust, to lie,
Sans Wine, sans Song, sans Singer, and — sans End!

Alike for those who for To-day prepare,
And those that after a To-morrow stare,
   A Muezzin from the Tower of Darkness cries,
'Fools! your Reward is neither Here nor There!'

Why, all the Saints and Sages who discuss'd
Of the Two Worlds so learnedly, are thrust
   Like foolish Prophets forth; their Words to Scorn
Are scatter'd and their Mouths are stopt with Dust.

Oh, come with old Khayyám, and leave the Wise
To talk; one thing is certain, that Life flies;
   One thing is certain, and the Rest is Lies;
The Flower that once has blown for ever dies . . .

Edward FitzGerald

A rivery field spread out below,
An odour of the new-mown hay
In his nostrils, the great lord of Chou
Cried, casting off the mountain snow,
'Let all things pass away.'

Wheels by milk-white asses drawn
Where Babylon or Nineveh
Rose; some conqueror drew rein
And cried to battle-weary men,
'Let all things pass away.'

From man's blood-sodden heart are sprung
Those branches of the night and day
Where the gaudy moon is hung.
What's the meaning of all song?
'Let all things pass away . . .'

W. B. Yeats

LONG I HAVE LOVED TO STROLL

Long I have loved to stroll among the hills and marshes,
And take my pleasure roaming the woods and fields.
Now I hold hands with a train of nieces and nephews,
Parting the hazel growth we tread the untilled wastes –
Wandering to and fro amidst the hills and mounds
Everywhere around us are dwellings of ancient men.
Here are vestiges of their walls and hearthstones,
There the rotted stumps of bamboo and mulberry groves.
I stop and ask a faggot-gatherer:
'These men – what has become of them?'
The faggot-gatherer turns to me and says:
'Once they were dead that was the end of them.'
In the same world men lead different lives;
Some at the court, some in the market-place.
Indeed I know these are no empty words:
The life of man is like a shadow-play
Which must in the end return to nothingness.

T'ao Ch'ien (translated by
William Acker)

Fear no more the heat o' the sun,
　　Nor the furious winter's rages;
Thou thy worldly task hast done,
　　Home art gone, and ta'en thy wages.
Golden lads and girls all must,
As chimney-sweepers, come to dust.

Fear no more the frown o' the great,
　　Thou art past the tyrant's stroke;
Care no more to clothe and eat,
　　To thee the reed is as the oak.
The sceptre, learning, physic, must,
All follow this, and come to dust.

Fear no more the lightning-flash,
　　Nor the all-dreaded thunder-stone;
Fear not slander, censure rash;
　　Thou hast finished joy and moan.
All lovers young, all lovers must
Consign to thee, and come to dust.

William Shakespeare

A DIRGE

Why were you born when the snow was falling?
You should have come to the cuckoo's calling,
Or when grapes are green in the cluster,
Or at least when lithe swallows muster
　　　　For their far off flying
　　　　From summer dying.

Why did you die when the lambs were cropping?
You should have died at the apples' dropping,
When the grasshopper comes to trouble,
And the wheat-fields are sodden stubble,
　　　　And all winds go sighing
　　　　For sweet things dying.

Christina Rossetti

332

22. THE CRIES OF WAR

The Cries of War

War is always the same, always abominable, always cruel, finding some of the best and much of the worst in men, always hated by good poets, yet always impressing them. Of the poets in this section, Wilfred Owen (page 349) was killed in the First World War, Henry Vaughan (page 347) and James Shirley (page 350) lived through the Civil War, and Jeremiah (page 344) cries of the fall of Jerusalem. Tu Fu, greatest poet of China (pages 342 and 344), lived twelve hundred years ago through most terrible years of invasion, rebellion, and ravage. So did the love poet Li Po (page 341), who was Tu Fu's friend (and was named T'ai-Po, or Evening Star, because his mother, before he was born, dreamt that the Evening Star fell into her lap).

Walt Whitman (page 338) saw horrors of fighting in the Civil War in the United States, and cried aloud over scenes of fighting, scenes in hospitals, scenes among the million dead, noting how the summer moon would look mildly on to an engagement: *The many conflicts in the dark, those shadowy-tangled, flashing moonbeam'd woods — the writhing groups and squads — the cries, the din, the cracking guns and pistols — the distant cannon — the cheers and calls and threats and awful music of the oaths — the indescribable mix — the devils fully rous'd in human hearts — the strong shout, Charge, men, charge — the flash of the naked sword, and rolling flame and smoke. And still the broken, clear and clouded heaven — and still again the moonlight pouring silvery soft its radiant patches over all.*

The woodcut, prickly with pride and weapons, comes from a German chronicle of 1486.

THE VALLEY OF THE BLACK PIG

The dews drop slowly and dreams gather: unknown spears
Suddenly hurtle before my dream-awakened eyes,
And then the crash of fallen horsemen and the cries
Of unknown perishing armies beat about my ears.
We who still labour by the cromlech on the shore,
The grey cairn on the hill, when day sinks drowned in dew,
Being weary of the world's empires, bow down to you,
Master of the still stars and of the flaming door.

W. B. Yeats

THE BLOODY CONQUESTS OF MIGHTY
TAMBURLAINE

Now crouch, ye kings of greatest Asia,
And tremble when ye hear this scourge will come,
That whips down cities, and controleth crowns,
Adding their wealth and treasure to my store.
The Euxine sea north to Natolia,
The Terrene west, the Caspian north north-east,
And on the south Senus Arabicus,
Shall all be loden with the martial spoils
We will convey with us to Persea.
Then shall my native city Samarcanda
And crystal waves of fresh Iaertis stream,
The pride and beauty of her princely seat,
Be famous through the furthest continents,
For there my Palace royal shall be plac'd:
Whose shining turrets shall dismay the heavens,
And cast the fame of Ilion's tower to hell.
Thorough the streets with troops of conquered kings,
I'll ride in golden armour like the Sun,
And in my helm a triple plume shall spring,
Spangled with diamonds dancing in the air,
To note me Emperour of the threefold world,
Like to an almond tree ymounted high,

335

Upon the lofty and celestial mount,
Of ever green Selinus quaintly deck'd
With blooms more white than Hericina's brows,
Whose tender blossoms tremble every one,
At every little breath that thorough heaven is blowen:
Then in my coach like Saturn's royal son,
Mounted in his shining chariot, gilt with fire,
And drawn with princely eagles through the path,
Pav'd with bright crystal, and enchas'd with stars,
When all the Gods stand gazing at his pomp,
So will I ride through Samarcanda streets,
Until my soul dissevered from this flesh,
Shall mount the milk-white way and meet him there.
To Babylon, my lords, to Babylon . . .

Christopher Marlowe

ALLITERATION, OR THE SIEGE OF BELGRADE

An Austrian army, awfully array'd,
Boldly by battery besiege Belgrade;
Cossack commanders cannonading come,
Deal devastation's dire destructive doom;
Ev'ry endeavour engineers essay,
For fame, for freedom, fight, fierce furious fray.
Gen'rals 'gainst gen'rals grapple – gracious God!
How honours Heav'n heroic hardihood!
Infuriate, indiscriminate in ill,
Just Jesus, instant innocence instil!
Kinsmen kill kinsmen, kindred kindred kill.
Labour low levels longest, loftiest lines;
Men march 'midst mounds, moats, mountains,
    murd'rous mines.
Now noisy, noxious numbers notice nought,
Of outward obstacles o'ercoming ought;
Poor patriots perish, persecution's pest!
Quite quiet Quakers 'Quarter, quarter' quest;
Reason returns, religion, right, redounds:
Suwarrow, stop such sanguinary sounds!
Truce to thee, Turkey, terror to thy train!
Unwise, unjust, unmerciful Ukraine!
Vanish vile vengeance, vanish victory vain!
Why wish we warfare? wherefore welcome won
Xerxes, Xantippus, Xavier, Xenophon?

Yield, ye young Yaghier yeomen, yield your yell!
Zimmerman's, Zoroaster's, Zeno's zeal
Again attract; art against arms appeal.
All, all ambitious aims, avaunt, away!
Et cætera, et cætera, et cætera.

BEFORE AGINCOURT
(From 'Henry the Fifth')

From camp to camp, through the foul womb of night
The hum of either army stilly sounds;
That the fix'd sentinels almost receive
The secret whispers of each other's watch.
Fire answers fire, and through their paly flames
Each battle sees the other's umber'd face;
Steed threatens steed, in high and boastful neighs
Piercing the Night's dull ear; and from the tents,
The armourers, accomplishing the knights,
With busy hammers closing rivets up,
Give dreadful note of preparation.
The country cocks do crow, the clocks do toll:
And the third hour of drowsy morning name.
Proud of their numbers, and secure in soul,
The confident and over-lusty French
Do the low-rated English play at dice;
And chide the cripple tardy-gaited Night
Who, like a foul and ugly witch, doth limp
So tediously away. The poor condemned English,
Like sacrifices, by their watchful fires
Sit patiently, and inly ruminate
The morning's danger; and their gesture sad,
Investing lank-lean cheeks and war-worn coats,
Presenteth them unto the gazing moon
So many horrid ghosts. O now, who will behold
The royal captain of this ruin'd band
Walking from watch to watch, from tent to tent,
Let him cry, 'Praise and glory on his head!'
For forth he goes, and visits all his host,
Bids them good morrow with a modest smile,
And calls them brothers, friends, and countrymen.
Upon his royal face there is no note
How dread an army hath enrounded him;

M

Nor doth he dedicate one jot of colour
Unto the weary and all-watched night,
But freshly looks, and over-bears attaint
With cheerful semblance and sweet majesty;
That every wretch, pining and pale before,
Beholding him, plucks comfort from his looks.
A largess universal, like the sun,
His liberal eye doth give to every one,
Thawing cold fear, that mean and gentle all
Behold, as may unworthiness define,
A little touch of Harry in the night . . .

William Shakespeare

BIVOUAC ON A MOUNTAINSIDE

I see before me now a travelling army halting,
Below a fertile valley spread, with barns and the orchards of
summer,
Behind, the terraced sides of a mountain, abrupt, in places
rising high,
Broken, with rocks, with clinging cedars, with tall shapes
dingily seen,
The numerous camp-fires scatter'd near and far, some away up
on the mountain,
The shadowy forms of men and horses, looming, large-sized,
flickering,
And over all the sky – the sky! far, far out of reach, studded,
breaking out, the eternal stars.

Walt Whitman

CAVALRY CROSSING A FORD

A line in long array where they wind betwixt green islands,
They take a serpentine course, their arms flash in the sun –
hark to the musical clank,
Behold the silvery river, in it the splashing horses loitering
stop to drink,
Behold the brown-faced men, each group, each person a
picture, the negligent rest on the saddles,
Some emerge on the opposite bank, others are just entering the
ford – while,
Scarlet and blue and snowy white,
The guidon flags flutter gayly in the wind.

Walt Whitman

338

On Linden, when the sun was low,
All bloodless lay the untrodden snow,
And dark as winter was the flow
  Of Iser, rolling rapidly.

But Linden saw another sight
When the drum beat at dead of night,
Commanding fires of death to light
  The darkness of her scenery.

By torch and trumpet fast arrayed,
Each horseman drew his battle blade,
And furious every charger neighed
  To join the dreadful revelry.

Then shook the hills with thunder riven,
Then rushed the steed to battle driven,
And louder than the bolts of heaven
  Far flashed the red artillery.

But redder yet that light shall glow
On Linden's hills of stainèd snow,
And bloodier yet the torrent flow
  Of Iser, rolling rapidly.

'Tis morn, but scarce yon level sun
Can pierce the war-clouds, rolling dun,
Where furious Frank and fiery Hun
  Shout in their sulphurous canopy.

The combat deepens. On, ye brave,
Who rush to glory, or the grave!
Wave, Munich! all thy banners wave,
  And charge with all thy chivalry!

Few, few shall part where many meet!
The snow shall be their winding-sheet,
And every turf beneath their feet
  Shall be a soldier's sepulchre.

Thomas Campbell

THE NIGHT OF TRAFALGÁR

i

In the wild October night-time, when the wind raved round
    the land,
And the Back-sea met the Front-sea, and our doors were
    blocked with sand,
And we heard the drub of Dead-man's Bay, where bones of
    thousands are,
We knew not what the day had done for us at Trafalgár.
                Had done,
                Had done,
            For us at Trafalgár.

ii

'Pull hard, and make the Nothe, or down we go!' one says,
    says he.
We pulled; and bedtime brought the storm; but snug at home
    slept we.
Yet all the while our gallants after fighting through the day,
Were beating up and down the dark, sou'-west of Cadiz Bay.
                The dark,
                The dark,
            Sou'-west of Cadiz Bay!

iii

The victors and the vanquished then the storm it tossed and
    tore,
As hard they strove, those worn-out men, upon that surly
    shore;
Dead Nelson and his half-dead crew, his foes from near and
    far,
Were rolled together on the deep that night at Trafalgár!
                The deep,
                The deep,
            That night at Trafalgár!

                                        Thomas Hardy

UNDER THE FRONTIER POST

We cross a stream and my horse
drinks up the autumn water; cold
water now, and the wind cuts like a knife.
Over the desert sand the sun sets;

through the haze I can barely see
the distant walls of Lintao; and I think
of all the battles fought beside the Great Wall
and of the tales of battles once
on all men's lips;
tales that have vanished
with the yellow dust storms of the ages; and now
at times come desert winds that blow
amongst the grasses
uncovering scattered bones.

Wang Chang-Ling
(translated by Rewi Alley)

WAR

Last year the war was in the northeast,
this year we fight in the far northwest,
grinding our weapons on the stones by
a highland lake; grazing our horses among snow-drifts
on Tienshan slopes; over the vast border front our men
grow ever older, wearier.

But to our enemy, the Hsiung Nu, killing
is as ploughing to us;
over the wide desert the only crops
are whitening bones;
here the people of Chin tried to wall out the tribesmen;
but we of Han must go on
burning beacon fires for ever,
as there seems no end
to this war.

In the madness of the battlefield, men fight and die
with abandon; horses riderless
neigh madly, the piercing sound
reaching to the heavens; crows
and eagles tear the intestines from the corpses,
fly heavily with them so that they catch up
in the branches of dead trees
and hang there.

Fragments of what once were men
scattered over the desert —
and in the end, it seems, the generals
have settled nothing.

War is a horrible thing —
only in sheer self-defence
would our wise men of old
ever resort to it.

Li Po (translated by
Rewi Alley)

THE BURIAL OF SIR JOHN MOORE
AFTER CORUNNA

Not a drum was heard, not a funeral note,
    As his corse to the rampart we hurried;
Not a soldier discharged his farewell shot
    O'er the grave where our hero we buried.

We buried him darkly at dead of night,
    The sods with our bayonets turning,
By the struggling moonbeam's misty light
    And the lanthorn dimly burning.

No useless coffin enclosed his breast,
    Not in sheet or in shroud we wound him;
But he lay like a warrior taking his rest
    With his martial cloak around him.

Few and short were the prayers we said,
    And we spoke not a word of sorrow;
But we steadfastly gazed on the face that was dead,
    And we bitterly thought of the morrow.

We thought, as we hollow'd his narrow bed
    And smooth'd down his lowly pillow,
That the foe and the stranger would tread o'er his head,
    And we far away on the billow!

Lightly they'll talk of the spirit that's gone,
    And o'er his cold ashes upbraid him —
But little he'll reck, if they let him sleep on
    In the grave where a Briton has laid him.

But half of our heavy task was done
    When the clock struck the hour for retiring;
And we heard the distant and random gun
    That the foe was sullenly firing.

Slowly and sadly we laid him down,
  From the field of his fame fresh and gory;
We carved not a line, and we raised not a stone,
  But we left him alone with his glory.

Charles Wolfe

THE WHITE HORSE

Out of the Northeast
galloped a white charger
with saddle empty, but
sticking into it, two arrows.

Pity the rider lost!
For who can now admire
his spirited prancing?

Last night he was the general
giving orders for battle;
just now he was killed;

war and its disorder bring death
through many doors,

cries of bitterness, and tears
like sleet in a winter's storm.

Tu Fu (translated by
Rewi Alley)

DAVID'S LAMENT

And David lamented with this lamentation over Saul and over Jonathan his son.

The beauty of Israel is slain upon thy high places: how are the mighty fallen!

Tell it not in Gath, publish it not in the streets of Askelon; lest the daughters of the Philistines rejoice, lest the daughters of the uncircumcised triumph.

Ye mountains of Gilboa, let there be no dew, neither let there be rain, upon you, nor fields of offerings: for there the shield of the mighty is vilely cast away, the shield of Saul, as though he had not been anointed with oil.

From the blood of the slain, from the fat of the mighty, the bow of Jonathan turned not back, and the sword of Saul returned not empty.

343

Saul and Jonathan were lovely and pleasant in their lives, and in their death they were not divided: they were swifter than eagles, they were stronger than lions.

Ye daughters of Israel, weep over Saul, who clothed you in scarlet, with other delights, who put on ornaments of gold upon your apparel.

How are the mighty fallen in the midst of battle! O Jonathan, thou wast slain in thine high places.

I am distressed for thee, my brother Jonathan: very pleasant hast thou been unto me: thy love to me was wonderful, passing the love of women.

How are the mighty fallen, and the weapons of war perished! . . .

The Second Book of Samuel

OVERNIGHT IN THE APARTMENT BY THE RIVER

While the evening here is approaching the mountain paths,
I come to this high up chamber, very close to the Water-Gate.
Thin clouds rest on the edges of cliffs;
A lonely moon turns among the waves.

A line of cranes in flight is silent;
A pack of wolves baying over their prey breaks the quiet.
I cannot sleep because I am concerned about wars,
Because I am powerless to amend the world.

Tu Fu

HOW IS THE GOLD BECOME DIM

How is the gold become dim! how is the most fine gold changed! the stones of the sanctuary are poured out in the tops of every street.

The precious sons of Zion, comparable to fine gold, how are they esteemed as earthen pitchers, the work of the hands of the potter!

Even the sea monsters draw out the breast, they give suck to their young ones: the daughter of my people is become cruel, like the ostriches in the wilderness.

344

The tongue of the sucking child cleaveth to the roof of his mouth for thirst: the young children ask bread, and no man breaketh it unto them.

They that did feed delicately are desolate in the streets: they that were brought up in scarlet embrace dunghills . . .

The Lamentations of Jeremiah

'AND THERE WAS A GREAT CALM'
(On the signing of the armistice, Nov. 11, 1918)

i

There had been years of Passion — scorching, cold,
And much Despair, and Anger heaving high,
Care whitely watching, Sorrows manifold,
Among the young, among the weak and old,
And the pensive Spirit of Pity whispered, 'Why?'

ii

Men had not paused to answer. Foes distraught
Pierced the thinned peoples in a brute-like blindness,
Philosophies that sages long had taught,
And Selflessness, were as an unknown thought,
And 'Hell!' and 'Shell!' were yapped at Lovingkindness.

iii

The feeble folk at home had grown full-used
To 'dug-outs', 'snipers', 'Huns', from the war-adept
In the mornings heard, and at evetides perused;
To day-dreamt men in millions, when they mused —
To nightmare-men in millions when they slept.

iv

Waking to wish existence timeless, null,
Sirius they watched above where armies fell;
He seemed to check his flapping when, in the lull
Of night a boom came thencewise, like the dull
Plunge of a stone dropped into some deep well.

v

So, when old hopes that earth was bettering slowly
Were dead and damned, there sounded 'War is done!'
One morrow. Said the bereft, and meek, and lowly,
'Will men some day be given to grace? yea, wholly,
And in good sooth, as our dreams used to run?'

Breathless they paused. Out there men raised their glance
To where had stood those poplars lank and lopped,
As they had raised it through the four years' dance
Of Death in the now familiar flats of France;
And murmured, 'Strange, this! How? All firing stopped?'

Aye: all was hushed. The about-to-fire fired not,
The aimed-at moved away in trance-lipped song.
One checkless regiment slung a clinching shot
And turned. The Spirit of Irony smirked out, 'What?
Spoil peradventures woven of Rage and Wrong?'

Thenceforth no flying fires inflamed the gray,
No hurtlings shook the dewdrop from the thorn,
No moan perplexed the mute bird on the spray;
Worn horses mused: 'We are not whipped to-day';
No weft-winged engines blurred the moon's thin horn.

Calm fell. From Heaven distilled a clemency;
There was peace on earth, and silence in the sky;
Some could, some could not, shake off misery:
The Sinister Spirit sneered: 'It had to be!'
And again the Spirit of Pity whispered, 'Why?'

Thomas Hardy

THE OLD KNIGHT

His golden locks Time hath to silver turned;
O Time too swift, O Swiftness never ceasing!
His youth 'gainst Time and Age hath ever spurned,
But spurned in vain; youth waneth by increasing:
    Beauty, Strength, Youth, are flowers but fading seen;
    Duty, Faith, Love, are roots, and ever green.

His helmet now, shall make a hive for bees;
And lovers' sonnets turned to holy psalms,
A man-at-arms must now serve on his knees,
And feed on prayers, which are Age his alms;
    But though from court to cottage he depart,
    His saint is sure of his unspotted heart.

And when he saddest sits in homely cell,
He'll teach his swains this carol for a song:
Blest be the hearts that wish my sovereign well,
Curst be the souls that think her any wrong.
 Goddess, allow this aged man his right,
 To be your beadsman now, that was your knight.

George Peele

PEACE

My Soul, there is a country
 Afar beyond the stars,
Where stands a wingéd sentry
 All skilful in the wars.
There, above noise and danger,
 Sweet peace sits, crown'd with smiles,
And One born in a manger
 Commands the beauteous files.
He is thy gracious friend
 And (O my Soul awake!)
Did in pure love descend,
 To die here for thy sake.
If thou canst get but thither,
 There grows the flower of peace,
The rose that cannot wither,
 Thy fortress, and thy ease.
Leave then thy foolish ranges;
 For none can thee secure,
But One, who never changes,
 Thy God, thy Life, thy Cure.

Henry Vaughan

PEACE

Sweet Peace, where dost thou dwell? I humbly crave,
 Let me once know.
I sought thee in a secret cave,
 And ask'd, if Peace was there,
A hollow wind did seem to answer, No:
 Go seek elsewhere.

I did; and going did a rainbow note:
  Surely, thought I,
 This is the lace of Peace's coat:
  I will search out the matter.
But while I looked the clouds immediately
  Did break and scatter.

Then went I to a garden and did spy
  A gallant flower,
 The crown imperial: Sure, said I,
  Peace at the root must dwell.
But when I digg'd, I saw a worm devour
  What show'd so well.

At length I met a rev'rend good old man;
  Whom when for Peace
 I did demand, he thus began:
  There was a Prince of old
At Salem dwelt, who liv'd with good increase
  Of flock and fold.

He sweetly liv'd; yet sweetness did not save
  His life from foes.
 But after death out of his grave
  There sprang twelve stalks of wheat:
Which many wondring at, got some of those
  To plant and set.

It prosper'd strangely, and did soon disperse
  Through all the earth:
 For they that taste it do rehearse,
  That virtue lies therein;
A secret virtue, bringing peace and mirth
  By flight of sin.

Take of this grain, which in my garden grows,
  And grows for you;
 Make bread of it: and that repose
  And peace, which ev'ry where
With so much earnestness you do pursue,
  Is only there.

George Herbert

THE SWORD AND THE SICKLE

The sword sung on the barren heath,
The sickle in the fruitful field:
The sword he sung a song of death,
But could not make the sickle yield.

William Blake

ANTHEM FOR DOOMED YOUTH

What passing-bells for these who die as cattle?
  Only the monstrous anger of the guns.
  Only the stuttering rifles' rapid rattle
Can patter out their hasty orisons.
No mockeries for them from prayers or bells,
  Nor any voice of mourning save the choirs, —
The shrill, demented choirs of wailing shells;
  And bugles calling for them from sad shires.

What candles may be held to speed them all?
  Not in the hands of boys, but in their eyes
Shall shine the holy glimmers of good-byes.
  The pallor of girls' brows shall be their pall;
Their flowers the tenderness of silent minds,
And each slow dusk a drawing-down of blinds.

Wilfred Owen

ALL, ALL OF A PIECE THROUGHOUT

All, all of a piece throughout:
  Thy chase had a beast in view;
Thy wars brought nothing about;
  Thy lovers were all untrue.
'Tis well an old age is out,
  And time to begin a new . . .

John Dryden

The glories of our blood and state
  Are shadows, not substantial things,
There is no armour against fate,
  Death lays his icy hand on Kings.
      Sceptre and Crown
      Must tumble down,
And in the dust be equal made
With the poor crooked scythe and spade.

Some men with swords may reap the field,
  And plant fresh laurels where they kill,
But their strong nerves at last must yield,
  They tame but one another still;
      Early or late,
      They stoop to fate,
And must give up their murmuring breath,
When they pale captives creep to death.

The garlands wither on your brow,
  Then boast no more your mighty deeds.
Upon Death's purple altar now
  See where the victor-victim bleeds.
      Your heads must come
      To the cold tomb;
Only the actions of the just
Smell sweet, and blossom in the dust.

James Shirley

23. O MORTAL MAN

O Mortal Man

The first English prayer-book of 1549 prayed that the dead
'escaping the gates of hell and paynes of eternall derkenesse,
may ever dwel in the region of lighte . . . in the place where
is no wepyng, sorowe, nor heaviness'. From that sixteenth
century of plague, torture, and execution come several of the
next poems. *O Death, Rock Me On Sleep* (page 357) is an execution
poem, though I doubt if it was written by Anne Boleyn. More
likely it was written about her. (Other execution poems are to
be found on pages 283 by Ralegh; page 324 by Chidiock
Tichborne; page 378 by Marvell; page 381 by Ralegh
again; and page 383.) Plague causes the sickness of death in
Thomas Nashe's poem (on page 358). Older still, *The Lyke-Wake
Dirge* (on page 366), from Yorkshire and the northern counties,
was sung or crooned by a woman over the 'lyke', which is the
dead body, at wakes, which were the vigils over the dead
between death and burial. The song guided the dead man's
soul over the gorse-covered moor, and across the narrow
bridge, to purgatory, to be purged of sin. How the refrains at
the end of each stanza in these poems – *Timor mortis conturbat me,
And Christ receive thy saule, For now I die,* and *Lord, have mercy on us*
(this one from the litany in the prayer-book) – toll out the
life; and how they match, as the writers intended they should,
the heavy tenor bell, the passing bell, which tolls from the
church tower.

> *Never send to know for whom the bell tolls: It tolls for thee.*
>
> (John Donne)

As for the woodcut, a French one of 1500, mankind is
broken on the wheel, and Fate watches in a hood, his back
turned to us, his face hidden.

AFTERWARDS

When the Present has latched its postern behind my tremulous
    stay,
  And the May month flaps its glad green leaves like wings,
Delicate-filmed as new-spun silk, will the neighbours say,
  'He was a man who used to notice such things'?

If it be in the dusk when, like an eyelid's soundless blink,
  The dewfall-hawk comes crossing the shades to alight
Upon the wind-warped upland thorn, a gazer may think,
  'To him this must have been a familiar sight.'

If I pass during some nocturnal blackness, mothy and warm,
  When the hedgehog travels furtively over the lawn,
One may say, 'He strove that such innocent creatures should
    come to no harm,
  But he could do little for them; and now he is gone.'

If, when hearing that I have been stilled at last, they stand at
    the door,
  Watching the full-starred heavens that winter sees,
Will this thought rise on those who will meet my face no
    more,
  'He was one who had an eye for such mysteries'?

And will any say when my bell of quittance is heard in the
    gloom,
  And a crossing breeze cuts a pause in its outrollings,
Till they rise again, as they were a new bell's boom,
  'He hears it not now, but used to notice such things'?

                        Thomas Hardy

MAN THAT IS BORN OF A WOMAN

Man that is born of a woman, hath but a short time to live,
  and is full of misery: he cometh up and is cut down like a
  flower; he flyeth as it were a shadow, and never continueth
  in one stay . . .

                        The Book of Job

UPON A MAID

Here she lies (in bed of spice)
Fair as Eve in Paradise:
For her beauty it was such
Poets could not praise too much.
Virgins come, and in a ring
Her supremest requiem sing;
Then depart, but see ye tread
Lightly, lightly o'er the dead.

Robert Herrick

LAMENT FOR THE MAKARIS

When He was Sek

I that in heill wes and gladness,
Am trublit now with gret seiknes,
And feblit with infermite;
    Timor mortis conturbat me.

Our plesance heir is all vane glory,
This fals warld is bot transitory,
The flesche is brukle, the Fend is sle;
    Timor mortis conturbat me.

The stait of man dois change and vary,
Now sound, now seik, now blith, now sary,
Now dansand mery, now like to dee;
    Timor mortis conturbat me.

No stait in erd heir standis sickir;
As with the wynd wavis the wickir,
Wavis this warldis vanite;
    Timor mortis conturbat me.

On to the ded gois all Estatis,
Princis, Prelotis, and Potestatis,
Baith riche and pur of all degre;
    Timor mortis conturbat me.

He takis the knychtis in to feild,
Anarmit under helme and scheild;
Victour he is at all mellie;
    Timor mortis conturbat me.

That strang unmercifull tyrand
Takis, on the moderis breist sowkand,
The bab full of benignitie;
    Timor mortis conturbat me.

He takis the campion in the stour,
The capitane closit in the tour,
The lady in bour full of bewte;
    Timor mortis conturbat me.

He sparis no lord for his piscence,
Na clerk for his intelligence;
His awful strak may no man fle;
    Timor mortis conturbat me.

Art, magicianis, and astrologgis,
Rethoris, logicianis, and theologgis,
Thame helpis no conclusionis sle;
    Timor mortis conturbat me.

In medicyne the most practicianis,
Lechis, surrigianis, and phisicianis,
Thame self fra ded may not supplè;
    Timor mortis conturbat me.

I se that makaris amang the laif
Playis heir ther pageant, syne gois to graif;
Sparit is nocht ther faculte;
    Timor mortis conturbat me.

He hes done petuously devour,
The noble Chaucer, of makaris flour,
The Monk of Bery, and Gower, all thre;
    Timor mortis conturbat me.

The gude Syr Hew of Eglintoun,
And eik Heryot, and Wyntoun,
He hes tane out of this cuntre;
    Timor mortis conturbat me.

That scorpion fell hes done infek
Maister Johne Clerk, and James Afflek,
Fra balat making and tragidie;
    Timor mortis conturbat me.

Holland and Barbour he hes berevit;
Allace! that he nocht with us levit
Schir Mungo Lokert of the Le;
    Timor mortis conturbat me.

Clerk of Tranent eik he hes tane,
That maid the Anteris of Gawane;
Schir Gilbert Hay endit hes he;
    Timor mortis conturbat me.

He hes Blind Hary and Sandy Traill
Slaine with his schour of mortall haill,
Whilk Patrik Johnestoun mycht nocht fle;
    Timor mortis conturbat me . . .

And he hes now tane, last of aw,
Gud gentill Stobo and Quintyne Schaw,
Of wham all wichtis hes pete;
    Timor mortis conturbat me.

Gud Maister Walter Kennedy
In poynt of dede lyis veraly,
Gret reuth it wer that so suld be;
    Timor mortis conturbat me.

Sen he hes all my brether tane,
He will nocht lat me lif alane,
On forse I man his nyxt pray be;
    Timor mortis conturbat me.

Sen for the deid remeid is none,
Best is that we for dede dispone,
Eftir our dede that lif may we;
    Timor mortis conturbat me.

                             William Dunbar

makaris: *makers, i.e. poets*; heill: *health*; Timor mortis conturbat me : *Fear of death disturbs me*; brukle: *brittle*; fend: *fiend, devil*; sle: *sly, cunning*; sickir: *safe*; wickir: *willow tree*; anarmit: *armed*; campion in the stour: *champion in the fight*; piscence: *puissance, power*; supple: *help*; the laif: *the rest*; syne: *then*; hes done infek: *has disabled, barred*; Anteris: *adventures*; whilk: *which*; wichtis: *wights, persons*; on forse: *perforce*; man: *must*; sen: *since*; dispone: *dispose ourselves*

Hung be the heavens with black, yield day to night!
Comets, importing change of times and states,
Brandish your crystal tresses in the sky,
And with them scourge the bad revolting stars
That have consented unto Henry's death . . .

William Shakespeare

O DEATH, ROCK ME ON SLEEP

O Death, rock me on sleep,
  Bring me on quiet rest:
Let pass my very guiltless ghost
  Out of my careful breast.
  Toll on the passing bell,
  Ring out the doleful knell:
  Let the sound my death tell,
    For I must die,
    There is no remedy;
    For now I die.

My pains who can express?
  Alas! they are so strong,
My dolour will not suffer strength
  My life for to prolong
  Toll on the passing bell,
  Ring out the doleful knell:
  Let the sound my death tell,
    For I must die,
    There is no remedy;
    For now I die.

Alone in prison strong
  I wail my destiny;
Woe worth this cruel hap that I
  Should taste this misery.
  Toll on the passing bell,
  Ring out the doleful knell:
  Let the sound my death tell,
    For I must die,
    There is no remedy;
    For now I die.

Farewell, my pleasures past,
    Welcome, my present pain:
I feel my torments so increase
    That life cannot remain.
    Cease now the passing bell,
    Rung is my doleful knell,
For the sound my death doth tell.
    Death doth draw nigh:
    Sound my end dolefully,
    For now I die.

Ascribed to Anne Boleyn

LORD, HAVE MERCY ON US

Adieu, farewell earth's bliss,
This world uncertain is;
Fond are life's lustful joys,
Death proves them all but toys,
None from his darts can fly.
I am sick, I must die:
    Lord, have mercy on us.

Rich men, trust not in wealth,
Gold cannot buy you health;
Physic himself must fade,
All things to end are made.
The plague full swift goes by.
I am sick, I must die:
    Lord, have mercy on us.

Beauty is but a flower
Which wrinkles will devour;
Brightness falls from the air,
Queens have died young and fair,
Dust hath closed Helen's eye.
I am sick, I must die:
    Lord, have mercy on us.

Strength stoops unto the grave,
Worms feed on Hector brave,
Swords may not fight with fate,
Earth still holds ope her gate.

Come! Come! the bells do cry.
I am sick, I must die:
　　　Lord, have mercy on us.

Wit with his wantonness
Tasteth death's bitterness;
Hell's executioner
Hath no ears for to hear
What vain art can reply.
I am sick, I must die:
　　　Lord, have mercy on us.

Haste, therefore, each degree,
To welcome destiny:
Heaven is our heritage,
Earth but a players' stage,
Mount we unto the sky.
I am sick, I must die:
　　　Lord, have mercy on us.

Thomas Nashe

FUNERAL SONG

Urns and odours, bring away,
Vapours, sighs, darken the day;
Our dole more deadly looks than dying
Balms, and gums, and heavy cheers,

Sacred vials fill'd with tears,
And clamours through the wild air flying:

Come all sad and solemn shows,
That are quick-ey'd pleasure's foes;
We convent nought else but woes.
　　We convent nought else but woes.

John Fletcher

cheers: looks; convent: summon

THE DUKE OF GRAFTON

As two men were a-walking, down by the sea-side,
O the brave Duke of Grafton they straightway espied,
Said the one to the other, and thus did they say,
'It is the brave Duke of Grafton that is now cast away

359

They brought him to Portsmouth, his fame to make known,
And from thence to fair London, so near to the throne;
They pulled out his bowels, and they stretched forth his feet,
They embalmed his body with spices so sweet.

All things were made ready, his funeral for to be,
Where the royal Queen Mary came there for to see,
Six Lords went before him, six bore him from the ground,
Six Dukes walked before him in black velvet gowns.

So black was their mourning, so white were their bands!
So yellow were their flamboys they carried in their hands!
The drums they did rattle, the trumpets sweetly sound,
While the muskets and cannons did thunder all around.

In Westminster Abbey 'tis now called by name,
There the great Duke of Grafton does lie in great fame;
In Westminster Abbey he lies in cold clay
Where the royal Queen Mary went weeping away.

From THE DUCHESS OF MALFI

(Daniel de Bosola, Gentleman of the Horse to the Duchess of Malfi, enters a
room in her lodging where he finds the Duchess and her maid Cariola)

Bosola. I am come to make thy tomb.

Duchess. Hah, my tomb?
    Thou speak'st, as if I lay upon my death bed,
    Gasping for breath: dost thou perceive me sick?

Bosola. Yes, and the more dangerously, since thy sickness is
insensible.

Duchess. Thou art not mad, sure. Dost know me?

Bosola. Yes.

Duchess. Who am I?

Bosola. Thou art a box of worm-seed, at best but a little
salvatory of green mummy. What's this flesh? a little
crudded milk, phantastical puff-paste: our bodies are
weaker than those paper prisons boys use to keep flies in;
more contemptible – since ours is to preserve earth-
worms. Didst thou ever see a lark in a cage? Such is the
soul in the body: this world is like her little turf of grass,
and the heaven o'er our heads, like her looking-glass,
only gives us a miserable knowledge of the small compass
of our prison.

Duchess. Am not I – thy duchess?

Bosola. Thou art some great woman sure, for riot begins to
sit on thy forehead (clad in gray hairs) twenty years
sooner than on a merry milkmaid's. Thou sleep'st worse
than if a mouse should be forc'd to take up her lodging
in a cat's ear: a little infant that breeds its teeth, should it
lie with thee, would cry out, as if thou were the more
unquiet bedfellow.

Duchess. I am the Duchess of Malfi still.

Bosola. That makes thy sleep so broken:
'Glories (like glow-worms) afar off shine bright,
But look'd too near, have neither heat nor light.'

Duchess. Thou art very plain.

Bosola. My trade is to flatter the dead, not the living – I am a
tomb-maker.

Duchess. And thou com'st to make my tomb?

Bosola. Yes.

Duchess. Let me be a little merry –
Of what stuff wilt thou make it?

Bosola. Nay, resolve me first, of what fashion?

Duchess. Why, do we grow phantastical in our death-bed?
Do we affect fashion in the grave?

Bosola. Most ambitiously: Princes' images on their tombs
Do not lie, as they were wont, seeming to pray
Up to heaven; but with their hands under their cheeks,
(As if they died of the toothache) – they are not carved
With their eyes fix'd upon the stars; but as
Their minds were wholly bent upon the world,
The selfsame way they seem to turn their faces.

Duchess. Let me know fully therefore the effect
Of this thy dismal preparation,
This talk, fit for a charnel?

Bosola. Now, I shall –
(*Enter Executioners, with a coffin, cord, and a bell*)
Here is a present from your princely brothers,
And may it arrive welcome, for it brings
Last benefit, last sorrow.

Duchess. Let me see it –
I have so much obedience in my blood,
I wish it in their veins, to do them good.

Bosola. This is your last presence chamber.

Cariola. O my sweet lady!

Duchess. Peace, it affrights not me.

Bosola. I am the common bell-man,
    That usually is sent to condemn'd persons
    The night before they suffer.
Duchess. Even now thou said'st,
    Thou wast a tomb-maker?
Bosola.   'Twas to bring you
    By degrees to mortification: Listen.
       Hark, now every thing is still —
       The scritch-owl and the whistler shrill
       Call upon our Dame, aloud,
       And bid her quickly don her shroud:
       Much you had of land and rent,
       Your length in clay's now competent.
       A long war disturb'd your mind,
       Here your perfect peace is sign'd —
       Of what is't fools make such vain keeping?
       Sin their conception, their birth, weeping:
       Their life a general mist of error,
       Their death, a hideous storm of terror —
       Strew your hair, with powders sweet:
       Don clean linen, bath your feet,
       And (the foul fiend more to check)
       A crucifix let bless your neck.
       'Tis now full tide, 'tween night, and day,
       End your groan, and come away.
Cariola. Hence, villains, tyrants, murderers: alas!
    What will you do with my lady? Call for help.
Duchess. To whom, to our next neighbours? they are mad folks.
Bosola.   Remove that noise.
Duchess. Farewell, Cariola.
    In my last will I have not much to give —
    A many hungry guests have fed upon me.
    Thine will be a poor reversion.
Cariola. I will die with her.
Duchess. I pray thee, look thou giv'st my little boy
    Some syrup, for his cold, and let the girl
    Say her prayers, ere she sleep. Now what you please,
    What death?
Bosola.   Strangling, here are your executioners.
Duchess. I forgive them:
    The apoplexy, cathar, or cough o' th' lungs,
    Would do as much as they do.
Bosola.   Doth not death fright you?

Duchess. Who would be afraid on't?
    Knowing to meet such excellent company
    In th'other world.
Bosola.   Yet, me thinks,
    The manner of your death should much afflict you,
    This cord should terrify you?
Duchess. Not a whit —
    What would it pleasure me, to have my throat cut
    With diamonds? or to be smothered
    With cassia? or to be shot to death, with pearls?
    I know death hath ten thousand several doors
    For men to take their exits: and 'tis found
    They go on such strange geometrical hinges
    You may open them both ways: any way (for heaven
      sake),
    So I were out of your whispering. Tell my brothers
    That I perceive death (now I am well awake)
    Best gift is they can give, or I can take —
    I would fain put off my last woman's fault,
    I'd not be tedious to you.
Executioner. We are ready.
Duchess. Dispose my breath how please you, but my body
    Bestow upon my women, will you?
Executioner. Yes.
Duchess. Pull, and pull strongly, for your able strength
    Must pull down heaven upon me:
    Yet stay, heaven-gates are not so highly arch'd
    As princes' palaces — they that enter there
    Must go upon their knees: Come, violent death,
    Serve for mandragora, to make me sleep;
    Go tell my brothers, when I am laid out,
    They then may feed in quiet . . .
            (*They strangle her*)

                         John Webster

CALL FOR THE ROBIN-REDBREAST

    Call for the robin-redbreast and the wren
    Since o'er shady groves they hover,
    And with leaves and flowers do cover
    The friendless bodies of unburied men.

Call unto his funeral dole
The ant, the field-mouse and the mole
To rear him hillocks that shall keep him warm,
And when gay tombs are robb'd, sustain no harm,
But keep the wolf far thence, that's foe to men,
For with his nails he'll dig them up again.

John Webster

PROUD MAISIE

Proud Maisie is in the wood,
   Walking so early:
Sweet Robin sits on the bush,
   Singing so rarely.

Tell me, thou bonny bird,
   When shall I marry me?
When six braw gentlemen
   Kirkward shall carry ye.

Who makes the bridal bed,
   Birdie, say truly?
The grey-headed sexton
   That delves the grave duly.

The glow-worm o'er grave and stone
   Shall light thee steady;
The owl from the steeple sing
   'Welcome, proud lady!'

Sir Walter Scott

THE DREE NIGHT

'T were a dree night, a dree night, as the squire's end drew
   nigh,
A dree night, a dree night, to watch, and pray, and sigh.

When the stream runs dry, and the dead leaves fall, and the
   ripe ear bends its head,
And the blood with lithing seems fair clogged, and one kens
   one's named with the dead;

When the eye grows dim, and folk draw nigh from the other
   side of the grave,
It's late to square up old accounts a ganging soul to save.

364

The priest may come, and the priest may go, his well-worn
    tale to chant,
When the death-smear clams a wrinkled brow, it does not
    fetch one's want.

No book, no candle, bell, nor mass, nor priest of any land,
When the dree night comes, can patch a soul, or the tottering
    make to stand.

'T were a dree night, a dree night, for a soul to gang away,
A dree night, a dree night, but a ganging soul can't stay.

And the window-shuts they rattled sore, and the mad wild
    wind did shill,
And the Gabriel ratchets yelped above, a ganging soul to chill.

'T were a dree night, a dree night, for death to don his cowl,
To staup abroad with whimly tread, to claim a ganging soul.

But little death recks how dree the night be, or how a soul may
    pray,
When the sand runs out, his sickle reaps; a ganging soul can't
    stay.

'T were a dree night, a dree night, ower Whinny-moor to
    trake,
Wi' shoonless feet, ower flinty stones, through many a thorny
    brake.

A dree night, a dree night, with nowt noways to mark
The gainest tread to the Brig o' Dead; a lone lost soul in the
    dark.

A dree night, a dree night, at the brig foot there to meet
Little souls that he were the father of, with no good dame in
    seet.

At the altar steps he never stayed, though many a vow he
    made,
Now the debt he owes to many a lass at the brig foot must be
    paid.

They face him now with other deeds, like black spots on a
    sheet,
They now unscape, they egg him on, on the brig his doom to
    meet.

No doves have settled on his sill, but a flittermouse to greet
Came thrice times through the casement and flackered round
    his feet.

And thrice times did a raven croak, and the same-like thrice
    came the hoot
From the ullet's tree; down chimneys three, there came a
    shroud of soot.

And round the candle two times came a dark-winged moth to
    the light,
But the third it swirled right into the flame, where gangs
    his soul this night.

'T were a dree night, a dree night, for one to lait to pray,
A dree night, a dree night, but a ganging soul can't stay.

    dree: *doleful*; lithing: *thickening*; shill: *shrill*; staup: *stalk*;
    whimly: *quietly*; gainest: *shortest*; good dame: *wife*; seet:
    sight; lait: *seek to*

A LYKE-WAKE DIRGE

This ae night, this ae night,
    Every night and alle,
Fire, and sleet, and candle light,
    And Christ receive thy saule.

When thou from hence away are passed,
    Every night and alle,
To Whinny-muir thou comest at last,
    And Christ receive thy saule.

If ever thou gavest hosen and shoon,
    Every night and alle,
Sit thee down and put them on,
    And Christ receive thy saule.

If hosen and shoon thou ne'er gavest nane,
    Every night and alle,
The whinnes shall prick thee to the bare bane,
    And Christ receive thy saule.

From Whinny-muir when thou mayst pass,
    Every night and alle,
To Brigg o' Dread thou comest at last,
    And Christ receive thy saule.

From Brigg o' Dread when thou mayst pass,
   Every night and alle.
To purgatory fire thou comest at last,
   And Christ receive thy saule.

If ever thou gavest meat or drink,
   Every night and alle,
The fire shall never make thee shrink,
   And Christ receive thy saule.

If meat or drink thou never gavest nane,
   Every night and alle,
The fire will burn thee to the bare bane,
   And Christ receive thy saule.

This ae night, this ae night,
   Every night and alle,
Fire, and sleet, and candle light,
   And Christ receive thy saule.

THE GRAVE

When the turf is thy tower,
And thy put is thy bower,
Thy wel and thy wite throte
Ssulen wormês to note.
What helpit thee thenne
All the worildê wenne?

put: pit, grave; wel: skin; ssulen wormes to note: *shall be
enjoyment for worms*; worilde wenne: *world's pleasure*

OUT, OUT, BRIEF CANDLE!

To-morrow, and to-morrow, and to-morrow,
Creeps in this petty pace from day to day,
To the last syllable of recorded time;
And all our yesterdays have lighted fools
The way to dusty death. Out, out, brief candle!
Life's but a walking shadow, a poor player
That struts and frets his hour upon the stage,
And then is heard no more; it is a tale
Told by an idiot, full of sound and fury,
Signifying nothing . . .

                  William Shakespeare

OF THE DEATH OF KINGS

For God's sake, let us sit upon the ground,
And tell sad stories of the death of kings: —
How some have been deposed; some slain in war;
Some haunted by the ghosts they have deposed;
Some poison'd by their wives; some sleeping kill'd;
All murder'd: — for within the hollow crown
That rounds the mortal temples of a king
Keeps Death his court; and there the antick sits,
Scoffing his state, and grinning at his pomp;
Allowing him a breath, a little scene,
To monarchize, be fear'd, and kill with looks;
Infusing him with self and vain conceit, —
As if this flesh, which walls about our life,
Were brass impregnable; and humour'd thus,
Comes at the last, and with a little pin
Bores through his castle-wall, and — farewell king! . . .

William Shakespeare

24. LIFE AND DEATH

Life and Death

Our habit of living is strong, so most of mankind has believed in some variety of living after death, a continuance grey sometimes, sometimes peaceful and gentle, sometimes tortured, sometimes splendid and perpetual.

John Donne, writer of life and death poems of a very strong splendour (on pages 381, 382, and 383), thought much about the death of his body, but much as well about his life afterwards. Cold and ill in his study in London, a fire blazing on the hearth, Donne posed in his winding sheet to the sculptor Nicholas Stone, whose pale statue of him, rising from the dead at the last trump, you can still see in St Paul's Cathedral (since it survived the burning of Old St Paul's). But read the poems: – *Death, thou shalt die.* Read John Donne exclaiming, in a sermon about himself and his god, *I shall finde my self, and all my sins enterred, and entombed in his wounds, and like a Lily in Paradise, out of red earth, I shall see my soule rise out of his blade, in a candor, and in an innocence, contracted there, acceptable in the sight of his Father.*

Other poets believe in the gleam of enduring excellence, as Stephen Spender in his poem on page 377; and every good poem is a piece of the poet still alive, still enduring.

I have taken the woodcut of a king being carried to burial, with black-hooded attendants and mourners in black –

> *Here are sands (ignoble things)*
> *Dropt from the ruin'd sides of kings*

– out of the *Croniques de France*, which were printed in 1514.

MUCH KNOWLEDGE, LITTLE REASON

What is this knowledge but the sky-stolen fire,
  For which the thief still chained in ice doth sit,
And which the poor rude Satyr did admire,
  And needs would kiss, but burnt his lips with it?

What is it but the cloud of empty rain,
  Which when Jove's guest embraced, he monsters got,
Or the false pails, which oft being filled with pain
  Received the water, but retained it not?

Shortly, what is it but the fiery coach,
  Which the youth sought, and sought his death withal,
Or the boy's wings, which when he did approach
  The sun's hot beams, did melt and let him fall?

And yet, alas! when all our lamps are burned,
  Our bodies wasted, and our spirits spent;
When we have all the learned volumes turned,
  Which yield men's wits both help and ornament:

What can we know, or what can we discern,
  When error chokes the windows of the mind?
The divers forms of things how can we learn,
  That have been ever from our birthday blind?

When Reason's lamp, which, like the sun in sky,
  Throughout man's little world her beams did spread,
Is now become a sparkle, which doth lie
  Under the ashes, half extinct, and dead:

How can we hope, that through the eye and ear,
  This dying sparkle, in this cloudy place,
Can recollect these beams of knowledge clear,
  Which were infused in the first minds by grace? . . .

                                        Sir John Davies

I KNOW MYSELF A MAN

I know my body's of so frail a kind
  As force without, fevers within, can kill;
I know the heavenly nature of my mind,
  But 'tis corrupted both in wit and will;

I know my soul hath power to know all things,
    Yet is she blind and ignorant in all;
I know I am one of nature's little kings,
    Yet to the least and vilest things am thrall.

I know my life's a pain and but a span,
    I know my sense is mocked with everything;
And to conclude, I know myself a man,
    Which is a proud, and yet a wretched thing . . .

                              Sir John Davies

THE LIE

Go, soul, the body's guest,
    Upon a thankless arrant,
Fear not to touch the best,
    The truth shall be thy warrant:
Go, since I needs must die,
    And give the world the lie.

Say to the Court it glows,
    And shines like rotten wood,
Say to the Church it shows
    What's good, and doth no good.
If Church and Court reply,
    Then give them both the lie.

Tell potentates they live
    Acting by others' action,
Not loved unless they give,
    Not strong but by affection.
If potentates reply,
    Give potentates the lie.

Tell men of high condition
    That manage the estate,
Their purpose is ambition,
    Their practice only hate:
And if they once reply,
    Then give them all the lie.

Tell them that brave it most,
    They beg for more by spending,
Who in their greatest cost
    Seek nothing but commending.

And if they make reply,
   Then give them all the lie.

Tell zeal it wants devotion,
   Tell love it is but lust,
Tell time it metes but motion,
   Tell flesh it is but dust,
And wish them not reply,
   For thou must give the lie.

Tell age it daily wasteth,
   Tell honour how it alters.
Tell beauty how she blasteth,
   Tell favour how it falters,
And as they shall reply,
   Give every one the lie.

Tell wit how much it wrangles
   In tickle points of niceness,
Tell wisdom she entangles
   Herself in over wiseness.
And when they do reply
   Straight give them both the lie.

Tell physic of her boldness,
   Tell skill it is prevention:
Tell charity of coldness,
   Tell law it is contention,
And as they do reply
   So give them still the lie.

Tell fortune of her blindness,
   Tell nature of decay,
Tell friendship of unkindness,
   Tell justice of delay.
And if they will reply,
   Then give them all the lie.

Tell arts they have no soundness,
   But vary by esteeming,
Tell schools they want profoundness
   And stand too much on seeming.
If arts and schools reply,
   Give arts and schools the lie.

Tell faith it's fled the City,
   Tell how the country erreth,
Tell manhood shakes off pity,
   Tell virtue least preferreth
And if they do reply,
   Spare not to give the lie.

So when thou hast as I
   Commanded thee, done blabbing,
Although to give the lie
   Deserves no less than stabbing,
Stab at thee he that will,
   No stab thy soul can kill.

                              Sir Walter Ralegh

THE PEOPLE OF TAO-CHOU

In the land of Tao-chou
Many of the people are dwarfs;
The tallest of them never grow to more than three feet.
They were sold in the market as dwarf slaves and yearly sent
   to Court;
Described as 'an offering of natural products from the land of
   Tao-chou.'
A strange 'offering of natural products'; I never heard of one
   yet
That parted men from those they loved, never to meet again!
Old men – weeping for their grandsons; mothers for their
   children!
One day – Yang Ch'ēng came to govern the land;
He refused to send up dwarf slaves in spite of incessant
   mandates.
He replied to the Emperor: 'Your servant finds in the Six
   Canonical Books
In offering products, one must offer what is there, and not
   what isn't there.
On the waters and lands of Tao-chou, amongst all the things
   that live
I only find dwarfish *people*; no dwarfish *slaves*.'
The emperor's heart was deeply moved and he sealed and sent
   a scroll
'The yearly tribute of dwarfish slaves is henceforth annulled.'

374

The people of Tao-chou,
Old ones and young ones, how great their joy!
Father with son and brother with brother henceforward kept
    together;
From that day for ever more they lived as free men.
The people of Tao-chou
Still enjoy this gift.
And even now when they speak of the Governor
Tears start to their eyes.
And lest their children and their children's children should
    forget the Governor's name,
When boys are born the syllable 'Yang' is often used in their
    forename.

Po Chu-i (translated by
Arthur Waley)

THE SOUL'S DARK COTTAGE

The Soul's dark cottage, batter'd and decay'd,
Lets in new light through chinks that time has made.
Stronger by weakness, wiser men become
As they draw near to their eternal home:
Leaving the Old, both worlds at once they view,
That stand upon the threshold of the New . . .

Edmund Waller

IT IS NOT GROWING LIKE A TREE

It is not growing like a tree
In bulk, doth make man better be;
Or standing long an oak, three hundred year,
To fall a log, at last, dry, bald, and sere:
A lily of a day,
Is fairer far, in May,
Although it fall, and die that night;
It was the plant and flower of light.
In small proportions, we just beauties see:
And in short measures, life may perfect be . . .

Ben Jonson

THE DOOR OF DEATH

The Door of Death is made of gold,
That mortal eyes cannot behold;
But when the mortal eyes are clos'd,
And cold and pale the limbs repos'd,
The soul awakes; and, wond'ring, sees
In her mild hand the golden keys . . .

William Blake

LET US NOW PRAISE FAMOUS MEN

Let us now praise famous men, and our fathers that begat us.

The Lord hath wrought great glory by them through his great power from the beginning.

Such as did bear rule in their kingdoms, men renowned for their power, giving counsel by their understanding, and declaring prophecies:

Leaders of the people by their counsels, and by their knowledge of learning meet for the people, wise and eloquent in their instructions:

Such as found out musical tunes, and recited verses in writing:

Rich men furnished with ability, living peaceably in their habitations:

All these were honoured in their generations, and were the glory of their times.

There be of them, that have left a name behind them, that their praises might be reported.

And some there be, which have no memorial; who are perished as though they had never been; and are become as though they had never been born; and their children after them.

But these were merciful men, whose righteousness hath not been forgotten.

With their seed shall continually remain a good inheritance, and their children are within the covenant.

Their seed standeth fast, and their children for their sakes.

Their seed shall remain for ever, and their glory shall not be blotted out.

Their bodies are buried in peace; but their name liveth for evermore . . .

Ecclesiasticus

THE NOBLE

There is
One great society alone on earth:
The noble Living and the noble Dead . . .

William Wordsworth

I THINK CONTINUALLY OF THOSE

I think continually of those who were truly great.
Who, from the womb, remembered the soul's history
Through corridors of light where the hours are suns
Endless and singing. Whose lovely ambition
Was that their lips, still touched with fire,
Should tell of the Spirit clothed from head to foot in song.
And who hoarded from the Spring branches
The desires falling across their bodies like blossoms.

What is precious is never to forget
The essential delight of the blood drawn from ageless springs
Breaking through rocks in worlds before our earth.
Never to deny its pleasure in the morning simple light
Nor its grave evening demand for love.
Never to allow gradually the traffic to smother
With noise and fog the flowering of the spirit.

Near the snow, near the sun, in the highest fields
See how these names are fêted by the waving grass
And by the streamers of white cloud
And whispers of wind in the listening sky.
The names of those who in their lives fought for life
Who wore at their hearts the fire's centre.
Born of the sun they travelled a short while towards the sun,
And left the vivid air signed with their honour.

Stephen Spender

DEATH OF SAMSON

Come, come, no time for lamentation now,
Nor much more cause, Samson hath quit himself
Like Samson, and heroically hath finish'd
A life heroic, on his enemies
Fully reveng'd, hath left them years of mourning,
And lamentation to the Sons of Caphtor
Through all Philistian bounds. To Israel
Honour hath left, and freedom, let but them
Find courage to lay hold on this occasion,
To himself and father's house eternal fame;
And which is best and happiest yet, all this
With God not parted from him, as was fear'd,
But favouring and assisting to the end.
Nothing is here for tears, nothing to wail
Or knock the breast, no weakness, no contempt,
Dispraise, or blame, nothing but well and fair,
And what may quiet us in a death so noble.
Let us go find the body where it lies
Soak'd in his enemies' blood, and from the stream
With lavers pure and cleansing herbs wash off
The clotted gore . . .

John Milton

ON THE ARMY OF SPARTANS, WHO DIED
AT THERMOPYLAE

Tell them in Lacedaemon, passer-by,
We kept the Spartan code, and here we lie.

Simonides of Ceos

KING CHARLES UPON THE SCAFFOLD

He nothing common did or mean
Upon that memorable scene:
But with his keener eye
The axe's edge did try:
Nor call'd the Gods with vulgar spite
To vindicate his helpless right,
But bow'd his comely head,
Down as upon a bed . . .

Andrew Marvell

CROMWELL DEAD

I saw him dead, a leaden slumber lies,
And mortal sleep, over those wakeful eyes:
Those gentle rays under the lids were fled,
Which through his looks that piercing sweetness shed;
That port which so majestic was and strong,
Loose and depriv'd of vigour, stretch'd along:
All wither'd, all discolour'd, pale and wan,
How much another thing, no more than man?
Oh human glory, vain, Oh death, oh wings,
Oh worthless world, Oh transitory things!
Yet dwelt that greatness in his shape decay'd
That still though dead, greater than death he lay'd;
And in his alter'd face you something fain
That threatens death he yet will live again . . .

                                        Andrew Marvell

EPITAPH FOR A GODLY MAN'S TOMB

Here lies a piece of Christ; a star in dust;
A vein of gold; a china dish that must
Be used in heaven, when God shall feast the just.

                                        Robert Wild

GO THOU TO ROME
(The Grave of Keats — from Adonais)

Go thou to Rome, — at once the Paradise,
The grave, the city, and the wilderness;
And where its wrecks like shattered mountains rise,
And flowering weeds, and fragrant copses dress
The bones of Desolation's nakedness,
Pass, till the Spirit of the spot shall lead
Thy footsteps to a slope of green access,
Where, like an infant's smile, over the dead
A light of laughing flowers along the grass is spread,

And grey walls moulder round, on which dull Time
Feeds, like slow fire upon a hoary brand;
And one keen pyramid with wedge sublime,
Pavilioning the dust of him who planned

This refuge for his memory, doth stand
Like flame transformed to marble; and beneath
A field is spread, on which a newer band
Have pitched in Heaven's smile their camp of death,
Welcoming him we lose with scarce extinguished breath.

Here pause: these graves are all too young as yet
To have outgrown the sorrow which consigned
Its charge to each; and if the seal is set,
Here, on one fountain of a mourning mind,
Break it not thou! too surely shalt thou find
Thine own well full, if thou returnest home,
Of tears and gall. From the world's bitter wind
Seek shelter in the shadow of the tomb.
What Adonais is, why fear we to become?

The One remains, the many change and pass;
Heaven's light for ever shines, Earth's shadows fly;
Life, like a dome of many-coloured glass,
Stains the white radiance of Eternity,
Until Death tramples it to fragments. – Die,
If thou wouldst be with that which thou dost seek!
Follow where all is fled! – Rome's azure sky,
Flowers, ruins, statues, music, words, are weak
The glory they transfuse with fitting truth to speak.

Why linger, why turn back, why shrink, my Heart?
Thy hopes are gone before: from all things here
They have departed; thou shouldst now depart!
A light is passed from the revolving year,
And man, and woman; and what still is dear
Attracts to crush, repels to make thee wither.
The soft sky smiles, the low wind whispers near:
'Tis Adonais calls! oh, hasten thither,
No more let Life divide what Death can join together.

That Light whose smile kindles the Universe,
That Beauty in which all things work and move,
That Benediction which the eclipsing Curse
Of birth can quench not, that sustaining Love
Which through the web of being blindly wove
By man and beast and earth and air and sea,
Burns bright or dim, as each are mirrors of
The fire for which all thirst; now beams on me
Consuming the last clouds of cold mortality.

The breath whose might I have invoked in song
Descends on me; my spirit's bark is driven
Far from the shore, far from the trembling throng
Whose sails were never to the tempest given;
The massy earth and spherèd skies are riven!
I am borne darkly, fearfully, afar;
Whilst burning through the inmost veil of Heaven,
The soul of Adonais, like a star,
Beacons from the abode where the Eternal are.

Percy Bysshe Shelley

DEATH, BE NOT PROUD

Death, be not proud, though some have callèd thee
Mighty and dreadful, for, thou art not so,
For those whom thou think'st, thou dost overthrow,
Die not, poor death, nor yet canst thou kill me.
From rest and sleep, which but thy pictures be,
Much pleasure, then from thee much more must flow,
And soonest our best men with thee do go,
Rest of their bones, and souls' delivery.
Thou art slave to fate, chance, kings and desperate men,
And dost with poison, war, and sickness dwell,
And poppy, or charms can make us sleep as well,
And better than thy stroke; why swell'st thou then?
One short sleep past, we wake eternally,
And death shall be no more; death, thou shalt die.

John Donne

EVEN SUCH IS TIME

Even such is Time, which takes in trust
Our youth, our joys, and all we have,
And pays us but with age and dust:
Who in the dark and silent grave,
When we have wandred all our ways,
Shuts up the story of our days.
But from this earth, this grave, this dust,
The Lord shall raise me up, I trust.

Sir Walter Ralegh

EPITAPH OF GRAUNDE AMOURE

O mortal folk, you may behold and see
How I lie here, sometime a mighty knight;
The end of joy and all prosperity
Is death at last, thorough his course and might;
After the day there cometh the dark night;
For though the day be never so long,
At last the bells ringeth to evensong.

And my self called La Graunde Amoure,
Seeking adventure in the worldly glory,
For to attain the riches and honoure,
Did think full lytell that I should here lie,
Till death did mate me full right privily.
Lo what I am! and where to you must!
Like as I am, so shall you be all dust.

Then in your mind inwardly despise
The brittle world so full of doubleness,
With the vile flesh, and right soon arise
Out of your sleep of mortal heaviness;
Subdue the devil with grace and mekeness,
That after your life frail and transitory
You may then live in joy perdurably . . .

Stephen Hawes

BLOW YOUR TRUMPETS, ANGELS

At the round earths imagin'd corners, blow
Your trumpets, Angels, and arise, arise
From death, you numberless infinities
Of souls, and to your scattred bodies go,
All whom the flood did, and fire shall o'erthrow,
All whom war, dearth, age, agues, tyrannies,
Despair, law, chance, hath slain, and you whose eyes,
Shall behold God, and never taste deaths woe.
But let them sleep, Lord, and me mourn a space,
For, if above all these, my sins abound,
'Tis late to ask abundance of thy grace,
When we are there; here on this lowly ground,
Teach me how to repent; for that's as good
As if thou hadst seal'd my pardon, with thy blood.

John Donne

VERSES COMPOSED ON THE EVE OF
HIS EXECUTION

Let them bestow on every airth a limb,
Then open all my veins that I may swim
To thee, my Maker, in that crimson lake;
Then place my parboiled head upon a stake,
Scatter my ashes, strew them in the air —
Lord! since thou knowest where all these atoms are,
I'm hopeful thou'lt recover once my dust,
And confident thou'lt raise me with the just

James Graham, Marquis of Montrose

airth: *point of the compass*

HYMN TO GOD MY GOD, IN MY SICKNESS

Since I am coming to that holy room,
    Where, with thy choir of saints for evermore,
I shall be made thy music; as I come
    I tune the instrument here at the door,
    And what I must do then, think here before.

While my physicians by their love are grown
    Cosmographers, and I their map, who lie
Flat on this bed, that by them may be shown
    That this is my south-west discovery
    Per fretum febris, by these straits to die,

I joy, that in these straits, I see my West;
    For though their currents yield return to none,
What shall my West hurt me? As West and East
    In all flat maps (and I am one) are one,
    So death doth touch the Resurrection.

Is the Pacific Sea my home? Or are
    The eastern riches? Is Jerusalem?
Anyan, and Magellan, and Gibraltare,
    All straits, and none but straits, are ways to them,
    Whether where Japhet dwelt, or Cham, or Sem.

We think that Paradise and Calvary,
    Christ's Cross, and Adam's tree, stood in one place;
Look, Lord, and find both Adams met in me;
    As the first Adam's sweat surrounds my face,
    May the last Adam's blood my soul embrace.

So, in his purple wrapp'd receive me, Lord,
  By these his thorns give me his other crown;
And as to others' souls I preach'd thy word,
  Be this my text, my sermon to mine own,
  Therefore that he may raise the Lord throws down.

John Donne

THEY ARE ALL GONE INTO THE WORLD OF LIGHT

They are all gone into the world of light!
  And I alone sit ling'ring here!
Their very memory is fair and bright,
  And my sad thoughts doth clear.

It glows and glitters in my cloudy breast
  Like stars upon some gloomy grove,
Or those faint beams in which this hill is dressed
  After the Sun's remove.

I see them walking in an air of glory,
  Whose light doth trample on my days;
My days, which are at best but dull and hoary,
  Mere glimmering and decays.

O holy Hope! and high Humility!
  High as the Heavens above;
These are your walks, and you have shew'd them me
  To kindle my cold love.

Dear, beauteous death; the Jewel of the Just!
  Shining no where but in the dark;
What mysteries do lie beyond thy dust,
  Could man outlook that mark!

He that hath found some fledg'd bird's nest may know
  At first sight if the bird be flown;
But what fair dell or grove he sings in now,
  That is to him unknown.

And yet, as Angels in some brighter dreams
  Call to the soul when man doth sleep,
So some strange thoughts transcend our wonted themes,
  And into glory peep . . .

Henry Vaughan

Woefully arrayed,
My blood, man,
For thee ran,
It may not be nay'd:
My body blue and wan,
Woefully arrayed.

Behold me, I pray thee, with thy whole reason,
And be not so hard-hearted, and for this encheason,
Sith I for thy soul sake was slain in good season,
Beguiled and betrayed by Judas' false treason:
Unkindly entreated,
With sharp cord sore fretted,
The Jews me threated:
They mowed, they grinned, they scorned me,
Condemned to death, as thou may'st see,
Woefully arrayed.

Thus naked am I nailed, O man, for thy sake.
I love thee, then love me; why sleepest thou? Awake!
Remember my tender heart-root for thee brake,
With pains my veins constrained to crake.
Thus tugged to and fro,
Thus wrapped all in woe,
Whereas never man was so,
Entreated thus in most cruel wise,
Was like a lamb offered in sacrifice,
Woefully arrayed.

Of sharp thorn I have worn a crown on my head,
So pained, so strained, so rueful, so red,
Thus bobbed, thus robbed, thus for thy love dead,
Unfeigned I deigned my blood for to shed.
My feet and handës sore
The sturdy nailës bore:
What might I suffer more
Than I have done, O man, for thee?
Come when thou list, welcome to me,
Woefully arrayed.

Of record thy good Lord I have been and shall be:
I am thine, thou art mine, my brother I call thee.

Thee love I entirely – see what is befall'n me!
Sore beating, sore threating, to make thee, man, all free;
      Why art thou unkind?
      Why hast not me in mind?
      Come yet and thou shalt find
Mine endless mercy and grace –
See how a spear my heart did race,
      Woefully arrayed.

Dear brother, no other thing I of thee desire
But give me thine heart free to reward mine hire:
I wrought thee, I brought thee from eternal fire;
I pray thee array thee toward my high empire
      Above the orient,
      Whereof I am regent,
      Lord God omnipotent,
With me to reign in endless wealth:
Remember, man, thy soul's health.

      Woefully arrayed,
        My blood, man,
        For thee ran,
      It may not be nay'd:
        My body blue and wan,
      Woefully arrayed.

nay'd: *denied*; encheason: *cause*; threated: *vexed, mal-*
treated; mowed: *made faces*; bobbed: *struck or mocked*; race:
wound   ? John Skelton

HYMNUS

God be in my hede
   And in my understandyng,
God be in myne eyes
   And in my loking,
God be in my mouth
   And in my speaking,
God be in my harte
   And in my thynkyng,
God be at mine ende
   And at my departyng.

25. WINTER

Winter

Outdoors and Indoors are two different winters. On the next page you have Winter Outdoors in an Irish poem written – when? A thousand or eleven hundred years ago. The Irish said it was a poem by their hero Finn, the warrior, wizard, and poet of legend, and leader of the Fiana or Fenians. And Winter Indoors? In contrast to *The Words of Finn*, you have it, on page 395, celebrated by another Irish poet, in a poem of our own century. *Bolt and bar the door*, says W. B. Yeats. *Shut out the mist and snow*; and tonight, indoors, in winter, our bodies are idle, and our minds are best at work; which is the great pleasure of the winter-time.

The ancient Irish (and the Welsh as well) were especially good at poems of summer, autumn, winter, and nature, and I suppose that Walter de la Mare wrote his winter poems (on pages 390, 393, and 394), so cunningly rhythmical, so frosty and delicate, so strong at the same time, with such Irish winter poems in his head – particularly some English version of *The Words of Finn*.

The round woodcut – warming hands and feet at the fire – stands for February in a German calendar of about 1485. Pot and all, it would stand very well, too, for another Irish poem, which Kenneth Jackson has translated:

> . . . Sad are the birds of every meadow-plain
> (except the ravens that feed on crimson blood)
> at the clamour of fierce winter;
> it is rough, black, dark, misty.
> Dogs are vicious in cracking bones;
> the iron pot is put on the fire
> after the dark black day.

– Or for Shakespeare's winter poem of cold indoors and chilled noses on page 392.

THE WORDS OF FINN

My words for you:
Stag ruts and bells,
Winter pours down,
Summer has gone.

Wind's high and cold,
Low is the sun,
Briefer its run.
Runs the sea strong.

Turns red the fern,
Broken its form.
Habit is hearing
The wild goose's song.

Season of ice,
Wings of the birds
Caught by the cold.
These are my words.

From the Old Irish

THE HIGH WIND

Arthur o'Bower has broken his band
And he comes roaring up the land;
The King of Scots with all his power
Cannot stop Arthur of the Bower.

THE MORNING STAR

Cold, clear, and blue, the morning heaven
Expands its arch on high;
Cold, clear, and blue, Lake Werna's water
Reflects that winter's sky.
The moon has set, but Venus shines
A silent, silvery star.

Emily Brontë

ALONE

The abode of the nightingale is bare,
Flowered frost congeals in the gelid air,
The fox howls from his lair:
    Alas, my loved one is gone,
    I am alone:
    It is winter.

Once the pink cast a winy smell,
The wild bee hung in the hyacinth bell,
Light in effulgence of beauty fell:
    Alas, my loved one is gone,
    I am alone:
    It is winter.

My candle a silent fire doth shed,
Starry Orion hunts o'erhead;
Come moth, come shadow, the world is dead:
    Alas, my loved one is gone,
    I am alone;
    It is winter.

Walter de la Mare

WINTER'S TROOPS

Like an invader, not a guest,
He comes to riot, not to feast;
And in wild fury overthrows
Whatever does his march oppose.

With bleak and with congealing winds,
The earth in shining chains he binds;
And still as he doth farther pass,
Quarries his way with liquid glass.

Hark, how the blusterers of the Bear
Their gibbous cheeks in triumph tear,
And with continued shouts do ring
The entry of their palsy'd king.

The squadron nearest to your eye
Is his forlorn of infantry,
Bow-men of unrelenting minds,
Whose shafts are feathered with the winds.

Now you may see his vanguard rise
Above the beachy precipice,
Bold horse on bleakest mountains bred,
With hail instead of provend fed.

Their launces are the pointed locks
Torn from the brows of frozen rocks,
Their shields are crystal as their swords,
The steel the crusted rock affords.

See the main body now appears,
And hark the Aeolian trumpeters,
By their hoarse levets do declare
That the bold General rides there.

And look where mantled up in white
He sleds it like the Muscovite;
I know him by the port he bears,
And his life-guard of Mountaineers.

Their caps are furred with hoary frosts,
The bravery their cold kingdom boasts;
Their spumy plaids are milk-white frieze
Spun from the snowy mountain's fleece.

Their partizans are fine carved glass,
Fringed with the morning's spangled grass;
And pendant by their brawny thighs
Hang scimitars of burnished ice.

See, see, the rear-ward now has won
The promontory's trembling crown,
Whilst at their numerous spurs the ground
Groans out a hollow murmuring sound.

The forlorn now halts for the van;
The rear-guard draws up to the main;
And now they altogether crowd
Their troops into a threat'ning cloud.

Fly, fly; the foe advances fast;
Into our fortress let us haste
Where all the roarers of the North
Can neither storm, nor starve us forth . . .

Charles Cotton

WINTER

When icicles hang by the wall,
   And Dick the shepherd blows his nail,
And Tom bears logs into the hall,
   And milk comes frozen home in pail;
When blood is nipped, and ways be foul,
Then nightly sings the staring owl.
Tu-whit, tu-who! a merry note,
While greasy Joan doth keel the pot.

When all aloud the wind doth blow,
   And coughing drowns the parson's saw,
And birds sit brooding in the snow,
   And Marian's nose looks red and raw,
When roasted crabs hiss in the bowl,
Then nightly sings the staring owl,
Tu-whit, tu-who! a merry note,
While greasy Joan doth keep the pot.

William Shakespeare

A CHILD THAT HAS A COLD

A child that has a cold we may suppose
Like wintry weather — Why? — it blows its nose.

Thomas Dibdin

NO!

No sun — no moon!
No morn — no noon —
No dawn — no dusk — no proper time of day —
No sky — no earthly view —
No distance looking blue —
No road — no street — no 't'other side the way' —
No end to any Row —

392

No indications where the Crescents go —
No top to any steeple —
No recognitions of familiar people —
No courtesies for showing 'em —
No knowing 'em! —
No travelling at all — no locomotion,
No inkling of the way — no notion —
'No go' — by land or ocean —
No mail — no post —
No news from any foreign coast —
No Park — no Ring — no afternoon gentility —
No company — no nobility —
No warmth, no cheerfulness, no healthful ease,
No comfortable feel in any member —
No shade, no shine, no butterflies, no bees,
No fruits, no flowers, no leaves, no birds —
    November!

Thomas Hood

A ROBIN

Ghost-grey the fall of night,
    Ice-bound the lane,
Lone in the dying light
    Flits he again;
Lurking where shadows steal,
Perched in his coat of blood,
Man's homestead at his heel,
    Death-still the wood.

Odd restless child; it's dark;
    All wings are flown
But this one wizard's — hark!
    Stone clapped on stone!
Changeling and solitary,
Secret and sharp and small,
Flits he from tree to tree,
    Calling on all.

Walter de la Mare

A WINTER NIGHT

It was a chilly winter's night;
   And frost was glitt'ring on the ground,
And evening stars were twinkling bright;
   And from the gloomy plain around
      Came no sound,
But where, within the wood-girt tow'r,
The churchbell slowly struck the hour;

As if that all of human birth
   Had risen to the final day,
And soaring from the worn-out earth
   Were called in hurry and dismay,
      Far away;
And I alone of all mankind
Were left in loneliness behind.

William Barnes

WINTER

Green Mistletoe!
Oh, I remember now
A dell of snow,
Frost on the bough;
None there but I:
Snow, snow, and a wintry sky.

None there but I,
And footprints one by one,
Zigzaggedly,
Where I had run;
Where shrill and powdery
A robin sat in the tree.

And he whistled sweet;
And I in the crusted snow
With snow-clubbed feet
Jigged to and fro,
Till, from the day,
The rose-light ebbed away.

And the robin flew
Into the air, the air,
The white mist through;

And small and rare
The night-frost fell
Into the calm and misty dell.

And the dusk gathered low,
And the silver moon and stars
On the frozen snow
Drew taper bars,
Kindled winking fires
In the hooded briers.

And the sprawling Bear
Growled deep in the sky;
And Orion's hair
Streamed sparkling by:
But the North sighed low:
'*Snow, snow, more snow!*'

Walter de la Mare

RIDDLES

i

A white bird floats down through the air
And never a tree but he lights there.

ii

White bird featherless
Flew from Paradise,
Pitched on the castle wall;
Along came Lord Landless,
Took it up handless
And rode away horseless
To the king's white hall.

(*Snow*; *Snow and Sun*)

MAD AS THE MIST AND SNOW

Bolt and bar the shutter,
For the foul winds blow:
Our minds are at their best this night,
And I seem to know
That everything outside us is
Mad as the mist and snow.

Horace there by Homer stands,
Plato stands below,
And here is Tully's open page.
How many years ago
Were you and I unlettered lads
Mad as the mist and snow?

You ask what makes me sigh, old friend,
What makes me shudder so?
I shudder and I sigh to think
That even Cicero
And many-minded Homer were
Mad as the mist and snow.

W. B. Yeats

SNOWFLAKES

Out of the bosom of the Air,
  Out of the cloud-folds of her garments shaken,
Over the woodlands brown and bare,
  Over the harvest-fields forsaken,
    Silent, and soft, and slow
    Descends the snow.

Even as our cloudy fancies take
  Suddenly shape in some divine expression,
Even as the troubled heart doth make
  In white countenance confession,
    The troubled sky reveals
    The grief it feels.

This is the poem of the Air,
  Slowly in silent syllables recorded;
This is the secret of despair,
  Long in its cloudy bosom hoarded,
    Now whispered and revealed
    To wood and field.

H. W. Longfellow

26. MOON AND STARS

Moon and Stars

Do you ever feel like Thomas Traherne who looked not only at the ripe wheat in Herefordshire, but at the streets, the people, the moon, the stars, feeling that they were all new; and that no one saw them except himself?

The city seemed to stand in Eden, or to be built in Heaven. The streets were mine, the temple was mine, the people were mine, their clothes and gold and silver were mine, as much as their smiling eyes, fair skins and ruddy faces. The skies were mine and so were the sun and moon and stars, and all the world was mine; and I the only spectator and enjoyer of it.

The phases of the moon, risings and settings of planets, constellations and individual stars of the first magnitude wheeling around the Pole Star, shooting stars, which fall in their periods – all of these glitter in poems; and all of them (which is difficult if you live in a city, where the lights are strong), frosty in the winter sky, paler in the summer sky, need to be known and not taken for granted. To know frosty Orion and the Pleiades, yellow Arcturus, bright Vega in the summer zenith, the Dragon winding between the Great and Little Bears, Sirius, Altair, to know the great box of Pegasus rising up in the autumn sky, is at any rate both excitement and comfort. Coleridge used to gaze at the Evening Star from the leads of Christ's Hospital, his school; and this planet, the star of love since Babylonian times, comforted him all his life. Sometimes it is so bright that it will cast a shadow.

As for other planets, turn back to Walt Whitman, on page 197. Read him, too, on page 236.

TO THE EVENING STAR

Thou fair-hair'd angel of the evening,
Now, whilst the sun rests on the mountains, light
Thy bright torch of love; thy radiant crown
Put on, and smile upon our evening bed!
Smile on our loves, and, while thou drawest the
Blue curtains of the sky, scatter thy silver dew
On every flower that shuts its sweet eyes
In timely sleep. Let thy west wind sleep on
The lake; speak silence with thy glimmering eyes,
And wash the dusk with silver. Soon, full soon,
Dost thou withdraw; then the wolf rages wide,
And the lion glares thro' the dun forest:
The fleeces of our flocks are cover'd with
Thy sacred dew: protect them with thine influence.

William Blake

THE EVENING STAR

Hesperus! the day is gone,
Soft falls the silent dew,
A tear is now on many a flower
And heaven lives in you.

Hesperus! the evening mild
Falls round us soft and sweet.
'Tis like the breathings of a child
When day and evening meet.

Hesperus! the closing flower
Sleeps on the dewy ground,
While dews fall in a silent shower
And heaven breathes around.

Hesperus! thy twinkling ray
Beams in the blue of heaven,
And tells the traveller on his way
That Earth shall be forgiven!

John Clare

399

EVENING QUATRAINS

The day's grown old, the fainting sun
Has but a little way to run,
And yet his steeds, with all his skill,
Scarce lug the chariot down the hill.

With labour spent, and thirst opprest,
While they strain hard to gain the West,
From fetlocks hot drops melted light,
Which turns to meteors in the night.

The shadows now so long do grow,
That brambles like tall cedars show,
Mole-hills seem mountains, and the ant
Appears a monstrous elephant.

A very little, little flock
Shades thrice the ground that it would stock;
Whilst the small stripling following them,
Appears a mighty Polyphem.

These being brought into the fold,
And by the thrifty master told,
He thinks his wages are well paid,
Since none are either lost, or stray'd . . .

The hedge is stripped, the clothes brought in,
Nought's left without should be within,
The bees are hiv'd, and hum their charm,
Whilst every house does seem a swarm.

The cock now to the roost is prest;
For he must call up all the rest;
The sow's fast pegg'd within the sty,
To still her squeaking progeny.

Each one has had his supping mess,
The cheese is put into the press,
The pans and bowls clean scalded all,
Rear'd up against the milk-house wall.

And now on benches all are sat
In the cool air to sit and chat,
Till Phoebus, dipping in the West,
Shall lead the world the way to rest.

Charles Cotton

Stars, I have seen them fall,
   But when they drop and die
No star is lost at all
   From all the star-sown sky.
The toil of all that be
   Helps not the primal fault;
It rains into the sea,
   And still the sea is salt.

A. E. Housman

THE STARS

Stars of the superior class,
Which in magnitude surpass,
From the time they rose and shone,
Have their names and places known.

Mazaroth his circuit runs,
With Arcturus and his sons;
Pleiad twinkles o'er the streams
Of Orion's bolder beams.

But what glories in array
Brighten all the milky way,
Where innumerables vie,
Told alone by God Most High! . . .

Christopher Smart

THE MOON AND THE NIGHTINGALE

Now came still Ev'ning on, and Twilight gray
Had in her sober livery all things clad;
Silence accompanied, for beast and bird,
They to their grassy couch, these to their nests,
Were slunk, all but the wakeful nightingale;
She all night long her amorous descant sung;
Silence was pleas'd: now glow'd the firmament
With living sapphires: Hesperus that led
The starry host, rose brightest, till the Moon
Rising in clouded majesty, at length
Apparent Queen, unveil'd her peerless light,
And o'er the dark her silver mantle threw . . .

John Milton

RIDDLE

In Mornigan's park there is a deer,
Silver horns and golden ear,
Neither fish, flesh, feather nor bone,
In Mornigan's park she walks alone.

(The crescent moon)

ACQUAINTED WITH THE NIGHT

I have been one acquainted with the night.
I have walked out in rain — and back in rain.
I have outwalked the furthest city light.

I have looked down the saddest city lane.
I have passed by the watchman on his beat
And dropped my eyes, unwilling to explain.

I have stood still and stopped the sound of feet
When far away an interrupted cry
Came over houses from another street,

But not to call me back or say good-bye;
And further still at an unearthly height,
One luminary clock against the sky
Proclaimed the time was neither wrong nor right.
I have been one acquainted with the night.

Robert Frost

ETHINTHUS, QUEEN OF WATERS

Ethinthus, queen of water, how thou shinest in the sky!
My daughter, how do I rejoice! for thy children flock around
Like the gay fishes on the wave, when the cold moon drinks
the dew . . .

William Blake

NIGHT AIRS AND MOONSHINE

Night airs that make tree-shadows walk, and sheep
Washed white in the cold moonshine on grey cliffs.

Walter Savage Landor

402

Queen, and Huntress, chaste, and fair,
　　Now the Sun is laid to sleep,
Seated, in thy silver chair,
　　State in wonted manner keep:
Hesperus intreats thy light,
Goddess, excellently bright.

Earth, let not thy envious shade
　　Dare it self to interpose;
Cynthia's shining orb was made
　　Heaven to clear, when day did close;
Bless us then with wishèd sight,
Goddess, excellently bright.

Lay thy bow of pearl apart,
　　And thy crystal-shining quiver;
Give unto the flying hart
　　Space to breathe, how short soever:
Thou that mak'st a day of night,
Goddess, excellently bright.

　　　　　　　　　　　　　　　　　Ben Jonson

WELCOME TO THE MOON

Welcome, precious stone of the night,
Delight of the skies, precious stone of the night,
Mother of stars, precious stone of the night,
Child reared by the sun, precious stone of the night,
Excellency of stars, precious stone of the night.

　　　　　　　　　　　　　　　From the Gaelic

THE NIGHT-WIND

In summer's mellow midnight,
A cloudless moon shone through
Our open parlour window
And rose-trees wet with dew.

I sat in silent musing,
The soft wind waved my hair:
It told me Heaven was glorious,
And sleeping Earth was fair.

I needed not its breathing
To bring such thoughts to me,
But still it whispered lowly,
'How dark the woods will be!

'The thick leaves in my murmur
Are rustling like a dream,
And all their myriad voices
Instinct with spirit seem.'

I said, 'Go, gentle singer,
Thy wooing voice is kind,
But do not think its music
Has power to reach my mind.

'Play with the scented flower,
The young tree's supple bough,
And leave my human feelings
In their own course to flow.'

The wanderer would not leave me;
Its kiss grew warmer still —
'O come', it sighed so sweetly,
'I'll win thee 'gainst thy will.

'Have we not been from childhood friends?
Have I not loved thee long?
As long as thou hast loved the night
Whose silence wakes my song.

'And when thy heart is laid at rest
Beneath the church-yard stone
I shall have time enough to mourn
And thou to be alone.'

Emily Brontë

THE MOON HAS SET

The moon has set,
The Seven Stars have set as well:
It is the middle of the night,
The hour goes by,
And by myself I lie.

From the Greek of Sappho

Mellow the moonlight to shine is beginning,
Close by the window young Eileen is spinning;
Bent over the fire her blind grandmother, sitting,
Is crooning, and moaning, and drowsily knitting: —
'Eileen, achora, I hear someone tapping.'
''Tis the ivy, dear mother, against the glass flapping.'
'Eily, I surely hear somebody sighing.'
''Tis the sound, mother dear, of the summer wind dying.'
  Merrily, cheerily, noiselessly whirring,
  Swings the wheel, spins the wheel, while the foot's stirring;
  Sprightly and brightly and airily ringing
  Thrills the sweet voice of the young maiden singing.

'What's that noise that I hear at the window, I wonder?'
''Tis the little birds chirping the holly-bush under.'
'What makes you be shoving and moving your stool on,
And singing, all wrong, that old song of "The Coolin"?'
There's a form at the casement — the form of her true love —
And he whispers, with face bent, 'I'm waiting for you, love;
Get up on the stool, through the lattice step lightly,
We'll rove in the grove while the moon's shining brightly.'
  Merrily, cheerily, noiselessly whirring,
  Swings the wheel, spins the wheel, while the foot's stirring;
  Sprightly and brightly and airily ringing
  Thrills the sweet voice of the young maiden singing.

The maid shakes her head, on her lips lays her fingers,
Steals up from her seat — longs to go, and yet lingers:
A frightened glance turns to her drowsy grandmother,
Puts one foot on the stool, spins the wheel with the other.
Lazily, easily, swings now the wheel round,
Slowly and lowly is heard now the reel's sound;
Noiseless and light to the lattice above her
The maid steps — then leaps to the arms of her lover.
  Slower — and slower — and slower the wheel swings;
  Lower — and lower — and lower the reel rings;
  Ere the reel and the wheel stop their ringing and moving,
  Through the grove the young lovers by moonlight are
    roving.

John Francis Waller

I GAZED UPON THE CLOUDLESS MOON

I gazed upon the cloudless moon,
And loved her all the night,
Till morning came and radiant noon,
And I forgot her light —

No, not forget — eternally
Remains its memory dear;
But could the day seem dark to me
Because the night was fair?

Emily Brontë

PHASES OF THE MOON

Lo, the moon's self!
Here in London, yonder late in Florence,
Still we find her face, the thrice-transfigured.
Curving on a sky imbrued with colour,
Drifted over Fiesole by twilight,
Came she, our new crescent of a hair's-breadth
Full she flared it, lamping Samminiato,
Rounder 'twixt the cypresses and rounder,
Perfect, till the nightingales applauded.
Now, a piece of her old self, impoverished,
Hard to greet, she traverses the houseroofs,
Hurries with unhandsome thrift of silver,
Goes dispiritedly, glad to finish . . .

Robert Browning

TO THE MOON

'What have you looked at, Moon,
    In your time,
Now long past your prime?'
'O, I have looked at, often looked at
    Sweet, sublime,
Sore things, shudderful, night and noon
    In my time.'

'What have you mused on, Moon,
    In your day,
So aloof, so far away?'

'O, I have mused on, often mused on
    Growth, decay,
Nations alive, dead, mad, aswoon,
    In my day!'

  'Have you much wondered, Moon,
    On your rounds,
  Self-wrapt, beyond Earth's bounds?'
'Yea, I have wondered, often wondered
    At the sounds
Reaching me of the human tune
    On my rounds.'

  'What do you think of it, Moon,
    As you go?'
  Is Life much, or no?'
'O, I think of it, often think of it
    As a show
God ought surely to shut up soon,
    As I go.'

Thomas Hardy

THE NIGHT MAIL

This is the night mail crossing the border,
Bringing the cheque and the postal order,
Letters for the rich, letters for the poor,
The shop at the corner and the girl next door,
Pulling up Beattock, a steady climb —
The gradient's against her but she's on time.

Past cotton grass and moorland boulder,
Shovelling white steam over her shoulder,
Snorting noisily as she passes
Silent miles of wind-bent grasses;
Birds turn their heads as she approaches,
Stare from the bushes at her blank-faced coaches;
Sheepdogs cannot turn her course,
They slumber on with paws across;
In the farm she passes no one wakes
But a jug in a bedroom gently shakes.

Dawn freshens, the climb is done.
Down towards Glasgow she descends
Towards the steam tugs, yelping down the glade of cranes
Towards the fields of apparatus, the furnaces
Set on the dark plain like gigantic chessmen.
All Scotland waits for her;
In the dark glens, beside the pale-green sea lochs,
Men long for news.

Letters of thanks, letters from banks,
Letters of joy from the girl and boy,
Receipted bills and invitations
To inspect new stock or visit relations,
And applications for situations,
And timid lovers' declarations,
And gossip, gossip from all the nations,
News circumstantial, news financial,
Letters with holiday snaps to enlarge in,
Letters with faces scrawled on the margin.
Letters from uncles, cousins and aunts,
Letters to Scotland from the South of France,
Letters of condolence to Highlands and Lowlands,
Notes from overseas to the Hebrides;
Written on paper of every hue,
The pink, the violet, the white and the blue,
The chatty, the catty, the boring, adoring,
The cold and official and the heart's outpouring,
Clever, stupid, short and long,
The typed and the printed and the spelt all wrong.

Thousands are still asleep
Dreaming of terrifying monsters
Or a friendly tea beside the band at Cranston's or Crawford's;
Asleep in working Glasgow, asleep in well-set Edinburgh,
Asleep in granite Aberdeen.
They continue their dreams
But shall wake soon and long for letters.
And none will hear the postman's knock
Without a quickening of the heart,
For who can bear to feel himself forgotten?

                                        W. H. Auden

The mountain summits sleep: glens, cliffs, and caves
Are silent — all the black earth's reptile brood,
The bees, the wild beasts of the mountain wood:
In depths beneath the dark red ocean's waves
Its monsters rest, whilst, wrapt in bower and spray,
Each bird is hushed that stretched its pinions to the day.

Alcman (translated by
Thomas Campbell)

SLEEP

Sleep is a god too proud to wait in palaces
And yet so humble too as not to scorn
The meanest country cottages;
His poppy grows among the corn.
The Halcyon sleep will never build his nest
In any stormy breast.
'Tis not enough that he does find
Clouds and darkness in their mind;
Darkness but half his work will do:
'Tis not enough; he must find quiet too . . .

Abraham Cowley

TO SLEEP

O soft embalmer of the still midnight!
Shutting, with careful fingers and benign,
Our gloom-pleased eyes, embower'd from the light,
Enshaded in forgetfulness divine;
O soothest Sleep! if so it please thee, close,
In midst of this thine hymn, my willing eyes,
Or wait the amen, ere thy poppy throws
Around my bed its lulling charities;
Then save me, or the passèd day will shine
Upon my pillow, breeding many woes;
Save me from curious conscience, that still lords
Its strength for darkness, burrowing like a mole;
Turn the key deftly in the oilèd wards,
And seal the hushèd casket of my soul.

John Keats

*O

SLEEP IS A RECONCILING

Weep you no more, sad fountains;
  What need you flow so fast?
Look how the snowy mountains
  Heaven's sun doth gently waste.
    But my sun's heavenly eyes
      View not your weeping,
      That now lies sleeping
    Softly, now softly lies
        Sleeping.

Sleep is a reconciling,
  A rest that peace begets.
Doth not the sun rise smiling
  When fair at even he sets?
    Rest you then, rest, sad eyes,
      Melt not in weeping,
      While she lies sleeping
    Softly, now softly lies
        Sleeping.

GO TO BED

Go to bed first
A golden purse;
Go to bed second
A golden bezant;
Go to bed third
A golden bird.

27. THE DAYS OF CHRISTMAS

The Days of Christmas

In the fifteenth century the English made carols of innocence and delight about the birth of Christ. Those who wrote them were probably friars of the order of St Francis, who disliked a sour and heavy and always severe religion, and delighted as much in the birth of Christ in winter as ordinary people delighted in carols and dances about love (carols were at first a combination of singing and dancing). With their new carols about the Child and his Mother, the Ox and the Ass, the Star, and the Three Kings, Jasper, Balthazar, and Melchior, the friars invented a way of feeling about Christmas which we have never abandoned, and which poets have maintained.

> There cam thre kynges fro Galylee
> Onto Bethleem, that fayre cytee,
> To seke hym that shulde ever be,
> By ryght-a,
> Lorde and Kynge, and Knight-a.

In the huge cathedrals such as York Minster or the cathedrals of France and Germany, they performed a Star play or Office of the Star, on Epiphany morning, the Twelfth Day of Christmas. The clergy acted the Three Kings. In robes of silk, with crowns on their heads, they entered from three different directions, recognized the Star, a golden one aloft in the cathedral, and kissed at the high altar. Then they followed the Star as it was drawn through the nave on a string; they encountered Herod and the Shepherds, and at last, carrying their gold, frankincense, and myrrh in golden and jewelled vessels out of the cathedral treasury, they found Bethlehem by the west door, and Christ in his crib – under the Star – and the Ox and the Ass; and offered their gifts.

I wish the Star play had caused more English poems and better English carols to be written about Jasper, Balthazar, and Melchior. Their legend, which spread through the North from their shrine in Cologne Cathedral, rooted itself in England too late. Yet these Christmas poems come to an end on page 426 with two lines, which in my judgment are among the most delightful ever written in our language; and I suppose John Milton would never have written them, if it had not been for that Stella or Office of the Star, long before he was born.

CHRISTMAS

Some say that ever 'gainst that season comes
Wherein our Saviour's birth is celebrated,
The bird of dawning singeth all night long;
And then, they say, no spirit can walk abroad;
The nights are wholesome; then no planets strike,
No fairy takes, nor witch hath power to charm,
So hallow'd and so gracious is the time . . .

William Shakespeare

IN DULCI JUBILO

In dulci jubilo
Now let us sing with mirth and jo!
 Our hartis consolatioun
Lyis in praesepio,
 And schynis as the sone
Matris in gremio.
Alpha es et O,
Alpha es et O!

O Jesu parvule,
I thrist sore efter the;
 Confort my hart and mynde,
O puer optime!
 God of all grace sa kynde,
Et princeps gloriae,
Trahe me post te,
Trahe me post te!

Ubi sunt gaudia
In ony place bot thair
 Whair that the angellis sing
Nova cantica,
 Bot and the bellis ring
In Regis curia?
God gif I war thair,
God gif I war thair!

John Wedderburn (from
the fourteenth-century German)

413

SHINE OUT, FAIR SUN, WITH ALL YOUR HEAT

Shine out, fair sun, with all your heat,
  Show all your thousand-colour'd light!
Black Winter freezes to his seat;
  The grey wolf howls, he does so bite;
Crookt Age on three knees creeps the street.
  The boneless fish close quaking lies
And eats for cold his aching feet;
  The stars in icicles arise:
Shine out, and make this winter night
Our beauty's spring, our Prince of Light!

George Chapman (?)

AS I SAT ON A SUNNY BANK

As I sat on a sunny bank,
  A sunny bank, a sunny bank;
As I sat on a sunny bank
  On Christmas Day in the morning.

I saw three ships come sailing in,
  Come sailing in, come sailing in;
I saw three ships come sailing in
  On Christmas Day in the morning.

I askèd them what they had in,
  What they had in, what they had in;
I askèd them what they had in
  On Christmas Day. in the morning.

They said they had the Saviour in,
  The Saviour in, the Saviour in;
They said they had the Saviour in
  On Christmas Day in the morning.

I askèd them where they found him,
  Where they found him, where they found him;
I askèd them where they found him
  On Christmas Day in the morning.

They said they found him in Bethlehem,
  In Bethlehem, in Bethlehem;
They said they found him in Bethlehem
  On Christmas Day in the morning.

Now all the bells on earth shall ring,
  On earth shall ring, on earth shall ring;
Now all the bells on earth shall ring
  On Christmas Day in the morning.

And all the angels in heaven shall sing,
  In heaven shall sing, in heaven shall sing;
And all the angels in heaven shall sing
  On Christmas Day in the morning.

INSTEAD OF NEAT INCLOSURES

    Instead of neat inclosures
    Of inter-woven osiers,
    Instead of fragrant posies
    Of daffadils, and roses,
    Thy cradle, Kingly Stranger.
          As gospel tells,
          Was nothing els
    But, here, a homely manger.

    But we with silks (not crewels),
    With sundry precious jewels,
    And lily-work will dress thee;
    And as we dispossess thee
    Of clouts, we'll make a chamber,
          Sweet Babe, for thee,
          Of ivory,
    And plaister'd round with amber . . .

                              Robert Herrick

          crewel: woollen yarn

THE YULE DAYS

The king sent his lady on the first Yule day,
A papingo-aye;
Wha learns my carol and carries it away?

The king sent his lady on the second Yule day,
Three partridges, a papingo-aye;
Wha learns my carol and carries it away?

The king sent his lady on the third Yule day,
Three plovers, three partridges, a papingo-aye;
Wha learns my carol and carries it away?

The king sent his lady on the fourth Yule day,
A goose that was gray,
Three plovers, three partridges, a papingo-aye;
Wha learns my carol and carries it away?

The king sent his lady on the fifth Yule day,
Three starlings, a goose that was gray,
Three plovers, three partridges, and a papingo-aye;
Wha learns my carol and carries it away?

The king sent his lady on the sixth Yule day,
Three goldspinks, three starlings, a goose that was gray,
Three plovers, three partridges, and a papingo-aye;
Wha learns my carol and carries it away?

The king sent his lady on the seventh Yule day,
A bull that was brown, three goldspinks, three starlings,
A goose that was gray,
Three plovers, three partridges, and a papingo-aye;
Wha learns my carol and carries it away?

The king sent his lady on the eighth Yule day,
Three ducks a-merry laying, a bull that was brown,
Three goldspinks, three starlings, a goose that was gray,
Three plovers, three partridges, and a papingo-aye;
Wha learns my carol and carries it away?

The king sent his lady on the ninth Yule day,
Three swans a-merry swimming, three ducks a-merry laying,
A bull that was brown,
Three goldspinks, three starlings, a goose that was gray,
Three plovers, three partridges, and a papingo-aye;
Wha learns my carol and carries it away?

The king sent his lady on the tenth Yule day,
An Arabian baboon,
Three swans a-merry swimming, three ducks a-merry laying,
A bull that was brown,
Three goldspinks, three starlings, a goose that was gray,
Three plovers, three partridges, and a papingo-aye;
Wha learns my carol and carries it away?

The king sent his lady on the eleventh Yule day,
Three hinds a-merry hunting,
An Arabian baboon, three swans a-merry swimming.
Three ducks a-merry laying, a bull that was brown,
Three goldspinks, three starlings, a goose that was gray,
Three plovers, three partridges, and a papingo-aye;
Wha learns my carol and carries it away?

The king sent his lady on the twelfth Yule day,
Three maids a-merry dancing, three hinds a-merry hunting, an
   Arabian baboon,
Three swans a-merry swimming, three ducks a-merry laying,
A bull that was brown, three goldspinks, three starlings,
A goose that was gray,
Three plovers, three partridges, and a papingo-aye;
Wha learns my carol and carries it away?

The king sent his lady on the thirteenth Yule day,
Three stalks o' merry corn, three maids a-merry dancing,
Three hinds a-merry hunting, an Arabian baboon,
Three swans a-merry swimming,
Three ducks a-merry laying, a bull that was brown,
Three goldspinks, three starlings, a goose that was gray,
Three plovers, three partridges, a papingo-aye;
Wha learns my carol and carries it away?

papingo-aye: *peacock*

CHRISTMAS DAY

Nature's decorations glisten
   Far above their usual trim;
Birds on box and laurels listen,
   As so near the cherubs hymn.

Boreas now no longer winters
   On the desolated coast;
Oaks no more are riv'n in splinters
   By the whirlwind and his host.

Spinks and ouzles sing sublimely,
   'We too have a Saviour born,'
Whiter blossoms burst untimely
   On the blest Mosaic thorn.

God all-bounteous, all-creative,
　　Whom no ills from good dissuade,
　Is incarnate, and a native
　　Of the very world he made . . .

Christopher Smart

THE SHEPHERDS AT BETHLEHEM

First Shepherd　Hail, comely and clean! Hail, young child!
Hail, maker, as I mean, of a maiden so mild!
Thou has warid, I ween, the warlo so wild;
The false guiler of tene now goes he beguild.
　　Lo, he merries,
　　Lo, he laughs, my sweeting!
　A well fair meeting!
　I have holden my heting.
　　Have a bob of cherries!

Second Shepherd　Hail, sufferan Saviour! for thou has us sought.
Hail, frely fode and flower that all thing has
　　　　wrought!
Hail, full of favour, that made all of nought!
Hail! I kneel and I cower. A bird have I brought
　　To my barne.
　Hail, little tiny mop!
　Of our creed thou art crop.
　I would drink on thy cop,
　　Little day starne.

Third Shepherd　Hail, darling dear, full of godhede!
I pray thee be near when that I have need.
Hail! Sweet is thy cheer! My heart would bleed
To see thee sit here in so poore weed,
　　With no pennies.
　Hail! Put forth thy dall!
　I bring thee bot a ball:
Have and play thee withall,
　　And go to the tennis.

From the 'Second Shepherds' Play'

warid: *put a curse on*; warlo: *devil*; tene: *grief*; heting:
promise; sufferan: *sovereign*; frely fode: *noble child*; barne:
baby; mop: *baby*; crop: *head*; on thy cop: *of thy cup*; starne:
star; dall: *hand*

Nowell sing we now all and some,
For rex pacificus is come.

In Bethlem, in that fair city,
A child was born of maiden free,
That shall a lord and princë be;
    A solis ortus cardine.

Children were slain full great plenty,
Jesus for the love of thee;
Wherefore their soules saved be,
    Hostis Herodis impie.

As the sunne shineth through the glass,
So Jesu in his mother was;
Thee to serve now grant us grace,
    O lux beata Trinitas.

Now God is comen to worshipen us;
Now of Mary is born Jesus;
Make we merry amonges us;
    Exultet caelum laudibus.

MASTERS, IN THIS HALL

'To Bethlem did they go, the shepherds three;
To Bethlem did they go to see whe'r it were so or no,
Whether Christ were born or no
    To set men free.'

    Masters, in this hall,
        Hear ye news to-day
    Brought over sea,
        And ever I you pray.
        Nowell! Nowell! Nowell! Nowell!
          Sing we clear!
        Holpen are all folk on earth,
          Born is God's Son so dear.

Going over the hills,
    Through the milk-white snow,
Heard I ewes bleat
    While the wind did blow.
      Nowell, etc.

Shepherds many an one
  Sat among the sheep;
No man spake more word
  Than they had been asleep.
    Nowell, etc.

Quoth I 'Fellows mine,
  Why this guise sit ye?
Making but dull cheer,
  Shepherds though ye be?
    Nowell, etc.

'Shepherds should of right
  Leap and dance and sing;
Thus to see ye sit
  Is a right strange thing.'
    Nowell, etc.

Quoth these fellows then
  'To Bethlem town we go,
To see a Mighty Lord
  Lie in manger low.'
    Nowell, etc.

'How name ye this Lord,
  Shepherds?' then said I.
'Very God', they said,
  'Come from Heaven high.'
    Nowell, etc.

Then to Bethlem town
  We went two and two,
And in a sorry place
  Heard the oxen low.
    Nowell, etc.

Therein did we see
  A sweet and goodly May,
And a fair old man;
  Upon the straw she lay.
    Nowell, etc.

And a little Child
  On her arm had she;
'Wot ye who this is?'
  Said the hinds to me.
    Nowell, etc.

420

Ox and ass him know,
  Kneeling on their knee:
Wondrous joy had I
  This little Babe to see.
    Nowell, etc.

This is Christ the Lord,
  Masters, be ye glad!
Christmas is come in,
  And no folk should be sad.
    Nowell! Nowell! Nowell! Nowell!
      Sing we clear!
    Holpen are all folk on earth,
      Born is God's Son so dear.

William Morris

THE HOLLY AND THE IVY

The holly and the ivy,
When they are both full grown,
Of all the trees that are in the wood,
The holly bears the crown:
  The rising of the sun
  And the running of the deer
  The playing of the merry organ,
  Sweet singing in the choir.

The holly bears a blossom
As white as the lily flower,
And Mary bore sweet Jesus Christ
To be our sweet Saviour:
  The rising of the sun . . .

The holly bears a berry
As red as any blood,
And Mary bore sweet Jesus Christ
To do poor sinners good:
  The rising of the sun . . .

The holly bears a prickle
As sharp as any thorn,
And Mary bore sweet Jesus Christ
On Christmas Day in the morn:
  The rising of the sun . . .

The holly bears a bark
As bitter as any gall,
And Mary bore sweet Jesus Christ
For to redeem us all:
   The rising of the sun . .

The holly and the ivy,
When they are both full grown,
Of all the trees that are in the wood,
The holly bears the crown
   The rising of the sun
   And the running of the dear,
   The playing of the merry organ,
   Sweet singing in the choir.

A CHRISTMAS CAROL

In the bleak mid-winter
   Frosty wind made moan,
Earth stood hard as iron,
   Water like a stone;
Snow had fallen, snow on snow,
   Snow on snow,
In the bleak mid-winter
   Long ago.

Our God, Heaven cannot hold him
   Nor earth sustain;
Heaven and earth shall flee away
   When he comes to reign:
In the bleak mid-winter
   A stable-place sufficed
The Lord God Almighty
   Jesus Christ.

Enough for him, whom cherubim
   Worship night and day,
A breastful of milk
   And a mangerful of hay;
Enough for him, whom angels
   Fall down before,
The ox and ass and camel
   Which adore.

Angels and archangels
   May have gathered there,
Cherubim and seraphim
   Thronged the air;
But only his mother
   In her maiden bliss
Worshipped the Beloved
   With a kiss.

What can I give him,
   Poor as I am?
If I were a shepherd
   I would bring a lamb,
If I were a Wise Man
   I would do my part, —
Yet what I can I give him,
   Give my heart.

Christina Rossetti

ANE SANG OF THE BIRTH OF CHRIST, WITH THE TUNE OF BAW LULA LOW

My saull and lyfe, stand up and see
Wha lyis in ane cribbe of tre:
What babe is that, sa gude and fair?
It is Christ, Goddis sone and air.

Welcome now, gracious God of mycht,
To sinnaris vyle, pure and unrycht.
Thow come to saif us from distres,
How can we thank thy gentilnes!

O God that maid all creature,
How art thow now becumit sa pure,
That on the hay and stray will ly,
Amang the assis, oxin and ky?

And war the warld ten tymes sa wyde,
Cled ouer with gold, and stanis of pryde,
Unworthie it war yet to thee,
Under thy feit ane stule to be.

The sylk and sandell thee to eis,
Ar hay, and sempill sweilling clais,
Wharin thow gloris, greitest King,
As thow in hevin war in thy ring.

Thow luke sic panis temporall,
To mak me ryche perpetuall.
For all this warldis welth and gude,
Can na thing ryche thy celsitude.

O my deir hart, yung Jesus sweit,
Prepair thy creddil in my spreit,
And I sall rock thee in my hart,
And never mair fra thee depart.

But I sall praise thee ever moir,
With sangis sweit unto thy gloir:
The kneis of my hart sall I bow,
And sing that rycht Balulalow.

John *Wedderburn* (after the German of Luther)

pure: *poor*; unrycht: *unrighteous*; stanis: *stones*; sandell: *silk*; eis: *ease*; sweilling: *swaddling*; gloris: *gloriest*; ring: *kingdom*; panis: *pains*; ryche: *reach*

THE KINGS FROM THE EAST

'Dear children', they asked in every town,
    Three kings from the land of the sun,
'Which is the road to Bethlehem?'
    But neither the old nor the young

Could tell, and the kings rode on;
    Their guide was a star in the air,
Of gold, which glittered ahead of them,
    So clear, so clear.

The star stood still over Joseph's house,
    They all of them stepped in;
The good ox lowed and the little child cried,
    And the kings began to sing.

From the German of Heinrich Heine

WASSAIL, WASSAIL

Wassail, wassail, out of the milk pail,
Wassail, wassail, as white as my nail,
Wassail, wassail, in snow, frost and hail,
Wassail, wassail, with partridge and rail,
Wassail, wassail, that much doth avail,
Wassail, wassail, that never will fail.

John Bale

THE MONTHS

Januar	By thys fyre I warme my handys;
Februar	And with my spade I delfe my landys.
Marche	Here I sette my thynge to sprynge;
Aprile	And here I here the fowlis synge.
Maij	I am as lyght as byrde in bowe;
Junij	And I wede my corne well inow.
Julij	With my sythe my mede I mawe;
Auguste	And here I shere my corne full lowe.
September	With my flayll I erne my brede;
October	And here I sawe my whete so rede.
November	At Martynesmasse I kylle my swyne;
December	And at Cristesmasse I drynke redde wyne.

delfe: delve; thynge: seed; sawe: sow; rede: red

THE MYSTIC MAGI

It is chronicled in an old Armenian myth, that the Wise Men of the
East were none other than the three sons of Noe, and that they were
raised from the dead to represent, and to do homage for, all mankind in
the cave of Bethlehem.

i

Three ancient men in Bethlehem's cave
  With awful wonder stand:
A voice had called them from their grave,
  In some far Eastern land.

ii

They lived: they trod the former earth,
  When the old waters swelled,
The Ark, that womb of second birth,
  Their house and lineage held.

Pale Japhet bows the knee with gold,
  Bright Sem sweet incense brings,
And Cham the myrrh his fingers hold:
  Lo! the three orient Kings.

Types of the total earth, they hailed
  The signal's starry frame:
Shuddering with second life, they quailed
  At the Child Jesu's Name.

Then slow the Patriarchs turned and trod,
  And this their parting sigh:
'Our eyes have seen the living God,
  And now — once more to die.'

Robert Stephen Hawker

TAKE FRANKINCENSE, O GOD

Take frankincense, O God, take gold, O King,
Take myrrh, O Man, from those who can them bring:
Poor I, nor gold, nor myrrh, nor frankincense,
Have to present, such is mine indigence;
Yet will I with these noble Persians bring
Some present still, when I salute my King:
I'll give myself. A gift too vile, too base
To be presented to so high a grace.
But thou who all thou tak'st doest better make,
Render me better than thou didst me take.
  Myself a worm, no man, I give to thee,
  Restore myself a man, a saint, to me . . .

Charles Fitz-Geffry

THE MAGI

See how from far upon the eastern road
The star-led Wizards haste with odours sweet . . .

John Milton

28. THE POET'S VOICE

The Poet's Voice

The image of the woodcut is the poet by himself in the wood; and in this section near the end of the book, poets, so to say, are by themselves, speaking of their most particular concerns, their particular admirations, or of their craft or intention as poets. Stars are not as durable as men used to believe, constellations change their shape, however slowly, poems do not last for ever, and wonderful poems must have been lost. Yet poets have a strong and justified sense that in a world of waste and cheapness they make things which are durable; which they hope will be read, not by everyone, but by you and others of a like feeling through the centuries. So John Milton, blind, and still writing *Paradise Lost* (just half-way through its 10,578 lines) asked Urania, his heavenly inspirer, to find him 'fit audience . . . though few' (page 464).

There are still poets (Robert Graves for one) who believe in a goddess of poetry, a powerful Muse, who demands their devotion. Ben Jonson, Shakespeare's friend, looked at the coloured intricate pompous Jacobean tombs newly made in the churches in his day, and wrote:

> It is the Muse, alone, can raise to heaven,
> And at her strong arms' end hold up and even
> The souls she loves. Those other glorious notes
> Inscrib'd in touch or marble, or the coats
> Painted or carved upon our great men's tombs,
> Or in their windows, do but prove the wombs
> That bred them graves: when they were born, they died
> That had no Muse to make their fame abide.

He thought of the constellations, and went on:

> Who heaved Hercules
> Unto the stars? or the Tyndarides?
> Who placed Jason's Argo in the sky?
> Or set bright Ariadne's crown so high?
> Who made a lamp of Berenice's hair?
> Or lifted Cassiopea in her chair?
> But only poets, rapt with rage divine?

The woodcut, again, is from the *Hypnerotomachia Poliphili* referred to on page 266.

A MUSE OF FIRE

O for a Muse of fire, that would ascend
The brightest heaven of invention . . .

William Shakespeare

THE POET'S VOICE

Hear the voice of the Bard!
Who Present, Past, and Future, sees;
Whose ears have heard
The Holy Word
That walk'd among the ancient trees,

Calling the lapsèd Soul,
And weeping in the evening dew;
That might control
The starry pole,
And fallen, fallen light renew!

'O Earth, O Earth, return!
Arise from out the dewy grass;
Night is worn,
And the morn
Rises from the slumbrous mass.

'Turn away no more;
Why wilt thou turn away?
The starry floor,
The wat'ry shore,
Is giv'n thee till the break of day.'

William Blake

TO VERSE LET KINGS GIVE PLACE

To verse let kings give place, and kingly shows,
And banks o'er which gold-bearing Tagus flows.
Let base conceited wits admire vile things,
Fair Phoebus lead me to the Muses' springs.

429

About my head be quivering myrtle wound,
And in sad lovers' heads let me be found.
The living, not the dead, can envy bite,
For after death all men receive their right.
Then, though death rakes my bones in funeral fire,
I'll live, and as he pulls me down, mount higher . . .

Ovid (translated by
Christopher Marlowe)

TO THE MUSES

Whether on Ida's shady brow
  Or in the chambers of the East,
The chambers of the sun, that now
  From antient melody have ceas'd;

Whether in Heav'n ye wander fair,
  Or the green corners of the earth,
Or the blue regions of the air,
  Where the melodious winds have birth;

Whether on chrystal rocks ye rove,
  Beneath the bosom of the sea
Wand'ring in many a coral grove,
  Fair Nine, forsaking Poetry!

How have you left the antient love
  That bards of old enjoy'd in you!
The languid strings do scarcely move!
  The sound is forc'd, the notes are few!

William Blake

CHRISTOPHER MARLOWE

Next Marlowe, bathed in the Thespian springs,
Had in him those brave translunary things
That the first poets had; his raptures were
All air and fire, which made his verses clear;
For that fine madness still he did retain
Which rightly should possess a poet's brain . . .

Michael Drayton

If all the pens that ever poets held,
Had fed the feeling of their maisters' thoughts,
And every sweetness that inspir'd their hearts,
Their minds, and muses on admired themes:
If all the heavenly quintessence they still
From their immortal flowers of Poesy,
Wherein as in a mirror we perceive
The highest reaches of a humain wit –
If these had made one poem's period
And all combin'd in Beauty's worthiness,
Yet should there hover in their restless heads,
One thought, one grace, one wonder at the least,
Which into words no virtue can digest . . .

Christopher Marlowe

IN MEMORY OF W. B. YEATS

Earth, receive an honoured guest;
William Yeats is laid to rest:
Let the Irish vessel lie
Emptied of its poetry.

Time that is intolerant
Of the brave and innocent,
And indifferent in a week
To a beautiful physique,

Worships language and forgives
Everyone by whom it lives;
Pardons cowardice, conceit,
Lays its honours at their feet.

Time that with this strange excuse
Pardoned Kipling and his views,
And will pardon Paul Claudel,
Pardons him for writing well.

In the nightmare of the dark
All the dogs of Europe bark,
And the living nations wait,
Each sequestered in its hate;

Intellectual disgrace
Stares from every human face,
And the seas of pity lie
Locked and frozen in each eye.

Follow, poet, follow right
To the bottom of the night,
With your unconstraining voice
Still persuade us to rejoice;

With the farming of a verse
Make a vineyard of the curse,
Sing of human unsuccess
In a rapture of distress;

In the deserts of the heart
Let the healing fountain start,
In the prison of his days
Teach the free man how to praise . . .

W. H. Auden

TO THE MEMORY OF MY BELOVED;
THE AUTHOR MR WILLIAM SHAKESPEARE

Sweet Swan of Avon! what a sight it were
   To see thee in our waters yet appear,
And make those flights upon the banks of Thames,
   That so did take Eliza, and our James!
But stay, I see thee in the Hemisphere
   Advanc'd, and made a constellation there!
Shine forth, thou star of Poets, and with rage,
   Or influence, chide, or cheer the drooping stage;
Which, since thy flight from hence, hath mourn'd like
   night,
   And despairs day, but for thy volume's light . . .

Ben Jonson

THEL'S MOTTO

Does the Eagle know what is in the pit?
Or wilt thou go ask the Mole?
Can Wisdom be put in a silver rod?
Or Love in a golden bowl?

William Blake

I who am dead a thousand years,
    And wrote this sweet archaic song,
Send you my words for messengers
    The way I shall not pass along.

I care not if you bridge the seas,
    Or ride secure the cruel sky,
Or build consummate palaces
    Of metal or of masonry.

But have you wine and music still,
    And statues and a bright-eyed love,
And foolish thoughts of good and ill,
    And prayers to them who sit above?

How shall we conquer? Like a wind
    That falls at eve our fancies blow,
And old Maeonides the blind
    Said it three thousand years ago.

O friend unseen, unborn, unknown,
    Student of our sweet English tongue,
Read out my words at night, alone:
    I was a poet, I was young.

Since I can never see your face,
    And never shake you by the hand,
I send my soul through time and space
    To greet you. You will understand.

                                    James Elroy Flecker

LOVE

Love bade me welcome: yet my soul drew back,
        Guilty of dust and sin.
But quick-ey'd Love, observing me grow slack
        From my first entrance in,
Drew nearer to me, sweetly questioning,
        If I lack'd any thing.

A guest, I answer'd, worthy to be here:
　　Love said, you shall be he.
I the unkind, ungrateful? Ah my dear,
　　I cannot look on thee.
Love took my hand, and smiling did reply,
　　Who made the eyes but I?

Truth Lord, but I have marr'd them: let my shame
　　Go where it doth deserve.
And know you not, says Love, who bore the blame?
　　My dear, then I will serve.
You must sit down, says Love, and taste my meat:
　　So I did sit and eat.

　　　　　　　　　　　　　　George Herbert

MY LORD AND KING

Love is and was my Lord and King,
　　And in his presence I attend
　　To hear the tidings of my friend,
Which every hour his couriers bring.

Love is and was my King and Lord,
　　And will be, tho' as yet I keep
　　Within his court on earth, and sleep
Encompass'd by his faithful guard,

And hear at times a sentinel
　　Who moves about from place to place,
　　And whispers to the world of space,
In the deep night, that all is well.

　　　　　　　　　　　　　Alfred, Lord Tennyson

ON HIS BLINDNESS

When I consider how my light is spent,
　Ere half my days, in this dark world and wide,
　And that one talent which is death to hide,
　Lodg'd with me useless, though my soul more bent
To serve therewith my Maker, and present
　My true account, lest he returning chide,
　Doth God exact day-labour, light deny'd,
　I fondly ask; but patience to prevent

That murmur, soon replies, God doth not need
  Either man's work or his own gifts, who best
  Bear his mild yoke, they serve him best, his state
Is kingly. Thousands at his bidding speed
  And post o'er land and ocean without rest:
  They also serve who only stand and wait.

John Milton

I STROVE WITH NONE

I strove with none, for none was worth my strife,
Nature I loved, and, next to Nature, Art;
I warmed both hands before the fire of Life;
It sinks, and I am ready to depart.

Walter Savage Landor

WHY DID I WRITE?

i

Why did I write? what sin to me unknown
Dipt me in ink, my parents' or my own?
As yet a child, nor yet a fool to fame,
I lisp'd in numbers, for the numbers came.
I left no calling for this idle trade,
No duty broke, no father disobey'd.
The Muse but serv'd to ease some friend, not wife,
To help me thro' this long disease, my life . . .

ii

I nod in company, I wake at night,
Fools rush into my head, and so I write . . .

Alexander Pope

A LITTLE LEARNING

A little learning is a dang'rous thing;
Drink deep, or taste not the Pierian spring:
There shallow draughts intoxicate the brain,
And drinking largely sobers us again.
Fired at first sight with what the Muse imparts,
In fearless youth we tempt the heights of Arts,
While from the bounded level of our mind,
Short views we take, nor see the lengths behind;

435

But more advanced, behold with strange surprize
New distant scenes of endless science rise!
So pleased at first the tow'ring Alps we try,
Mount o'er the vales, and seem to tread the sky,
Th'eternal snows appear already past,
And the first clouds and mountains seem the last:
But, those attained, we tremble to survey
The growing labours of the lengthened way,
Th'increasing prospect tires our wand'ring eyes,
Hills peep o'er hills, and Alps on Alps arise! . . .

Alexander Pope

A DIVINE IMAGE

Cruelty has a human heart,
And Jealousy a human face;
Terror the human form divine,
And Secrecy the human dress.

The human dress is forgèd iron,
The human form a fiery forge,
The human face a furnace seal'd,
The human heart its hungry gorge.

William Blake

INTIMATIONS OF IMMORTALITY

Our birth is but a sleep and a forgetting:
The Soul that rises with us, our life's Star,
    Hath had elsewhere its setting,
        And cometh from afar:
    Not in entire forgetfulness,
    And not in utter nakedness,
But trailing clouds of glory do we come
    From God, who is our home:
Heaven lies about us in our infancy!
Shades of the prison-house begin to close
    Upon the growing Boy,
But He beholds the light, and whence it flows,
    He sees it in his joy;
The Youth, who daily farther from the east
    Must travel, still is Nature's Priest,
    And by the vision splendid
    Is on his way attended;

436

At length the Man perceives it die away,
And fade into the light of common day.

Earth fills her lap with pleasures of her own;
Yearnings she hath in her own natural kind,
And, even with something of a Mother's mind,
    And no unworthy aim,
    The homely Nurse doth all she can
To make her Foster-child, her Inmate Man,
    Forget the glories he hath known,
And that imperial palace whence he came . . .

William Wordsworth

A VISION

I lost the love of heaven above,
    I spurned the lust of earth below,
I felt the sweets of fancied love,
    And hell itself my only foe.

I lost earth's joys, but felt the glow
    Of heaven's flame abound in me,
Till loveliness and I did grow
    The bard of immortality.

I loved but woman fell away,
    I hid me from her faded fame,
I snatch'd the sun's eternal ray
    And wrote till earth was but a name.

In every language upon earth,
    On every shore, o'er every sea,
I gave my name immortal birth
    And kept my spirit with the free.

John Clare

THE ISLES OF GREECE

i

The isles of Greece, the isles of Greece!
    Where burning Sappho loved and sung,
Where grew the arts of war and peace,
    Where Delos rose, and Phoebus sprung!
Eternal summer gilds them yet,
But all, except their sun, is set.

437

ii

The Scian and the Teian muse,
  The hero's harp, the lover's lute,
Have found the fame your shores refuse:
  Their place of birth alone is mute
To sounds which echo further west
Than your sires' 'Islands of the Blest.'

iii

The mountains look on Marathon —
  And Marathon looks on the sea;
And musing there an hour alone,
  I dream'd that Greece might still be free;
For standing on the Persians' grave,
I could not deem myself a slave.

iv

A king sate on the rocky brow
  Which looks o'er sea-born Salamis;
And ships, by thousands, lay below,
  And men in nations; — all were his!
He counted them at break of day —
And when the sun set where were they?

v

And where are they? and where art thou,
  My country? On thy voiceless shore
The heroic lay is tuneless now —
  The heroic bosom beats no more!
And must thy lyre, so long divine,
Degenerate into hands like mine?

vi

'Tis something, in the dearth of fame,
  Though link'd among a fetter'd race,
To feel at least a patriot's shame,
  Even as I sing, suffuse my face;
For what is left the poet here?
For Greeks a blush — for Greece a tear.

vii

Must *we* but weep o'er days more blest?
  Must *we* but blush? — Our fathers bled.
Earth! render back from out thy breast
  A remnant of our Spartan dead!

Of the three hundred grant but three,
To make a new Thermopylae!

viii

What, silent still? and silent all?
   Ah! no; — the voices of the dead
Sound like a distant torrent's fall,
   And answer, 'Let one living head,
But one arise, — we come, we come!'
'Tis but the living who are dumb.

ix

In vain — in vain: strike other chords;
   Fill high the cup with Samian wine!
Leave battles to the Turkish hordes,
   And shed the blood of Scio's vine!
Hark! rising to the ignoble call —
How answers each bold Bacchanal!

x

You have the Pyrrhic dance as yet;
   Where is the Pyrrhic phalanx gone?
Of two such lessons, why forget
   The nobler and the manlier one?
You have the letters Cadmus gave —
Think ye he meant them for a slave?

xi

Fill high the bowl with Samian wine!
   We will not think of themes like these!
It made Anacreon's song divine:
   He served — but served Polycrates —
A tyrant; but our masters then
Were still, at least, our countrymen.

xii

The tyrant of the Chersonese
   Was freedom's best and bravest friend;
That tyrant was Miltiades!
   Oh! that the present hour would lend
Another despot of the kind!
Such chains as his were sure to bind.

Fill high the bowl with Samian wine!
  On Suli's rock, and Parga's shore,
Exists the remnant of a line
  Such as the Doric mothers bore;
And there, perhaps, some seed is sown,
The Heracleidan blood might own.

Trust not for freedom to the Franks —
  They have a king who buys and sells;
In native swords, and native ranks,
  The only hope of courage dwells:
But Turkish force, and Latin fraud,
Would break your shield, however broad.

Fill high the bowl with Samian wine!
  Our virgins dance beneath the shade —
I see their glorious black eyes shine;
  But gazing on each glowing maid,
My own the burning tear-drop laves,
To think such breasts must suckle slaves.

Place me on Sunium's marbled steep,
  Where nothing, save the waves and I,
May hear our mutual murmurs sweep;
  There, swan-like, let me sing and die:
A land of slaves shall ne'er be mine —
Dash down yon cup of Samian wine!

George Gordon, Lord Byron

TO HELEN

Helen, thy beauty is to me
  Like those Nicean barks of yore,
That gently, o'er a perfumed sea,
  The weary, wayworn wanderer bore
  To his own native shore.

On desperate seas long wont to roam,
  Thy hyacinth hair, thy classic face,
Thy Naiad airs have brought me home
  To the glory that was Greece
  And the grandeur that was Rome.

Lo! in yon brilliant window-niche
   How statue-like I see thee stand,
The agate lamp within thy hand!
   Ah, Psyche, from the regions which
   Are Holy Land!

Edgar Allan Poe

HELLAS

The world's great age begins anew,
   The golden years return,
The earth doth like a snake renew
   Her winter weeds outworn:
Heaven smiles, and faiths and empires gleam,
Like wrecks of a dissolving dream.

A brighter Hellas rears its mountains
   From waves serener far;
A new Peneus rolls his fountains
   Against the morning star.
Where fairer Tempes bloom, there sleep
Young Cyclads on a sunnier deep.

A loftier Argo cleaves the main,
   Fraught with a later prize;
Another Orpheus sings again,
   And loves, and weeps, and dies.
A new Ulysses leaves once more
Calypso for his native shore.

Oh, write no more the tale of Troy,
   If earth Death's scroll must be!
Nor mix with Laian rage the joy
   Which dawns upon the free:
Although a subtler sphinx renew
Riddles of death Thebes never knew.

Another Athens shall arise,
   And to remoter time
Bequeath, like sunset to the skies,
   The splendour of its prime;
And leave, if nought so bright may live,
All earth can take or Heaven can give.

Saturn and Love, their long repose
    Shall burst, more bright and good
Than all who fell, than One who rose,
    Than many unsubdued:
Not gold, not blood, their altar dowers,
But votive tears and symbol flowers.

Oh, cease! must hate and death return?
    Cease! must men kill and die?
Cease! drain not to its dregs the urn
    Of bitter prophecy.
The world is weary of the past,
Oh, might it die or rest at last! . . .

P. B. Shelley

TO VIRGIL

Written at the request of the Mantuans for the
nineteenth centenary of Virgil's death

Roman Virgil, thou that singest
    Ilion's lofty temples robed in fire,
Ilion falling, Rome arising,
    wars, and filial faith, and Dido's pyre;

Landscape-lover, lord of language
    more than he that sang the 'Works and Days',
All the chosen coin of fancy
    flashing out from many a golden phrase;

Thou that singest wheat and woodland,
    tilth and vineyard, hive and horse and herd;
All the charm of all the Muses
    often flowering in a lonely word;

Poet of the happy Tityrus
    piping underneath his beechen bowers;
Poet of the poet-satyr
    whom the laughing shepherd bound with flowers;

Chanter of the Pollio, glorying
    in the blissful years again to be,
Summers of the snakeless meadow,
    unlaborious earth and oarless sea;

Thou that seëst Universal
    Nature moved by Universal Mind;
Thou majestic in thy sadness
    at the doubtful doom of human kind;

Light among the vanish'd ages;
    star that gildest yet this phantom shore;
Golden branch amid the shadows,
    kings and realms that pass to rise no more;

Now thy Forum roars no longer,
    fallen every purple Caesar's dome –
Tho' thine ocean roll of rhythm
    sound for ever of Imperial Rome –

Now the Rome of slaves hath perish'd,
    and the Rome of freemen holds her place,
I, from out the Northern Island
    sunder'd once from all the human race,

I salute thee, Mantovano,
    I that loved thee since my day began,
Wielder of the stateliest measure
    ever moulded by the lips of man.

Alfred, Lord Tennyson

ON FIRST LOOKING INTO CHAPMAN'S HOMER

Much have I travell'd in the realms of gold,
    And many goodly states and kingdoms seen;
    Round many western islands have I been
Which bards in fealty to Apollo hold.
Oft of one wide expanse had I been told,
    That deep-brow'd Homer ruled as his demesne:
    Yet did I never breathe its pure serene
Till I heard Chapman speak out loud and bold:
Then felt I like some watcher of the skies
    When a new planet swims into his ken;
Or like stout Cortez when with eagle eyes
    He stared at the Pacific – and all his men
Look'd at each other with a wild surmise –
    Silent, upon a peak in Darien.

John Keats

'FRATER AVE ATQUE VALE'

Row us out from Desenzano, to your Sirmione row!
So they row'd, and there we landed – 'O venusta Sirmio!'
There to me thro' all the groves of olive in the summer glow,
There beneath the Roman ruin where the purple flowers grow,
Came that 'Ave atque Vale' of the Poet's hopeless woe,
Tenderest of Roman poets nineteen hundred years ago,
'Frater Ave atque Vale' – as we wander'd to and fro
Gazing at the Lydian laughter of the Garda-lake below
Sweet Catullus's all-but-island, olive-silvery Sirmio!

Alfred, Lord Tennyson

BLOW, BUGLE, BLOW

The splendour falls on castle walls
  And snowy summits old in story:
The long light shakes across the lakes,
  And the wild cataract leaps in glory.
Blow, bugle, blow, set the wild echoes flying,
Blow, bugle; answer, echoes, dying, dying, dying.

O hark, O hear! how thin and clear,
  And thinner, clearer, farther, going!
O sweet and far from cliff and scar
  The horns of Elfland faintly blowing!
Blow, let us hear the purple glens replying:
Blow, bugle; answer, echoes, dying, dying, dying.

O love, they die in yon rich sky,
  They faint on hill or field or river:
Our echoes roll from soul to soul,
  And grow for ever and for ever.
Blow, bugle, blow, set the wild echoes flying,
And answer, echoes, answer, dying, dying, dying.

Alfred, Lord Tennyson

CALLICLES' SONG

Through the black, rushing smoke-bursts,
Thick breaks the red flame;
All Etna heaves fiercely
Her forest-clothed frame.

Not here, O Apollo!
Are haunts meet for thee.
But, where Helicon breaks down
In cliff to the sea,

Where the moon-silver'd inlets
Send far their light voice
Up the still vale of Thisbe,
O speed, and rejoice!

On the sward at the cliff-top
Lie strewn the white flocks,
On the cliff-side the pigeons
Roost deep in the rocks.

In the moonlight the shepherds,
Soft lull'd by the rills,
Lie wrapt in their blankets
Asleep on the hills.

— What forms are these coming
So white through the gloom?
What garments out-glistening
The gold-flower'd broom?

What sweet-breathing presence
Out-perfumes the thyme?
What voices enrapture
The night's balmy prime? —

'Tis Apollo comes leading
His choir, the Nine.
— The leader is fairest,
But all are divine.

They are lost in the hollows!
They stream up again!
What seeks on this mountain
The glorified train? —

They bathe on this mountain,
In the spring by their road;
Then on to Olympus,
Their endless abode.

– Whose praise do they mention?
Of what is it told? –
What will be for ever;
What was from of old.

First hymn thcy the Father
Of all things; and then,
The rest of immortals,
The action of men.

The day in his hotness,
The strife with the palm;
The night in her silence,
The stars in their calm . . .

Matthew Arnold

LAUDATE DOMINUM

(Psalm 150)

O praise God in his holiness: praise him in the firmament of
his power.

Praise him in his noble acts: praise him according to his
excellent greatness.

Praise him in the sound of the trumpet: praise him upon the
lute and harp.

Praise him in the cymbals and dances:
Praise him upon the strings and pipe.

Praise him upon the well-tuned cymbals:
Praise him upon the loud cymbals.

Let everything that hath breath:
Praise the Lord.

PRAISE

O poet, what do you do? I praise.
But the murderous and the monstrous –
How endure it and submit? I praise.
But the nameless and anonymous –
How invoke it, though? I praise.

From where your right, in every dress,
In every mask, to truth? I praise.
And how like star and storm,
Do quiet and the impetuous know you? —
  Because I praise.

From the German of Rainer Maria Rilke

A SONG TO DAVID

i

O Thou, that sit'st upon a throne,
With harp of high majestic tone,
  To praise the King of kings;
And voice of heaven-ascending swell,
Which, while its deeper notes excel,
  Clear, as a clarion, rings:

ii

To bless each valley, grove, and coast,
And charm the cherubs to the post
  Of gratitude in throngs;
To keep the days on Zion's Mount,
And send the year to his account,
  With dances and with songs:

iii

O Servant of God's holiest charge,
The minister of praise at large,
  Which thou mayst now receive;
From thy blest mansion hail and hear,
From topmost eminence appear
  To this the wreath I weave.

iv

Great, valiant, pious, good, and clean,
Sublime, contemplative, serene,
  Strong, constant, pleasant, wise!
Bright effluence of exceeding grace;
Best man! — the swiftness and the race,
  The peril, and the prize!

v

Great – from the lustre of his crown,
From Samuel's horn and God's renown,
  Which is the people's voice;
For all the host, from rear to van,
Applauded and embraced the man –
  The man of God's own choice.

vi

Valiant – the word and up he rose –
The fight – he triumphed o'er the foes,
  Whom God's just laws abhor;
And, arm'd in gallant faith, he took
Against the boaster, from the brook,
  The weapons of the war.

vii

Pious – magnificent and grand;
'Twas he the famous temple plann'd,
  (The seraph in his soul;)
Foremost to give the Lord his dues,
Foremost to bless the welcome news,
  And foremost to condole.

viii

Good – from Jehudah's genuine vein,
From God's best nature good in grain,
  His aspect and his heart;
To pity, to forgive, to save,
Witness En-gedi's conscious cave,
  And Shimei's blunted dart.

ix

Clean – if perpetual prayer be pure,
And love, which could itself innure
  To fasting and to fear –
Clean in his gestures, hands, and feet,
To smite the lyre, the dance complete,
  To play the sword and spear.

x

Sublime – invention ever young,
Of vast conception, tow'ring tongue,
  To God the eternal theme;

Notes from yon exaltations caught,
Unrivall'd royalty of thought,
    O'er meaner strains supreme.

xi

Contemplative — on God to fix
His musings, and above the six
    The sabbath-day he blest;
'Twas then his thoughts self-conquest prun'd
And heavenly melancholy tun'd,
    To bless and bear the rest.

xii

Serene — to sow the seeds of peace,
Rememb'ring, when he watch'd the fleece,
    How sweetly Kidron purl'd —
To further knowledge, silence vice,
And plant perpetual paradise,
    When God had calmed the world.

xiii

Strong — in the Lord, who could defy
Satan, and all his powers that lie
    In sempiternal night;
And hell, and horror, and despair
Were as the lion and the bear
    To his undaunted might.

xiv

Constant — in love to God, the truth,
Age, manhood, infancy, and youth —
    To Jonathan his friend
Constant, beyond the verge of death;
And Ziba, and Mephibosheth,
    His endless fame attend.

xv

Pleasant — and various as the year;
Man, soul, and angel, without peer,
    Priest, champion, sage and boy;
In armour, or in ephod clad,
His pomp, his piety was glad;
    Majestic was his joy.

xvi

Wise — in recovery from his fall,
Whence rose his eminence o'er all,
  Of all the most revil'd;
The light of Israel in his ways,
Wise are his precepts, prayer and praise,
  And counsel to his child.

xvii

His muse, bright angel of his verse,
Gives balm for all the thorns that pierce,
  For all the pangs that rage;
Blest light, still gaining on the gloom,
The more than Michal of his bloom,
  The Abishag of his age.

xviii

He sung of God — the mighty source
Of all things — the stupendous force
  On which all strength depends;
From whose tight arm, beneath whose eyes,
All period, pow'r, and enterprise
  Commences, reigns, and ends.

xix

Angels — their ministry and meed,
Which to and fro with blessings speed,
  Or with their citterns wait;
Where Michael with his millions bows,
Where dwells the seraph and his spouse,
  The cherub and her mate.

xx

Of man — the semblance and effect
Of God and Love — the Saint elect
  For infinite applause —
To rule the land, and briny broad,
To be laborious in his laud,
  And heroes in his cause.

xxi

The world — the clust'ring spheres he made,
The glorious light, the soothing shade,
  Dale, champaign, grove, and hill;

The multitudinous abyss,
Where secrecy remains in bliss,
    And wisdom hides her skill.

xxii

Trees, plants, and flow'rs — of virtuous root;
Gem yielding blossom, yielding fruit,
    Choice gums and precious balm;
Bless ye the nosegay in the vale,
And with the sweetness of the gale
    Enrich the thankful psalm.

xxiii

Of fowl — e'en ev'ry beak and wing
Which cheer the winter, hail the spring,
    That live in peace or prey;
They that make music, or that mock,
The quail, the brave domestic cock,
    The raven, swan, and jay.

xxiv

Of fishes — ev'ry size and shape,
Which nature frames of light escape,
    Devouring man to shun:
The shells are in the wealthy deep,
The shoals upon the surface leap,
    And love the glancing sun.

xxv

Of beasts — the beaver plods his task;
While the sleek tigers roll and bask,
    Nor yet the shades arouse;
Her cave the mining coney scoops;
Where o'er the mead the mountain stoops,
    The kids exult and browse.

xxvi

Of gems — their virtue and their price,
Which hid in earth from man's device,
    Their darts of lustre sheathe;
The jasper of the master's stamp,
The topaz blazing like a lamp
    Among the mines beneath.

xxvii

Blest was the tenderness he felt
When to his graceful harp he knelt,
  And did for audience call;
When Satan with his hand he quell'd,
And in serene suspence he held
  The frantic throes of Saul.

xxviii

His furious foes no more malign'd
As he such melody divin'd,
  And sense and soul detain'd;
Now striking strong, now soothing soft,
He sent the godly sounds aloft,
  Or in delight refrain'd.

xxix

When up to heaven his thoughts he pil'd
From fervent lips fair Michal smil'd,
  As blush to blush she stood;
And chose herself the queen, and gave
Her utmost from her heart, 'so brave
  And plays his hymns so good'.

xxx

The pillars of the Lord are seven,
Which stand from earth to topmost heav'n;
  His wisdom drew the plan;
His WORD accomplished the design,
From brightest gem to deepest mine,
  From CHRIST enthron'd to man.

xxxi

Alpha, the cause of causes, first
In station, fountain, whence the burst
  Of light, and blaze of day;
Whence bold attempt, and brave advance,
Have motion, life, and ordinance,
  And heaven itself its stay.

xxxii

Gamma supports the glorious arch
On which angelic legions march,
  And is with sapphire pav'd;

Thence the fleet clouds are sent adrift,
And thence the painted folds, that lift
    The crimson veil, are wav'd.

xxxiii

Eta with living sculpture breathes,
With verdant carvings, flow'ry wreaths,
    Of never-wasting bloom;
In strong relief his goodly base
All instruments of labour grace,
    The trowel, spade, and loom.

xxxiv

Next Theta stands to the Supreme –
Who formed, in number, sign, and scheme,
    Th'illustrious lights that are;
And one address'd his saffron robe,
And one, clad in a silver globe,
    Held rule with ev'ry star.

xxxv

Iota's tuned to choral hymns
Of those that fly, while he that swims
    In thankful safety lurks;
And foot, and chapitre, and niche,
The various histories enrich
    Of God's recorded works.

xxxvi

Sigma presents the social droves
With him that solitary roves,
    And man of all the chief;
Fair on whose face, and stately frame,
Did God impress his hallow'd name,
    For ocular belief.

xxxvii

OMEGA! GREATEST and the BEST,
Stands sacred to the day of rest,
    For gratitude and thought;
Which blessed the world upon his pole,
And gave the universe his goal,
    And clos'd th'infernal draught.

O DAVID, scholar of the Lord!
Such is thy science, whence reward
  And infinite degree;
O strength, O sweetness, lasting ripe!
God's harp thy symbol, and thy type
  The lion and the bee!

xxxix

There is but One who ne'er rebell'd,
But One by passion unimpell'd,
  By pleasures unenticed;
He from himself his semblance sent,
Grand object of his own content,
  And saw the God in CHRIST.

xl

Tell them, I am, JEHOVA said
To MOSES; while earth heard in dread,
  And, smitten to the heart,
At once above, beneath, around,
All Nature, without voice or sound,
  Replied, 'O Lord, THOU ART.'

xli

Thou art – to give and to confirm,
For each his talent and his term;
  All flesh thy bounties share:
Thou shalt not call thy brother fool:
The porches of the Christian school
  Are meekness, peace, and pray'r.

xlii

Open, and naked of offence,
Man's made of mercy, soul, and sense;
  God armed the snail and wilk;
Be good to him that pulls thy plough;
Due food and care, due rest, allow
  For her that yields thee milk.

xliii

Rise up before the hoary head,
And God's benign commandment dread,
  Which says thou shalt not die:

'Not as I will, but as thou wilt',
Prayed he, whose conscience knew no guilt;
  With whose bless'd pattern vie.

xliv

Use all thy passions! — love is thine,
And joy and jealousy divine;
  Thine hope's eternal fort,
And care thy leisure to disturb,
With fear concupiscence to curb,
  And rapture to transport.

xlv

Act simply, as occasion asks;
Put mellow wine in season'd casks;
  Till not with ass and bull:
Remember thy baptismal bond;
Keep from commixtures foul and fond,
  Nor work thy flax with wool.

xlvi

Distribute: pay the Lord his tithe,
And make the widow's heart-strings blithe;
  Resort with those that weep:
As you from all and each expect,
For all and each thy love direct,
  And render as you reap.

xlvii

The slander and its bearer spurn,
And propagating praise sojourn
  To make thy welcome last;
Turn from Old Adam to the New;
By hope futurity pursue;
  Look upwards to the past.

xlviii

Control thine eye, salute success,
Honour the wiser, happier bless,
  And for their neighbour feel;
Grudge not of mammon and his leaven,
Work emulation up to heaven
  By knowledge and by zeal.

O DAVID, highest in the list
Of worthies, on God's ways insist,
  The genuine word repeat:
Vain are the documents of men,
And vain the flourish of the pen
  That keeps the fool's conceit.

l

PRAISE above all — for praise prevails;
Heap up the measure, load the scales,
  And good to goodness add;
The generous soul her saviour aids,
But peevish obloquy degrades;
  The Lord is great and glad.

li

For ADORATION all the ranks
Of angels yield eternal thanks,
  And DAVID in the midst;
With God's good poor, which, last and least
In man's esteem, thou to thy feast,
  O blessed bridegroom, bidst.

lii

For ADORATION seasons change,
And order, truth, and beauty range,
  Adjust, attract, and fill:
The grass the polyanthus cheques,
And polish'd porphyry reflects,
  By the descending rill.

liii

Rich almonds colour to the prime
For ADORATION; tendrils climb,
  And fruit-trees pledge their gems;
And Ivis, with her gorgeous vest,
Builds for her eggs her cunning nest,
  And bell-flowers bow their stems.

liv

With vinous syrup cedars spout;
From rocks pure honey gushing out,
  For ADORATION springs:

All scenes of painting crowd the map
Of nature; to the mermaid's pap
    The scalèd infant clings.

lv

The spotted ounce and playsome cubs
Run rustling 'mongst the flow'ring shrubs,
    And lizards feed the moss;
For ADORATION beasts embark,
While waves upholding halcyon's ark
    No longer roar and toss.

lvi

While Israel sits beneath his fig,
With coral root and amber sprig
    The wean'd advent'rer sports;
Where to the palm the jasmin cleaves,
For ADORATION 'mongst the leaves
    The gale his peace reports.

lvii

Increasing days their reign exalt,
Nor in the pink and mottled vault
    The opposing spirits tilt;
And, by the coasting reader spied,
The silverlings and crusions glide
    For ADORATION gilt.

lviii

For ADORATION rip'ning canes,
And cocoa's purest milk detains
    The western pilgrim's staff;
Where rain in clasping boughs enclos'd,
And vines with oranges dispos'd,
    Embow'r the social laugh.

lix

Now labour his reward receives,
For ADORATION counts his sheaves,
    To peace, her bounteous prince;
The nectarine his strong tint imbibes,
And apples of ten thousand tribes,
    And quick peculiar quince.

lx

The wealthy crops of whit'ning rice,
'Mongst thyine woods and groves of spice,
   For ADORATION grow;
And, marshall'd in the fencèd land,
The peaches and pomegranates stand,
   Where wild carnations blow.

lxi

The laurels with the winter strive;
The crocus burnishes alive
   Upon the snow-clad earth:
For ADORATION myrtles stay
To keep the garden from dismay,
   And bless the sight from dearth.

lxii

The pheasant shows his pompous neck;
And ermine, jealous of a speck,
   With fear eludes offence;
The sable, with his glossy pride,
For ADORATION is descried,
   Where frosts the waves condense.

lxiii

The cheerful holly, pensive yew,
And holy thorn, their trim renew;
   The squirrel hoards his nuts:
All creatures batten o'er their stores,
And careful nature all her doors
   For ADORATION shuts.

lxiv

For ADORATION, DAVID'S Psalms
Lift up the heart to deeds of alms;
   And he, who kneels and chants,
Prevails his passions to control,
Finds meat and med'cine to the soul,
   Which for translation pants.

lxv

For ADORATION, beyond match,
The scholar bulfinch aims to catch
   The soft flute's iv'ry touch;

458

And, careless, on the hazel spray,
The daring redbreast keeps at bay
   The damsel's greedy clutch.

lxvi

For ADORATION, in the skies,
The Lord's philosopher espies
   The Dog, the Ram, and Rose;
The planet's ring, Orion's sword;
Nor is his greatness less ador'd
   In the vile worm that glows.

lxvii

For ADORATION on the strings
The western breezes work their wings,
   The captive ear to sooth. —
Hark! 'tis a voice — how still, and small —
That makes the cataracts to fall,
   Or bids the sea be smooth!

lxviii

For ADORATION, incense comes
From bezoar, and Arabian gums,
   And on the civet's furr:
But as for prayer, or e're it faints,
Far better is the breath of saints
   Than galbanum or myrrh.

lxix

For ADORATION from the down
Of dam'sins to th'anana's crown,
   God sends to tempt the taste;
And while the luscious zest invites,
The sense, that in the scene delights,
   Commands desire be chaste.

lxx

For ADORATION, all the paths
Of grace are open, all the baths,
   Of purity refresh;
And all the rays of glory beam
To deck the man of God's esteem,
   Who triumphs o'er the flesh.

459

For ADORATION, in the dome
Of CHRIST, the sparrows find an home;
   And on his olives perch:
The swallow also dwells with thee,
O man of God's humility,
   Within his Saviour CHURCH.

lxxii

Sweet is the dew that falls betimes,
And drops upon the leafy limes;
   Sweet, Hermon's fragrant air:
Sweet is the lilly's silver bell,
And sweet the wakeful tapers smell
   That watch for early pray'r.

lxxiii

Sweet the young nurse, with love intense,
Which smiles o'er sleeping innocence;
   Sweet when the lost arrive:
Sweet the musician's ardour beats,
While his vague mind's in quest of sweets,
   The choicest flow'rs to hive.

lxxiv

Sweeter, in all the strains of love,
The language of thy turtle dove,
   Pair'd to thy swelling chord;
Sweeter, with every grace endu'd,
The glory of thy gratitude,
   Respir'd unto the Lord.

lxxv

Strong is the horse upon his speed;
Strong in pursuit the rapid glede,
   Which makes at once his game:
Strong the tall ostrich on the ground;
Strong through the turbulent profound
   Shoots xiphias to his aim.

lxxvi

Strong is the lion – like a coal
His eyeball – like a bastion's mole
   His chest against the foes:

Strong, the gier-eagle on his sail,
Strong against tide, th'enormous whale
   Emerges as he goes.

lxxvii

But stronger still, in earth and air,
And in the sea, the man of pray'r,
   And far beneath the tide;
And in the seat to faith assign'd,
Where ask is have, where seek is find,
   Where knock is open wide.

lxxviii

Beauteous the fleet before the gale;
Beauteous the multitudes in mail,
   Ranked arms and crested heads:
Beauteous the garden's umbrage mild,
Walk, water, meditated wild,
   And all the bloomy beds.

lxxix

Beauteous the moon full on the lawn;
And beauteous, when the veil's withdrawn,
   The virgin to her spouse:
Beauteous the temple, deck'd and fill'd,
When to the heav'n of heav'ns they build
   Their heart-directed vows.

lxxx

Beauteous, yea beauteous more than these,
The shepherd king upon his knees,
   For his momentous trust;
With wish of infinite conceit,
For man, beast, mute, the small and great,
   And prostrate dust to dust.

lxxxi

Precious the bounteous widow's mite;
And precious, for extream delight,
   The largess from the churl:
Precious the ruby's blushing blaze,
And alba's blest imperial rays,
   And pure cerulean pearl.

lxxxii

Precious the penitential tear;
And precious is the sigh sincere;
  Acceptable to God:
And precious are the winning flow'rs,
In gladsome Israel's feast of bow'rs,
  Bound on the hallow'd sod.

lxxxiii

More precious that diviner part
Of David, even the Lord's own heart,
  Great, beautiful, and new:
In all things where it was intent,
In all extreams, in each event,
  Proof — answering true to true.

lxxxiv

Glorious the sun in mid career;
Glorious th'assembled fires appear;
  Glorious the comet's train:
Glorious the trumpet and alarm;
Glorious th'almighty stretched-out arm;
  Glorious th'enraptured main:

lxxxv

Glorious the northern lights a-stream;
Glorious the song, when God's the theme;
  Glorious the thunder's roar:
Glorious hosannah from the den;
Glorious the catholic amen;
  Glorious the martyr's gore:

lxxxvi

Glorious, — more glorious, is the crown
Of Him that brought salvation down,
  By meekness, called thy Son;
Thou that stupendous truth believ'd; —
And now the matchless deed's atchiev'd,
  DETERMINED, DARED, and DONE.

Christopher Smart

It's no joke at all, I'm not that sort of poet.
Though I adore the sheen of white quartz,
Though I love green pines, vast seas, the glimmer of sunset on
    a crow's back,
The dusky sky interwoven with the wings of bats,
Though I adore heroes and high mountains,
The flags of nations waving in the wind,
All colours from saffron to the heavy bronze of chrysanthe-
    mums,
Remember my food is a pot of old tea.
You should be afraid: there is another person in me:
His imagination is a gnat's and he crawls through muck.

Wen Yi-tuo

HOW PLEASANT TO KNOW MR LEAR

How pleasant to know Mr Lear!
    Who has written such volumes of stuff!
Some think him ill-tempered and queer,
    But a few think him pleasant enough.

His mind is concrete and fastidious,
    His nose is remarkably big;
His visage is more or less hideous,
    His beard it resembles a wig.

He has ears, and two eyes, and ten fingers,
    Leastways if you reckon two thumbs;
Long ago he was one of the singers,
    But now he is one of the dumbs.

He sits in a beautiful parlour,
    With hundreds of books on the wall;
He drinks a great deal of Marsala,
    But never gets tipsy at all.

He has many friends, laymen and clerical;
    Old Foss is the name of his cat;
His body is perfectly spherical,
    He weareth a runcible hat.

When he walks in a waterproof white,
　　The children run after him so!
Calling out, 'He's come out in his night-
　　Gown, that crazy old Englishman, oh!'

He weeps by the side of the ocean,
　　He weeps on the top of the hill;
He purchases pancakes and lotion,
　　And chocolate shrimps from the mill.

He reads but he cannot speak Spanish,
　　He cannot abide ginger-beer:
Ere the days of his pilgrimage vanish,
　　How pleasant to know Mr Lear!

Edward Lear

STANDING ON EARTH

Standing on Earth, not rapt above the Pole,
More safe I sing with mortal voice, unchang'd
To hoarse or mute, though fall'n on evil days,
On evil days though fall'n, and evil tongues;
In darkness, and with dangers compast round,
And solitude; yet not alone, while thou
Visit'st my slumbers nightly, or when Morn
Purples the East: still govern thou my song,
Urania, and fit audience find, though few.
But drive far off the barbarous dissonance
Of Bacchus and his revellers, the race
Of that wild rout that tore the Thracian Bard
In Rhodope, where woods and rocks had ears
To rapture, till the savage clamor drowned
Both harp and voice; nor could the Muse defend
Her son.　So fail not thou, who thee implores:
For thou art heav'nly, she an empty dream . . .

John Milton

29. I THINK
YOU STINK

I Think You Stink

Poets are dangerous. On the whole I believe it is their function to praise. But if they are crossed, or provoked, or if they are made indignant by nastiness or pretentious writing, they have the power to answer back, in epigrams and satires. A not very sensible judge said to a barrister, 'I have read your case, and I am no wiser now than when I started.' 'No wiser, my Lord,' replied the barrister, 'but far better informed.' Poets can make repartee of that kind much sharper by inventing it in rhythm and rhyme, and so ensuring that it will be always remembered; and since it is their business to see things more clearly than mose people dare to see them (or can afford to see them), they recognize the folly and the beastliness which are about always, in every age, including our own.

> We are a little age, where the blind pygmy treads
> In hypnotized crusades against all splendour,

wrote Wyndham Lewis, who died in 1957; and John Dryden said more than two centuries ago that there are always fools, and new fools:

> Fools change in England, and new fools arise;
> For tho' th'immortal species never dies,
> Yet ev'ry year new maggots make new flies.

Excellent – and necessary – to say such things. Yet these last pages offer only a taste of poets being sharp or indignant, or poking fun, as a contrast to what is, on the whole, their more admirable voice.

DOCTOR FELL

I do not like thee, Doctor Fell,
The reason why I cannot tell;
But this I know, and know full well,
I do not like thee, Doctor Fell.

Tom Brown

MR CROMEK

A pretty sneaking knave I knew —
O Mr Cromek, how do ye do?

William Blake

MINIVER CHEEVY

Miniver Cheevy, child of scorn,
  Grew lean while he assailed the seasons;
He wept that he was ever born,
  And he had reasons.

Miniver loved the days of old
  When swords were bright and steeds were prancing;
The vision of a warrior bold
  Would set him dancing.

Miniver sighed for what was not,
  And dreamed, and rested from his labors;
He dreamed of Thebes and Camelot,
  And Priam's neighbours.

Miniver mourned the ripe renown
  That made so many a name so fragrant;
He mourned Romance, now on the town,
  And Art, a vagrant.

Miniver loved the Medici,
  Albeit he had never seen one;
He would have sinned incessantly
  Could he have ever been one.

Miniver cursed the commonplace
   And eyed a khaki suit with loathing;
He missed the mediaeval grace
   Of iron clothing.

Miniver scorned the gold he sought,
   But sore annoyed was he without it;
Miniver thought, and thought, and thought,
   And thought about it.

Miniver Cheevy, born too late,
   Scratched his head and kept on thinking;
Miniver coughed and called it fate,
   And kept on drinking.

                              Edwin Arlington Robinson

HOW BEASTLY THE BOURGEOIS IS —

How beastly the bourgeois is
especially the male of the species —

Presentable, eminently presentable —
shall I make you a present of him?

Isn't he handsome? isn't he healthy? Isn't he a fine specimen?
doesn't he look the fresh clean englishman, outside?
Isn't it god's own image? tramping his thirty miles a day
after partridges, or a little rubber ball?
wouldn't you like to be like that, well off, and quite the
     thing?

Oh, but wait!
Let him meet a new emotion, let him be faced with another
     man's need,
Let him come home to a bit of moral difficulty, let life face
     him with a new demand on his understanding
and then watch him go soggy, like a wet meringue.
Watch him turn into a mess, either a fool or a bully.
Just watch the display of him, confronted with a new demand
     on his intelligence,
a new life-demand.

How beastly the bourgeois is
especially the male of the species —

Nicely groomed, like a mushroom
standing there so sleek and erect and eyeable –
and like a fungus, living on remains of bygone life
sucking his life out of the dead leaves of greater life than his
    own.

And even so, he's stale, he's been there too long.
Touch him, and you'll find he's all gone inside
just like an old mushroom, all wormy inside, and hollow
under a smooth skin and an upright appearance.

Full of seething, wormy, hollow feelings
rather nasty –
How beastly the bourgeois is!

Standing in their thousands, these appearances, in damp
    England
what a pity they can't all be kicked over
like sickening toadstools, and left to melt back, swiftly
into the soil of England.

D. H. Lawrence

LATIN

Latin is a dead tongue,
Dead as dead can be.
First it killed the Romans –
Now it's killing me.

SUM, ES, EST

Sum – I am a gentleman;
Es – thou art a fool;
Est – he is a crocodile
Sitting on a stool.

SALLY BIRKETT'S ALE

O mortal man, that lives by bread,
What is it makes thy nose so red?
Thou silly fool, that looks't so pale,
'Tis drinking Sally Birkett's ale.

AUNT ELIZA

In the drinking-well
    Which the plumber built her,
Aunt Eliza fell . . .
    We must buy a filter.

                              Harry Graham

THE STERN PARENT

Father heard his children scream,
So he threw them in the stream,
Saying, as he drowned the third,
'Children should be seen, not heard.'

                              Harry Graham

JACOB TONSON, HIS PUBLISHER

With leering looks, bull-fac'd, and freckl'd fair,
With two left legs, and Judas-colour'd hair,
And frowzy pores that taint the ambient air.

                              John Dryden

SOME OF WORDSWORTH

Dank, limber verses, stuft with lakeside sedges,
And propt with rotten stakes from broken hedges.

                              Walter Savage Landor

A REPLY TO LINES BY THOMAS MOORE

Will you come to the bower I have shaded for you?
Our couch shall be roses all spangled with dew.
Tommy Moore, Tommy Moore, I'll be hang'd if I do,
It would give me a cough, and a rheumatise too . . .

                              Walter Savage Landor

THOMAS SHADWELL THE POET

The midwife laid her hand on his thick skull,
With this prophetic blessing — *Be thou dull* . . .

                              John Dryden

SAMUEL HALL

Oh, my name is Samuel Hall,
Samuel Hall, Samuel Hall!
Oh, my name is Samuel Hall,
An' I hate you one an' all,
You're a gang of muckers all!
   Damn your hides!

Yes, I killed a man, 'twas said,
So 'twas said, so 'twas said,
Yes, I killed a man, 'twas said,
'Cause I shot him through the head,
An' I left him there for dead,
   Damn his hide!

Oh, the parson he has come,
He has come, he has come,
Oh, the parson he has come,
An' he looks so pious glum,
As he talks of kingdom come,
   Damn his hide!

An' the sheriff he's come too,
He's come too, he's come too,
Oh, the sheriff he's come too,
With his boys all dressed in blue,
They're a gang of muckers too,
   Damn their hides!

To the gallows I must go,
I must go, I must go,
To the gallows I must go,
With the crowd all there below
Shoutin' 'Sam, I told yer so!'
   Damn their hides!

Let this be my partin' knell,
Partin' knell, partin' knell,
Let this be my partin' knell,
Hope ter see yer all in hell,
Hope to see yer all in hell,
   Damn your hides!

471

A CRITIC

With much ado you fail to tell
The requisites for writing well;
But what bad writing is, you quite
Have proved by every line you write.

Walter Savage Landor

THE CURSE

To a sister of an enemy of the author's who disapproved of his
'Playboy of the Western World.'

Lord, confound this surly sister,
Blight her brow with blotch and blister,
Cramp her larynx, lung, and liver,
In her guts a galling give her.

Let her live to earn her dinners
In Mountjoy with seedy sinners:
Lord, this judgment quickly bring,
And I'm your servant, J. M. Synge.

J. M. Synge

THE BOOK-WORMS

Through and through the inspired leaves,
Ye maggots, make your windings;
But, oh! respect his lordship's taste,
And spare his golden bindings.

Robert Burns

LORD WATERFORD

Lord Waterford is dead, says the Shan Van Vocht,
Lord Waterford is dead, says the Shan Van Vocht,
Lord Waterford is dead, and the divil's at his head,
And hell shall be his bed, says the Shan Van Vocht.

When he went down below, says the Shan Van Vocht,
Where the landlords all do go, says the Shan Van Vocht,
Queen Bess she did appear, and says she, you're wanted here
For this five and fifty year, says the Shan Van Vocht.

Then the divil he came on, says the Shan Van Vocht,
And says he to Bess, Begone! says the Shan Van Vocht,
Says Lord George, How are you all, I think I've made an
    awkward call,
Says the divil, Not at all! says the Shan Van Vocht.

Then the next one he did see, says the Shan Van Vocht,
Was his bailiff, Black Magee, says the Shan Van Vocht,
He was sitting on the shelf, washing up the divil's delf,
Och, says George, is that yourself? says the Shan Van Vocht.

We'll not put him in the pit, says the Shan Van Vocht,
Where the common sinners sit, says the Shan Van Vocht,
But we'll build a brand-new grate, where his fathers bake in
    state,
With a nice resarvèd sate, says the Shan Van Vocht.

> the Shan Van Vocht: the poor old woman, a name for Ireland;
> delf: delft or glazed earthenware

IMPROMPTU ON CHARLES II

We have a pretty witty King
    Whose words no man relies on:
He never said a foolish thing,
    And never did a wise one.

John Wilmot, Earl of Rochester

QUEEN ANNE

I am Queen Anne, of whom 'tis said
I'm chiefly famed for being dead.
Queen Anne, Queen Anne, she sits in the sun,
As fair as a lily, as brown as a bun.

THE GEORGES

George the First was always reckoned
Vile, but viler George the Second;
And what mortal ever heard
Any good of George the Third?
When from earth the Fourth descended
(God be praised!) the Georges ended.

Walter Savage Landor

JACK AND ROGER

Jack, eating rotten cheese, did say,
'Like Samson I my thousands slay.'
'I vow', quoth Roger, 'so you do,
And with the self-same weapon, too!'

Benjamin Franklin

ON DEAN INGE

Hark the herald angels sing
Timidly, because Dean Inge
Has arrived and seems to be
Bored with immortality.

Humbert Wolfe

SPORUS

Let *Sporus* tremble — 'What? that thing of silk,
Sporus, that mere white curd of ass's milk?
Satire or sense alas! can *Sporus* feel?
Who breaks a butterfly upon a wheel?'
Yet let me flap this bug with gilded wings,
This painted child of dirt, that stinks and stings;
Whose buzz the witty and the fair annoys,
Yet wit ne'er tastes, and beauty ne'er enjoys:
So well-bred spaniels civilly delight
In mumbling of the game they dare not bite.
Eternal smiles his emptiness betray,
As shallow streams run dimpling all the way,
Whether in florid impotence he speaks,
Or, as the prompter breathes, the puppet squeaks,
Or at the ear of *Eve*, familiar toad,
Half froth, half venom, spits himself abroad,
In puns, or politicks, or tales, or lies,
Or spite, or smut, or rhymes, or blasphemies,
His wit all see-saw, between *that* and *this*,
Now high, now low, now master up, now miss,
And he himself one vile Antithesis . . .

Alexander Pope

THE LATEST DECALOGUE

Thou shalt have one God only; who
Would be at the expense of two?
No graven images may be
Worshipped, except the currency:
Swear not at all; for, for thy curse
Thine enemy is none the worse:
At church on Sunday to attend
Will serve to keep the world thy friend:
Honour thy parents; that is, all
From whom advancement may befall:
Thou shalt not kill; but need'st not strive
Officiously to keep alive:
Do not adultery commit;
Advantage rarely comes of it:
Thou shalt not steal; an empty feat,
When it's so lucrative to cheat:
Bear not false witness; let the lie
Have time on its own wings to flie:
Thou shalt not covet, but tradition
Approves all forms of competition.

Arthur Hugh Clough

ON THE REVEREND JONATHAN DOE

Here lies the Reverend Jonathan Doe,
Where he has gone to I don't know:
If haply to the realms above,
Farewell to happiness and love.
If haply to a lower level,
I can't congratulate the Devil.

OLD SAM'S WIFE

The children of Israel prayed for bread,
The Lord he sent them manna.
Old Sam prayed for a wife
And the devil sent him Anna.

TWO LIMERICKS

i. TOM AGNEW, BILL AGNEW

There are dealers in pictures named Agnew
Whose soft soap would make an old rag new:
　　The Father of Lies
　　With his tail to his eyes
Cries — 'Go to it, Tom Agnew, Bill Agnew!'

ii. ON THE POET O'SHAUGHNESSY

There's the Irishman Arthur O'Shaughnessy —
On the chessboard of poets a pawn is he:
　　Though bishop or king
　　Would be rather the thing
To the fancy of Arthur O'Shaughnessy.

D. G. Rossetti

BLOW, BLOW, THOU WINTER WIND

　　Blow, blow, thou winter wind,
　　Thou art not so unkind
　　　　As man's ingratitude;
　　Thy tooth is not so keen
　　Because thou art not seen,
　　　　Although thy breath be rude.
Heigh-ho! sing heigh-ho! unto the green holly:
Most friendship is feigning, most loving mere folly.
　　　　Then heigh-ho! the holly!
　　　　This life is most jolly.

　　Freeze, freeze, thou bitter sky,
　　That dost not bite so nigh
　　　　As benefits forgot:
　　Though thou the waters warp,
　　Thy sting is not so sharp
　　　　As friend remembered not.
Heigh-ho! sing heigh-ho! unto the green holly:
Most friendship is feigning, most loving mere folly.
　　　　Then heigh-ho! the holly!
　　　　This life is most jolly.

William Shakespeare

ACKNOWLEDGMENTS

For allowing the inclusion of copyright poems thanks are due to:

Mrs George Bambridge, Macmillan & Co. Ltd, and the Macmillan Company of Canada Ltd for 'Song of the Galley Slaves' by Rudyard Kipling, from *Many Inventions*; Robert Graves, for two poems from his *Collected Poems 1959* (Cassell & Co. Ltd); Siegfried Sassoon, for 'Phoenix' from his *Collected Poems* (Faber & Faber Ltd); the Marchesa Origo, for 'Frutta di Mare' by the late Geoffrey Scott; Mrs Geoffrey Taylor, for 'Cruel Clever Cat' by the late Geoffrey Taylor; Mrs Edward Thomas, for poems from Edward Thomas's *Collected Poems* (Faber & Faber Ltd); Rewi Alley, for translations from the Chinese, from his *Peace Through the Ages* (Guozi Shudian, Peking); Trustees of the Hardy Estate and Macmillan & Co Ltd, for Thomas Hardy's 'Night of Trafalgar' from *The Dynasts*, and three poems from his *Collected Poems*; Mrs Yeats, for poems from the *Collected Poems of W. B. Yeats* (Macmillan & Co. Ltd); Miss Anne Wolfe and Victor Gollancz Ltd, for a poem by Humbert Wolfe; Canon Andrew Young, for 'Bee Orchis', 'Go Now My Song', and 'Cuckoo'; Literary Trustees of Walter de la Mare and their representative the Society of Authors, for poems from Walter de la Mare's *Collected Poems* (Faber & Faber Ltd); the Society of Authors, as literary representatives of the Trustees of the Estate of A. E. Housman, and Jonathan Cape Ltd, for poems from A. E. Housman's *Collected Poems*; the Society of Authors, as representatives of the James Joyce Estate, for a poem by James Joyce from *Chamber Music* (Faber & Faber Ltd); Allan & Company (Pty) Ltd (Melbourne), and the Oxford University Press, for 'Waltzing Matilda' by A. B. Paterson; Edward Arnold Ltd, for two poems from Harry Graham's *Ruthless Rhymes*; Blackwell & Mott Ltd, for John Gray's *Flying Fish*; the translator and Cambridge University Press, for 'Arran' from Professor Kenneth Jackson's *Studies in Early Celtic Poetry*; the author, Jonathan Cape Ltd, and Henry Holt & Co. Inc., for three poems from *The Complete Poems of Robert Frost*; the author and Chatto & Windus Ltd, for 'Jonah' from Aldous Huxley's *Verses and a Comedy*; Chatto & Windus Ltd, for a poem by Wilfred Owen (*Collected Poems*); Clarendon Press, Oxford, for poems from *Poetical Works of Robert Bridges*; the author and Constable & Co. Ltd, for poems from Arthur Waley's *170 Chinese Poems*; Constable & Co. Ltd, for a poem from Gordon Bottomley's *Poems of Thirty Years*; J. M. Dent & Sons Ltd, for James Elroy Flecker's 'To a Poet a Thousand Years Hence' (*Collected Poems*, Secker & Warburg); Gerald Duckworth & Co. Ltd, for poems from Hilaire Belloc's *Cautionary Tales* and *Bad Child's Book of Beasts*; the author, Eyre & Spottiswoode Ltd, and Alfred A. Knopf Inc., for two poems from *Selected Poems of John Crowe Ransom*; the authors and Faber & Faber Ltd, for poems from W. H. Auden's *Collected Poems*, Stephen Spender's *Poems*, and Louis MacNeice's *Collected Poems*; the translator and Harvard University Press, for a poem from William Hung's *Tu Fu: China's Greatest Poet*; the Estate of the late Mrs Frieda Lawrence, and William Heinemann Ltd, for poems from *The Collected*

Poems of D. H. Lawrence; Macmillan Company, New York, for poems from *Collected Poems* of Vachel Lindsay, and 'An Inscription by the Sea' from *Collected Poems* of Edwin Arlington Robinson; Oxford University Press, London, for 'Hurrahing in Harvest', and part of 'The Vision of the Mermaids' from *The Poems of Gerard Manley Hopkins*; the author and Oxford University Press, London, for 'W' from James Reeves's *Blackbird in the Lilies*; H.M. Postmaster General and the author, for *Night Mail* by W. H. Auden; Routledge and Kegan Paul Ltd, for 'The Confession' by Wen Yi-Tuo from Robert Payne's *Contemporary Chinese Poets*; the translator and Rupert Hart-Davis Ltd, for 'Ophelia', from *The Drunken Boat*, translated by Brian Hill; Sidgwick & Jackson Ltd, for 'Garden Lion', from *A Garden in the Antipodes* by Evelyn Hayes; the translator and Thames & Hudson Ltd, for 'Long I Have Loved to Stroll', from William Acker's *Tao the Hermit*; Charles Scribners Sons, New York, for 'Miniver Cheevy', copyright 1907 Charles Scribners Sons; renewal copyright 1935. Reprinted from *The Town Down the River* by Edwin Arlington Robinson.

INDEX OF AUTHORS AND POEMS

attrib. Skelton (handwritten annotation in left margin)

486

494

495

INDEX OF FIRST LINES AND TITLES

R   497

507

November (handwritten marginal note)

508

The Strange Visitor 513

132

Walsingham - Lament p. 327 + "As you came.." p. 55

If sensuality were happiness, beasts were happier than men; but human felicity is lodged in the soul, not in the flesh. - Seneca